01

GENESIS

Ross Breitkreuz

Q830 Media Inc.
info@Q830.com
www.Q830.com

Cataloguing in Publication information may be obtained through Library and Archives Canada.

CONTENTS

EVERYONE LOVES A GOOD STORY.

Even though millions have been told and millions more will come, our appetite to hear another never subsides. Stories have a unique way of drawing us in and making us engage with the drama, and when they do, something happens in the process.

Suddenly, we can find ourselves captivated by the smallest details as we cheer for underdogs, demand justice, hope for a hero, and rejoice in happy endings.

WITHOUT QUESTION, STORIES HAVE AN EXCEPTIONAL WAY OF COMPELLING US AND, IN THE END, LEAVING US INSPIRED.

BUT I WONDER...

What if there was a story that did even *more* than this?

What if there was a story that didn't just entertain or inspire, but rather, it penetrated lives, lived beyond its pages, and made its story our own? What if there was a story that challenged everything we thought we knew and spoke to desires we didn't know we had? What if there was a story that could take us beyond cheering for characters by daring us to believe that, in fact, we are the heroes, we are the warriors, and we are part of its purpose?

A story like that would impact many; in fact, it already has. And *this* is the story of Q830—the story in the Bible. Though I did not write it, I will guide you through it. Though I am not in it, it's no less a record of my history. And though you think you know it, you've read nothing like it.

" I'm about to tell you your story... and I dare you to read it. **"**

"'Do you understand what you're reading?'...
'How can I unless someone guides
me [through it]?'" (ESV)
- Acts 8:30 (The Bible)

**RESPONDING TO THE QUESTION IN
ACTS CHAPTER 8 VERSE 30.**

Q830: YOUR GUIDE TO THE BIBLE.

As a guide to the Bible I have little to offer apart from it.

Q830 is a story, but it's a story of a story. As the Q830 logo appears in the chapters it's imperative that you read the corresponding passages.

PREFACE

Every book in a store gives you a peek at what's inside before you read it: an abstract of the story and an introduction to the author. *So why doesn't the Bible?* Flip over a Bible and chances are the back cover's empty.

The preface to Q830 is a simple solution to that blank space. This marks the beginning of our reintroduction to the Bible, a snapshot of what's inside, and a familiar place to start the story.

SYNOPSIS

In the greatest display of power, from inside deep darkness, the universe was born through the words of an author. At the heart of this creation was mankind—the centrepiece of all that the author had made.

Created to experience a relationship with their Creator, against all logic mankind rejected Him. Turning their backs and running, mankind had little interest in living the way they were designed to. As a result, life took a form it was never intended to. An evil disease infected the earth and threatened to destroy everyone. Mankind's fate was sealed.

However, not once startled by their ignorance, armed with a plan to restore them, the Creator chased His broken creation through continued rejection, war, famine, sexual promiscuity, and years of neglect. He was determined to love the hell out of them regardless of the cost. His love has left us with a story that always protects, always trusts, and always hopes. **Love never fails.**

ABOUT THE AUTHOR OF THE BIBLE

For reasons that will be explained, the author of the Bible is not easily described. Due to His uniqueness, His "About the Author" section will run slightly longer than normal. Regardless, when all is said and done, we will receive an introduction from our author as He answers the question "Who are You?"

To begin our "About the Author" section we must first explain the difference between writing the Bible and authoring it.

The Bible is composed of numerous books (sixty-six, to be exact). For most of the Bible, we know who wrote these books. However, though we know who was credited with writing the words, the *author* of the Bible was always God. This is likely an odd statement to read but true nonetheless. In fact, the Bible was actually composed using a method quite common in early society.

At earlier stages in history, most people lacked the skills required for reading and writing. If someone wanted something written down, they usually needed someone skilled in writing to record it while they told them what to write. In this process, though someone else wrote the words, the one dictating what the hand chronicled was known as the author. It is in this fashion that the Bible emerged. Authorship of the Bible is therefore credited to God, as He chose men to record what He desired.

" Penned by the hands of man but inspired by the heart of God. "

The inspiration these men received as they wrote came in numerous forms. On some occasions, God commanded that they write something specific (**Exodus 17:14**); other times He had events He wanted remembered (**Deuteronomy 6–8**). There are over 3,800 statements in the Old Testament where God inspired men and spoke to them through words, dreams, and visions and instructed them about the future (**Isaiah 1:2; Jeremiah 11:1; Psalm 84:2; 2 Peter 1:21; Hebrews 1:1**). On one particular occasion, God even wrote a portion of the Bible without the help of anyone (**Exodus 31:18**). The main point is, regardless of the "how," the "who" remained the same. This makes the Bible a book penned by the hands of man but inspired by the heart of God. Therefore, since it is common for authors to introduce themselves, we will now jump to a point in the Bible's story where God did just that.

In Exodus, a book about a nation's daring escape from slavery, the Bible records a discussion between God and a man named Moses. At the time of their conversation, Moses was tending sheep when suddenly a nearby bush was engulfed by flames. However, what was odd to Moses was the fact that this bush was not being consumed, and apparently seeing a not-burning burning bush was perplexing. As Moses moved in for a closer inspection, he found himself caught up in a conversation with our author.

At the time this took place Moses had been living as an alien in a foreign land for quite some time. Today his situation would be like an illegal immigrant hiding in another country. Originally from the land of Egypt, Moses had run away and had been gone for roughly forty years. Meanwhile, back in Egypt, his people, the Israelites, were trapped in slavery.

Aware of the situation, as Moses and God dialogued, God told Moses to go back to Egypt and lead his people out of slavery. No sooner did these words land on Moses' ears than he realized the magnitude of the request. The modern-day equivalent to what God told Moses would be to have the United States of America enslave an entire ethnic group, then have a descendant from this group (one who was hiding in another country and had no position of authority among his people) stomp into the Oval Office, point his finger at the president's nose, and demand— not ask for—the freedom of his people. All because the God he met at the not-burning burning bush told him to.

Undoubtedly, Moses knew this would sound odd, and although he agreed that the freedom of his people was a great idea, he quickly tried to pass the freedom-fighting mission off on a new recruit. However, God responded to Moses' hesitation by telling him he need not worry, because he wouldn't be going alone. God would be with him and was putting His stamp of approval on the task.

Still somewhat leery and wanting to leave no stone unturned, Moses sought clarity by asking God one simple question: *"Okay. If I go and tell these people I've been sent by God, they're gonna ask me 'which god'? So who are you exactly?"* Here, in response to Moses' question, our author finally introduced Himself. And what God told Moses was this: **"Tell them, 'I AM has sent me to you'"** (**Exodus 3:14**). Are you confused? Very few aren't.

To understand this odd reply, we need to remember that back in those days people were not skeptical about the existence of gods. Egyptian culture, in particular, was filled with gods and deities that represented every aspect of life. Due to Egypt's vast number of gods, it would be common to ask the question "Which god are you referring to?" Moses knew that telling people "God sent me" was as specific as standing in the Oval Office and telling the president, "Bob sent me." Since God knew this, He realized He would need to be specific. By introducing

Himself in the manner that He did, not only was He specific, He was exceedingly clear about who He was. The name "I AM" would have been unique, uncommon, and bold. Labelling Himself as the I AM was His way of implying that *"although there are many 'gods' in attendance at this party, I AM the host, and the Man of the House!"*

God's introduction to Moses (and now to us) as I AM is His way of answering the call to "Who is the God of all gods?" Boldly He answers, *"I AM. I am not like other gods. I AM the only true God. Capital 'G,' above all, superior to all, G-O-D."* In His name alone, He answers nearly every question we might have about God:

Who is love? **I AM.**
Who is forgiving? **I AM.**
Who is the answer to life's problems, pains, and trials? **I AM.**
Who is the one I can place my hope in? **I AM.**
Who is the God of all gods, King of all kings, and Lord of all lords? **I AM.**
Who is the author of the Bible? **I AM.**

A daring introduction, to say the least, but we will let our author speak for Himself.

For further introductions from I AM, feel free to read **Isaiah 43:10–13** and **1 Corinthians 8:5–6**.

NOW OUR STORY BEGINS...

CHAPTER 1

THE STORY I AM ABOUT TO TAKE PART IN TELLING YOU IS UNLIKE any other. In fact, it is so unique, the argument could be made that it's the original—the starting point of every story ever told, the beginning of us all.

Setting the stage for this epic is not easily done, because it did not start in a specific location or at a certain moment in time. No, to grasp the concept of where this story began, we must go back to before space and time existed. A moment so empty, defined by darkness, where nothing was everything. Like being lost in space, except someone turned off all the stars and removed every planet. No light, no life, no sound, just a darkness that knows no boundaries. We might think of such a state as a void, but for the author who breathed life into this story, it was a blank canvas with limitless potential and a galaxy of opportunities.

Absent of time, mass, colour, or life, without the need of tools or inspiration, into the darkness our author spoke, and earth came to life (**2 Peter 3:5; Psalm 24:1–2**). With His words our story began, and as it did, so did every story that has ever been told. Every canvas and every author traces their beginning back to this moment.

 **Genesis 1:1–25**

Well-written stories can begin with any number of scenes and draw readers into them. From quiet contemplative moments to the climax of a battle, strong opening paragraphs are captivating, enticing, and descriptive. Which raises the question, why does the Bible's introduction seem so poor?

Let's be serious—if the same God who designed the universe was actually inspiring the writers of this story, surely He could have given them something more entertaining to write.

Why are we not captivated by descriptions of what it was like to watch water burst to life? God could make Niagara Falls look like a bathroom sink. What about when light exploded into existence? The eruption of all earth's fireworks would be like a birthday cake sparkler in comparison. Considering, for a moment, everything the Bible says God made, we could have a much more intriguing first twenty-five verses. So why don't we? How can someone create the universe but not manage to author a captivating introduction? And why didn't the person recording all this tell God that good stories need hair-raising introductions?

"Every canvas and every author traces
their beginning back to
this moment...**"**

The man who failed to relay that message as he scribed this introduction (as well as the rest of Genesis) on God's behalf was named Moses. Many of us may be familiar with Moses and his life accomplishments, but for those who aren't, here is a quick synopsis, as well as some foreshadowing of things to come.

In his life, Moses went from being the prince of Egypt to being a lowly shepherd. He then returned to Egypt, where he butted heads with the most powerful nation on earth. He parted the ocean, climbed mountains, and led over a million people on a forty-year nature walk, and now we discover that he had been keeping a journal about creation in his downtime (assuming he had any). We can't definitively say what it was like for Moses as he wrote amidst all this, but to gain perspective we will venture a guess.

Thus far, the only thing the story has covered is that God created the universe and capped off the first five days of creation by looking at what He had done and calling it "good." Here is a point we can identify with.

Anyone who has built anything with the slightest degree of success can identify with the feeling of accomplishment that comes with a job well done. When we complete a project and it's good, we're excited about it. God is no different. In fact, the Bible will continue to show us that excitement and passion are common traits of His. In light of this, perhaps the story begins so simply and structured because Moses was overwhelmed with the information God enthusiastically told him. Recording Genesis 1:1–25 would have been a monumental task.

What if God had passionately recounted every design He had made with painstaking detail, providing in-depth explanations that didn't skip a feature? What if He told Moses about the intricate structure of molecules and particles, highlighted the birth of light, and explained its design and how it gathers speed? After that, what if God described the process He used to separate earth from sky and illustrated the way the mountains blossomed like flowers and birds appeared like bubbles from a wand? All of this before getting around to outlining the way He suspended the sun and calculated earth's orbit around it.

Had Moses been privy to any of that information, the details would have added up quickly. Before lining up his chisel or placing his feather into ink, he may have stopped to wonder, *Should I write out the explanation of an atom's structure or draw a diagram? And was it two hydrogen and one oxygen or the other way around?*

Trying to condense so many details and do justice to God's work would have been overwhelming. The story of creation would have read more like a science textbook, perhaps encouraging Moses to suggest, "God? Maybe I could just write You down as saying, 'Let there be light'...and then...there was light?"

Thinking about Moses' task shows us that he had a big responsibility. However, further study of the story reveals that the opening verses were *not* written with simplicity because Moses was overwhelmed or God was incapable of an adequate explanation. The flaw at the start of Genesis lies not with the author or the structure but with an audience merely searching for entertainment.

Maybe the real reason we don't think the Bible's account of creation is captivating is because it was never intended for entertainment purposes. The goal of creation was not to just impress us with what was created. The purpose was to highlight *who* created. Like beautiful architecture boasts about the architect, mountains, valleys, stars, and oceans boast about the work of God. If this is true, and the whole purpose of creation is to proclaim the majesty of God, the introduction no longer needs rewriting. This is why the Bible later describes creation as declaring the work of God's hands and proclaiming His glory (**Psalm 19; Romans 1:20**).

> **"** Creation was never meant to be an end in itself; it's a sign pointing to something greater, some*one* greater. **"**

No longer does the power of the ocean end with angry waves, but the waves point to someone powerful enough to control them (**Isaiah 51:15**). Earth's beauty challenges us to wonder who could be great enough to measure its dimensions, like a tailor fitting a groom for a tux (**Job 38:4–7**). The story might not begin by explaining everything about creation, but it communicates the most important information. In fact, the first sentence alone tells us all we need to know.

As long as we remember *who* created, we have the exciting opportunity to explore creation for ourselves. It's as if the story starts with a challenge to put down the book, go for a walk, and consider the possibility that everything we see was created by someone.

With our story momentarily paused during the sixth day of creation, it's apparent that God has more work to do. As He works at putting the finishing touches on His creation, we will soon be introduced to His greatest masterpiece yet...

HIS "PIÈCE DE RÉSISTANCE."

CHAPTER 2

SET ON ITS COURSE AND BOUND BY AN INVISIBLE LEASH, THE EARTH began its dependable journey around the sun, a voyage it continues to this day. With creation sitting on the cusp of completion, as marvellous as it was, it still required one final touch. Like all great masterpieces, it needed the marking of its Creator—an artist's signature and unique way of stating "This is My creation. I am the one who made it, and no one can take credit from Me." Formed with a level of intimacy nothing else had seen, this final design and marking would receive more attention than all five previous days of creation combined. And as Day 6 draws to a close, we are introduced to the crown jewel of creation, man.

 Genesis 1:26

"...man's arrival was a powerful scene...**"**

Though it may not seem significant at first, man's arrival was a powerful scene. In fact, all on its own, one small word brought so much meaning to man's creation that it had the potential to overwhelm Moses.

Before discovering that word, it's important to remember that man's creation meant so much to Moses primarily because he was not debating God's existence as he wrote. Moses had a strong faith in God, and more than that, he had a knowledge of what God is like and an understanding of God's character. Because of this, Moses understood the magnified meaning of man's creation when God used the word "our."

Though this word may seem misplaced to us, for Moses it would have looked like it was written in **bold**. He knew God's reference to plurality at the moment of man's design ("our image") was referring to the Trinity—the very nature of God's existence. The implications of this were tremendous.

For Moses (and Christians today), the Trinity refers to the nature of God's existence. The Bible reveals God as Father, Son, and Holy Spirit (Deuteronomy 6:9, Matthew 28:19, John 10:30, John 14:9, John 14:16-23, Romans 8:9). While each is it's own personage, there remains at all times, one God.

Trinity means, three separate forms remaining in infinite and constant existence in all forms at all times. Three-in-one. Three-united. Tri-unity. Trinity. This can feel like a lot of mental heavy lifting, but no need to worry. The story will progressively reveal the Trinity to us. For now, what's most important is understanding the relationship of the Trinity.

(As a disclaimer, by no means is the following an attempt to explain the Trinity and it's function. Greater minds have tried and fallen short. Rather, the intention of the analogy is to get us to envision the depth of interconnectedness and intimacy the Trinity represents.)

Perhaps it would be helpful to think of the Trinity's relationship this way: I am Ross Breitkreuz the writer, the husband, and the preacher. Though I am one man, I am revealed through these different roles. Ross Breitkreuz the writer reveals passion, the husband hopefully reveals selflessness (but you'd have to ask my wife), and the preacher gives you a glimpse at conviction and concern. Three separate roles showcase numerous characteristics in unique individual settings, yet, they are inseparable from one another under the single title of Ross Breitkreuz. That being said, one of the many ways this explanation falls short is that these are merely roles

I fulfill as an individual. More accurately, we would need three individual Ross Breitkreuzes, one who writes, one that's a husband, and one who preaches, but in the end, there would only be one Ross Breitkreuz.

It can still be hard to understand all this, but it could be said that the sheer difficulty of comprehending a relationship of this kind further reveals its beauty. Here on earth, no relationship contains such intimacy and perfect harmony that you cannot separate the individual parties. Though all earthly relationships (friendship, relationship, marriage) reflect aspects of selflessness, forgiveness, care, patience, and love, at no point are these relationships so flawlessly intermingled that you can't identify one lover from the other.

Yet, that's precisely the intimacy present in the Trinity. Inseparably united, unimaginably loving, and deeply intimate. The Trinity represents the best relationship and every characteristic of perfect unity, without measure. That's who God is.

This is the knowledge Moses possessed as he scribed the sentence "make man in OUR image." Immediately he gained insight into the way man was made to function. What he saw was that mankind was created for relationship. Relationship would be the heart and purpose of human life. We would long to be apart of an intense connection."Yet there was more.

In this design, God was also revealing that mankind's desire for relationship would be so intense, it could only be filled through unity with his Creator. Therefore, since mankind would have a need for its Creator, it meant God was making mankind for Himself. Man was not just an arrow to point to God; he was a creation to share His love.

The realization that God had chosen man above everything else to have a relationship with would have pierced Moses' heart. God was showing that He was mindful of man above all other creations (**Psalm 8:3–9**). Instantly Moses likely considered rewriting man's arrival in Genesis a second time, with a disclaimer that read, "Make sure you are sitting down prior to reading!"

As Moses continued to write, attempting to process all he had heard, he may have quickly experienced another wave of God's love as he thought, *Wait a minute. Not only did God give mankind the gift of life, He also gave him everything previously created so he could rule over it!*

This realization may have sent Moses back to reread about the first five days of creation. If what God said was true, and creation was a gift for man to enjoy, then those first five days were not the mindless placement of land and water; they were five days of cosmic gift wrapping—God's gift to man. The earth had not been designed to sit empty; it was made for inhabitants—it was made for man (**Isaiah 45:18**). Moses' heart would have wrenched over the details of a Creator so powerful, so authoritative, so magnificent, so free, yet so intimately loving.

Astonished by everything he had written, perhaps Moses took a moment to marinate in these truths, letting them set in slowly with rich meaning and flavour. As he meditated on man's design, it's possible that he sat back from his writing, face turned to the heavens, and exhaled a long, contemplative sigh. In that moment, as his chest gently fell, a spark ignited in his heart as the reality of man's design settled upon him once more. More conscious of his breathing than ever before, Moses closed his eyes and pictured air's journey into his lungs. And during a process he had performed millions of times without thinking, he felt great love. As if he was inhaling electricity, hungry for more, Moses pulled long conscious breaths as a smile grew on his face and moisture built in his eyes. In awe over the act of breathing, he sat mesmerized by the notion that God had placed that very breath inside of man. His very breath was God's doing.

The story does not reveal whether or not this is truly how Moses reacted, but given the fact that he was recording God's intimate love for creation, it's doubtful that he overlooked it.

Even the slightest glimpse into the intimacy and purpose behind man's design should cause a stir as we move through this story. Yet oftentimes we flip through this introduction unimpressed, as if it's a stack of mail that only contains bills.

Man's arrival was nothing short of momentous when we see the purpose and intention he was formed with. He received more splendour and ceremony than anything else God made. With man's arrival creation edged that much closer to completion. However, as spectacular as man was, Day 6 was still not over.

GOD'S PLANS WERE STILL UNFOLDING.

CHAPTER 3

ONE STEP CLOSER TO COMPLETION, EARTH MOVED THROUGH DAY 6 of its young life, now equipped with a passenger. As the details of creation continued to unfold, man's significance on earth was further revealed, expanding on his role in the created order.

 **Genesis 2:8-17**

Trees, rivers, and a garden. Wrapping our minds around these images is far simpler than picturing earth's arrival from nothing.

At the moment of his inception, Adam was the world's only human occupant, and he found himself placed in a garden with few concerns in life apart from the obligation to cultivate the land, enjoy its crops, and gallivant around naked—a way of life most men dream of.

Though it seems wild and free, Adam's life was not completely void of other responsibilities, which we discover through the introduction of two rather peculiar trees. One tree, in particular, has caused a great degree of confusion over the years, leading many people to wonder, *What was the purpose in planting a tree man was not allowed to eat from?* And *why would God plant this particular tree in the middle of the garden?*

This one tree has muddled this section of the story for years, usually because it alters our focus when we come to it. Oftentimes, when the story mentions this one tree, we instantly forget about every other tree present in the garden. Suddenly this tree takes centre stage, and we act like it's the point of the story. However, if we remember Adam's location inside a massive garden that God had just created and filled with organic life, the introduction of *one* tree shouldn't erase our awareness of *everything else* God made.

Viewing one tree from Adam's spot in the story actually makes his conversation with God about the non-edible tree significantly different. When we remember all five days of creation and the magnitude of all that was made, the tone of verses 16 and 17 shifts, and what Adam hears God tell him regarding the tree could have sounded much simpler. Maybe somewhat like this:

> *"Adam. You know I brought you to life and gave you the entire world. I created you to enjoy it and conquer it; but there is one stipulation. Though you can eat from every tree I created, and there are many, there is one tree you must not eat from. My reasoning for this is simple: eating from this tree will result in your death. I am warning you about this tree so that your death can be avoided, because I love you and have your best interest in mind. Now, since we are on the topic of this death tree, I should tell you that I took the liberty of installing a few precautionary measures so it doesn't catch you off guard. To minimize the risk of you stumbling upon this tree and eating from it unknowingly, I placed it precisely in the middle of the garden. Now you know where it is—no surprises. Beyond this, if you are still enticed by the thought of eating from the death tree, I conveniently planted another more beneficial tree in the middle of the garden as well. View this second tree as your emergency escape, a reminder of what I have told you. Sound good?"*

When we look at this one tree in the context of all God made and His love for His creation, this tree almost appears to be a non-issue. The scenario presents itself as clearly as 1+1=2. Example: Eat from every tree in the garden minus one, and it equals very good; *or* eat from one tree of death, and it equals death. It's simple!

> **"**Though this seems like a no-brainer,
> the question remains as to why
> this tree had to be planted
> in the first place.**"**

In order to understand why a non-edible tree was necessary, we must re-examine the reason for mankind's creation and how God made man. The story has revealed that God made mankind out of love, and He made him *for* love. God chose man over every other option. Choosing mankind to share a relationship with showcased the central ingredient to sincere love: the choice. Making the choice to embrace someone and refuse all others is what makes love so exhilarating, a truth that God clearly knew, since the story tells us that God is love (**1 John 4:8**). God exhibited true love first by choosing mankind, but He was not interested in forcing man to love Him in return. Therefore, He placed a tree inside the garden.

Without the presence of this one tree, mankind would have been incapable of showing sincere love back to God. To reciprocate the love he had been shown, mankind had to choose God above all others (or in the context of the story thus far, he had to choose God over the death tree). If man had been created without any other option apart from God, his love would have been forced, dry, and passionless. The absence of this tree would have made mankind into nothing more than a race of Interactive Elmos.

For those of you who don't know, Interactive Elmo is a toy created without the ability to choose what he actually loves. Elmo has no free will. This means we can kick him, drop him, throw him, punch him, or slap him. We can do anything we desire other than tickle him, yet we will always receive the same response, "I love you." Does Elmo really love being slapped? I guess we will never know.

Having someone in your life and never giving him or her the option to freely choose you over everyone else is not love. Attempting to force someone's love is wrong. In fact, there are laws against such things, and people who try are usually referred to as dictators, kidnappers, or stalkers—none of which are synonymous with true love. Give someone the freedom to choose whomever they want. Then pursue them, love them, protect them, and cherish them. Show them you truly are the best option in the world. When that individual freely chooses you over everybody else, that is sincere love. It is this choice and the anticipation of another's decision that makes love so electrifying and devastating.

Without the presence of this one tree, mankind would have been destined to a robotic way of life, void of knowing real love. So in an act of loving man first, God provided an opportunity for man to return the love He was revealing to them (**1 John 4:19**).

Although whether or not to return God's love seems as obvious a choice as whether to bungee jump with or without the cord, Adam still needed to make a decision—

AND HE WOULDN'T MAKE IT ALONE.

CHAPTER 4

UP TO THIS POINT IN THE STORY, ONE CHAPTER HAS BEEN USED to describe the first five-and-a-half days of creation. Now, three chapters later, we are still exploring Day 6, suggesting that its events were of utmost importance.

With God having already given Adam every reason to embrace His love, He then went one step further, blessing Adam with another gift. This gift, in particular, would prove to be cause for major celebration throughout the rest of the story, as its arrival brought with it certain "benefits," not only for Adam but for mankind in general.

With Adam inside the perfect garden, exploring the garden—no shirt, no shoes, no problem—enjoying uninterrupted community with God, he was unaware that God was about to take things from good to great.

Looking at His creation, God prepared to add one final ingredient, like the secret contents of a family recipe or that last pinch of salt needed to enhance flavour. He had one more thing to do.

 **Genesis 2:18–25**

What a design! Undoubtedly, Adam was ecstatic to receive such a blessing, and the story wants to capture that. Numerous translations of the story highlight Adam's excitement in that moment by describing it different ways. Reading him saying "now," "at last," or "finally," it can sound as if Adam had an "It's about time!" attitude. *Was he being ungrateful?*

Although his reaction may seem odd, perhaps another look at Day 6 and how it unfolded will help us understand Adam's eagerness. In fact, for anyone currently single, Adam's frustrations may feel eerily familiar.

Reflecting on what the story tells us about Day 6, we can only imagine the excitement Adam must have felt when God mentioned a suitable helper. Though many years separate us from Adam, and countless things have changed during those years, butterflies and nerves inspired by a significant other are not on that list.

As Adam anticipated the arrival of his helper, perhaps he experienced some blind-date-esque jitters, nervously preparing for the encounter by freshening up with a mint leaf and putting on his best...smile.

Standing in silent anticipation over the arrival of the helper God mentioned, he must have trembled with excitement as a new wave of life surged through his body, triggered by the sound of approaching footsteps. Instantly his palms began to sweat, and his mind raced through a list of possibilities. *Long hair? Short hair? Maybe no hair?!* There was really no way of anticipating what his helper might look like. As thoughts rushed through his mind the steps grew closer. Just then, some foliage nearby began to move, and Adam's anxiety peaked. Should he stand tall and confident or go for the shy look? Hands on his hips or modestly clasped in front?

Just then something broke into the clearing, and like the stereotypical in-walks-the-hot-girl scene that's been played out in countless movies since, Adam turned a slow-motion gaze towards the commotion. Excited to behold all that would be his, his eyes drank in the curves of...a rhino?

Understand what I am saying here. *Rhino* is not implying that the original woman was big. What I mean is, an actual animal came sauntering in—

whether or not it was a rhino, I'm not sure, but you get the idea. Either way, instantly this animal's arrival caused Adam to think, *This can't be right! My order got mixed up!*

How disheartening for Adam to hear God announce the arrival of a suitable helper (**Genesis 2:18**), only to have a parade of animals arrive instead. One after another, animal after animal, Adam experienced a roller coaster of emotions. Each set of footsteps brought with it the excitement of this potentially being "the one," only to conclude with the disappointing realization that once again this "creature" was far from what he desired. In light of some of our dating experiences, perhaps we can identify with Adam's disheartenment?

After going through the entire lineup of animals, Adam realized there wasn't one suitable helper. How sad he must have been, since he did not just *feel* like he had seen all the fish in the sea; he *had*. Luckily his next decision wasn't to pursue a suitable helper the way many of us do.

> **"**You need to slay a few dragons to get the princess.**"**

Had Adam been influenced by today's culture, there is no telling what would have transpired next. What would have happened if he'd been counselled with sayings like "You need to slay a few dragons to get the princess" or "Kiss a few frogs to get the prince?" Had Adam succumbed to match-making misfortune the way many of us do, Genesis 2:21 might have read more like this:

Unable to find a suitable helper for himself amidst the multitude of beasts he had seen, Adam grew disheartened. Afraid he might be alone forever, he decided he should improvise. Taking matters into his own hands, Adam said to himself, "Ya know, although this creature over here is not entirely, or remotely, what I am looking for in a suitable helper, we do hang out at the same watering hole. Sure, it's not the best design, but it's not the worst either. I think I could make this work because it's convenient, and God can't expect me to wait around forever!"

Sound familiar? Thankfully that's not what happened, and in his frustration Adam did not take it upon himself to go out cougar hunting. He did not start chasing quail or settle for any random piece of donkey. Instead, he named the animals, embraced the current absence of a suitable helper, and was drawn into a deep sleep. Figuratively speaking, he left the party alone, with no regrets or "I can't believe I did that" moments weighing heavy on his mind. And boy, was he in for a surprise when he woke up!

At this point in the story, we need another level of clarification. A common error in reading the word "helper" is assuming that it highlights women as nothing more than maids or servants. There could not be a more perverted view of the truth. This word does not refer to being below man; more accurately, it represents strength and power, which makes sense when you consider the strength and power men find to impress women.

So God created the perfect helper, and when Adam woke up and saw her, he knew she was for him. Like the moment Goldilocks locked eyes on her bowl of porridge, Adam saw his suitable helper and thought *"This one is juuuuust right,"* either that or *"Bow-chicka-wow-wow,"* given that they were both naked. Regardless, imagine the jubilation and excitement he felt when feasting his eyes on his wife for the very first time!

Given that some of these details don't come out after one cursory glance at these passages, you may want to go back and read this part again, because this was *not* a boring encounter. For Adam this was a **"Finally! It's about time!"** moment. This was his tickertape-parade World-Series-championship celebration, which essentially is how meeting our suitable helper should feel.

This chapter contains one of many pictures the story will give us of marriage: a moment of rejoicing and celebration, overflowing with energy and the intimacy that comes from being free of guilt, shame, and regret. This is where the chapter stops. As creation received its crown jewels, the arrival of man and woman marked the completion of God's created splendour.

No wonder creation was incomplete prior to their arrival. Man and woman were both designed in the nature and image of God! Built for relationship, created for love, now they had the love of one another as well as the love of God! They are God's greatest and most intimate design, which makes it obvious why their presence took creation from "good" to "very good."

There inside that flawless garden, the story truly began. With life designed to perfection, man and woman were placed in the garden with the task of subduing the earth and enjoying all it had to offer. They were designed for love and given the gift of each other, and populating the earth was one of their responsibilities. It didn't come with excruciating pain, inconvenience, bloating, or unnatural cravings—just the pleasure of baby making and the rapture of a child's arrival.

An existence of abundance is where the story sat, an existence made complete in relationship with God, a relationship they still needed to embrace. With Adam and his wife set to discover life, as well as each other, ending here is most appropriate, as further discussion regarding them getting "acquainted" might require a viewer rating.

As happy as things were, a decision was still required, a love reciprocated.

THE HONEYMOON DID NOT LAST LONG.

CHAPTER 5

WITH EARTH ACCOMMODATING TWO HUMAN INHABITANTS, creation lacked nothing. At this point in the story, life was perfect, free from the toil of finance-driven work, pain and suffering. Things could not have been better! In a moment when mankind, meaning Adam and his wife, were perfect, without fault, without sin, and without blemish, their flawless design allowed them to share in an intimate relationship with their flawless designer. Herein lay the splendour of their existence—not the absence of trials or having a carefree schedule, but the constant presence of the one they were made for.

THEY WERE FULFILLING THEIR CREATED PURPOSE.

Stepping back from the story's perfect state, we as readers find ourselves on the opposite side of such an existence. Reading this story from our worldview, with lives that are far from perfect, it's almost impossible to comprehend a perfect world. Many of our lives seem to orbit around unanswered questions, with one question, in particular, drawing the attention of many: **"What is our purpose?"** This question tends to ignite more wonder, such as *"What were we made for?"* and *"What is the meaning of life's stress and toil?"* Though this is our experience, Adam and his wife, due to the contentment they had in relationship with God, were oblivious to such questions.

Inside the garden, Adam and his wife had no perception of the question *"What's life all about?"* They knew. Walking and talking, laughing and loving with the one they were made for, they were consumed by life, like children lost in the rapture of playing their favourite game with their father. This is a harsh contrast to what we call "reality." Today, it sometimes feels tragic when we observe children experiencing moments of joy and elation. We can feel sad, wanting to protect their innocence, because we know that one day they will face the "real" world, and life will rob them of their carefree ways. Years of heartache and the stress of life have us so disconnected from the delight found in the garden that when we watch children tasting "garden moments," we view it as naive. We believe that *they* have it wrong and *they* are oblivious to reality. As if *they're* the ones who have yet to learn what it truly means to live.

There is no denying that our world is filled with confusion, hurt, brokenness, cheating, lying, betrayal, war, rape, murder, emptiness, disease, depression, and hunger. The atrocities seem endless. The sum of these things makes an existence beyond the pain hard to imagine. But what if the pain and anguish in our lives offer us a glimpse into a perfect world? What if there is something to learn from moments when we cry ourselves to sleep? Maybe our heartache contains insight, and our confusion brings a level of awareness. What if the cries that our hearts make when the chaos of life grabs us actually teach us about a perfect world? A world like the one Adam and his wife were experiencing in the garden.

The garden Adam and his wife were in contained no pain and provided answers to life's questions. Therefore, if God designed man and placed him inside such a perfect place, the story suggests that this is where man belongs. If this is true, it could be said that pain is actually our body's way of screaming and our heart's method of crying, "I am not meant for this world! I am homesick!"

Although no one wants to meditate on pain, it has the potential to paint a picture of how great garden life must have been. Like the darkest of nights makes the sunrise all the more radiant...

> **"**...the pain of this life makes the idea of being made for something different, something more, something better, something like Eden, astounding!**"**

What if our pain points towards the life Adam and his wife had? This could mean that all those times our bodies reacted, our hearts bled, and our eyes ran dry, we were longing for this story. Lost in our pain, our body's cry is really for the garden. Our tears are simply saying,

> *"Life is not supposed to hurt this much. I was not created to endure this. Nothing feels right! I'm confused, I'm lost, I'm lonely. If only I could live life the way I was designed to. If I just knew how it felt to truly be alive! But right now I don't feel it. All I feel is like I don't belong here. If I could just go home..."*

The life the story outlines is the kind we all dream of, especially when suffering and hopelessness feel like our closest companions. As Moses wrote about the perfect garden, he did so from a world similar to our own. He wrote longingly about such an existence, hungry for an escape from the pain and slavery of his people, desperate for a taste of the garden's beauty.

With a heightened awareness of the perfect lifestyle found in the garden, we arrive back at our story. Catching up with Adam and his wife, we find them faced with the perfect opportunity to embrace God's love and choose Him over everything else. In that moment, Adam and his wife stood at an intersection. Living with an abundance of blessings and aware that God had picked them, it was their turn to make a decision. The time had come for them to choose God.

 **Genesis 3:1–13**

What agony Moses would have felt as he recorded these events! Like him, we should feel frustration as we read this. Longingly we should wish to dive into the story and go to that moment. If only we could be there to plead with this man and woman, to save them from themselves. Knowing what we know now, we should be desperate to change the outcome, desperate to tell them to guard the garden life. But we are incapable of doing anything that might avoid this horrific conclusion. Helplessly we are left to sit and read, caged spectators to this atrocity, caught up in the aftermath.

With the man and woman making a decision that failed to return God's love...

...A RADICAL SHIFT WAS ABOUT TO TAKE PLACE ON THE WORLD.

CHAPTER 6

COMMANDS WERE IGNORED, PLANS SHATTERED, BLUEPRINTS rejected, and designs thwarted. How would God react to this?

As readers, had we faced the kind of rejection God did, we likely would have responded with outrage. How ungrateful mankind's decision was, turning away from all they had been given! As a result of their rebellion against God's instructions, the flawless creation was stained with sin.

No longer would mankind have unhindered access to their Creator. No longer would mankind know without hindrance how it felt to fulfill their created purpose. All this was only the beginning of the devastation.

Whether Adam and his wife understood the chain reaction their decision set off did not matter; it could not be undone. When they ate from that tree, they chose a new way of life, they embraced a new story, and they invited a new character into it—the serpent.

FULLY AWARE OF THE SERPENT'S BACKGROUND, MOSES LOATHED HIS ARRIVAL.

Before moving forward, one might ask, how is it that Moses was familiar with this character? How did he know the serpent had a background?

A number of sections in the Bible discuss events that took place at the beginning of creation. And similar to how knowledge of the Trinity shed light on God's purpose for man, knowledge of these events will help us understand the weight of Genesis chapter 3.

This parallel story begins by turning back the pages to "In the beginning" and re-examining Genesis chapter 1. This time, however, we look no further than the very first sentence. Locating the word "heavens," we peer inside this seemingly innocent word to discover a myriad of events that took place prior to the serpent's arrival in Genesis chapter 3. A story-within-our-story.

Though, without foreknowledge of the story, we did not see it at the time, that one word, "heavens," speaks of the creation of a multitude of beings.

Over the years, these created beings have received numerous titles, such as heavenly hosts, sons of God, cherubim, or seraphim. But most commonly they are known as angels.

" For one angel in particular, his beauty proved to be a great weakness. "

We discover that as God spoke the heavens into existence in Genesis 1:1, before moving on to the creation of earth He went about the task of filling the heavens. And with the arrival of heavenly hosts this parallel story began.

 Psalm 148:1–5

Although no specific time frame can be gathered for the filling of the heavens, the Bible tells us that God created them and suggests that they were around to witness the most spectacular show ever: creation.

 Job 38:4–7

With angels (the sons of God) on the scene at the time of earth's conception, a new story lies inside the one word "heavens."

Created before the arrival of man, angels do not hold the honour of bearing God's image like mankind does, but they are no less fantastic. In fact, most often their very presence promotes fear, and their beauty is among their many strengths. For one angel in particular, his beauty proved to be a great weakness.

Not once overlooking his splendour, the story's short record of the early events in heaven focus on one haughty angel known as Satan.

Satan was an angel bursting with pride. During his time in heaven, he set off on a quest for glory. Embracing a hunger for power and longing for recognition, he sought to receive honour above all others. His heart became so consumed by thoughts of praise that his delusions of grandeur had him aiming to overthrow his Creator, if it were possible.

 **Isaiah 14:12–15**

 **Ezekiel 28:14–17**

Banished from heaven and the presence of God, before the story of mankind began, Satan was torn from the place he was made for. Left to prowl like a restless wanderer, he found himself on earth, alongside a number of the heavenly hosts he had dragged with him. Seething with anger after his removal, he made it his objective to do what he could to defeat God's plans.

Meanwhile, in the garden, knowing not to eat from the tree, Adam and his wife were encouraged to ignore God's command. Their rejection of God's instructions was not simply a bad choice, it was a failure to return God's love. It was a choice that fused two rebellious stories together, as we discover the serpent's true identity.

 **Revelation 12:9**

THE SERPENT'S TRUE IDENTITY...

CHAPTER 7

SATAN, THE ARROGANT ANGEL WHO DESPISED GOD'S LOVE, WAS now responsible for the deception of mankind.

As humans, experiencing the level of rejection God endured from Satan and earth's first couple would leave our minds numb and our hearts aching. On some level or another we all know what rejection feels like. We are familiar with the suffocating emotions that heartache brings. Which leads us to wonder, *how would God respond after all He'd done for mankind?*

He designed the universe, brought mankind to life, and chose them as His own. He decorated the world in love, displayed His goodness in every corner, and offered it as a gift. After all that, He provided mankind with free will and the opportunity to choose Him in return. He made himself vulnerable to His creation. Though He had the authority to use them however He saw fit, He exposed Himself to potential rejection and patiently waited for them to embrace His love...

ONLY TO HAVE HIS PROPOSAL DENIED.

Though we may not grasp the full horror of this moment, we can identify with aspects of God's pain. Most of us have loved throughout our lives, pouring time and resources into those we adored, only to watch them walk away. We know on a small scale what it's like to place our hearts in the hands of another and walk the fragile wire between elation and heartache, allowing someone to determine the state of our heart, vulnerable to their response and unsure if the outcome will bring joy or devastation. Such a moment is fragile and sacred. Yet this was precisely where the story hung as Adam and his wife stood before the tree, weighing the serpent's words against God's. Like the audience at a baseball game watching a proposal on the big screen, creation watched Adam and his wife and held its breath—paralyzed with anticipation, desperately wanting their response to be "yes." But to creation's horror, "yes" was not the answer. God was not the one they embraced. As they grabbed the fruit from that tree and walked away from God, a hush washed over creation, robbing each spectator of breath as they ached for the one who was rejected. Meanwhile, on the sidelines of the heartache, one individual sat smugly with a smile.

As everyone else responded in shock, the villainous serpent began to smirk. He had just watched man and woman throw God's love on the ground so they could free up their hands to eat from the tree. Satan rejoiced in his deception, satisfied in knowing that since he himself could not overthrow God, he would belittle the ones who possessed God's image. He sat back, marvelling at this notion, and at that moment, mankind's rebellion had fused their story to his in a seemingly inseparable manner.

Trying to comprehend the pain involved in this moment brings our focus back to the question "How will God respond?" At one point, Satan had been one of the most beautiful creatures God had made, meant to stand in God's presence. As for mankind, they had been built for an intimate relationship with God, created to experience the splendour of all He had to offer. The combined rejection of them both was like your best friend rejecting you, brainwashing your fiancée into leaving as well, and then running off with her. Our emotional response to events of this nature would consume us. In the wake of our pain, we would respond with rage and vengeance. A desire to make them taste our heartache would become our obsession. Our goal, revenge; our fuel, retribution—believing that if they are not interested in our love, perhaps they would be interested in our wrath!

As we think of how we might react to such heartache, the story now stops, awaiting God's response. For a moment in time, Adam and his wife sat contemplating their future, unsure of what was to come. Meanwhile, God surveyed each aspect of His broken creation—studying it in pain, anger, faith, hope, and love...

BUT THE GREATEST OF THESE WAS LOVE.

CHAPTER 8

SENSING THE SHIFT THAT WAS TAKING PLACE ON EARTH, ADAM and his wife felt exposed and vulnerable. Incapable of knowing life as it had been, their minds filled with questions: *"What will life look like now? Is there any way we can make this right? What is our purpose if we are separated from the one we were made for?"*

Fear grew inside them as they realized they didn't have a solution to their problem. The reality that they couldn't fix what had been done stung.

Coming from an existence that knew no fear, they shuddered at its arrival. Their future looked dark. There was nothing they could do. Sin had entered their perfect world and taken away its purity and innocence. Like with an inoperable cancer destroying their bodies, they were left to suffer.

SUFFERING WOULD BE INEVITABLE.

" Fearfully they waited to hear God's response. And in the background, the serpent celebrated "

Sin's arrival had created a great divide that tore them apart and separated them from God's perfect loving nature,

> **"** ...like falling from the rapture
> and intimacy of a honeymoon
> into the emptiness and longing of divorce. **"**

Only in their innocent perfection had they been able to experience an unbroken relationship with God's heart, but now, through their rebellion and guilt, that would be impossible.

Carried away by emotions they had never felt before, Adam and his wife were incapable of verbalizing what they felt. They had never experienced anxiety. They had never walked in shame. They had never tasted guilt. It was the poisoning of their souls. Fearfully they waited to hear God's response. And in the background, the serpent celebrated.

Having meddled in the affairs of God before, the serpent was no stranger to all of this. However, unlike when he rejected God, this time he felt he had the upper hand.

Satan had seen God respond to rebellion before. Remembering his own rejection of the Creator, this time his confidence grew. He found comfort in assuming that God would respond to the humans the same way He had to him—with total and utter rejection. Not to mention, he had been one of the most beautiful creations in all the heavens—in fact, the most beautiful, far more lovely than these weak creatures. He had walked in the presence of God and shone like the stars. Yet God still saw fit to cast him out of heaven and remove him from His presence. As haunting as those memories were, they now served as source of encouragement as Satan anticipated a similar result for mankind. Such an outcome would mark the end for mankind and the beginning of everything Satan had sought in heaven. Upon God's rejection of mankind, God would effectively remove Himself from their presence entirely. Satan would be left with the opportunity to finally rule supreme, becoming the ultimate authority and symbol of beauty he so desperately longed to be.

As Satan's mind relished the thought of certain victory, the minds of Adam and his wife froze with uncertainty.

And not for a moment was a single one of these details overlooked by God. Aware of each thought and potential outcome, finally He responded.

It's paramount that we recognize the weight of God's words as we read the following section in the story. His authority was not weak and His voice was far from monotone. For it was from deep within His pain and overflowing with passion that He spoke these unanticipated words...

 Genesis 3:14–15

These verses appear to begin as we might hope, with wrath, doom, and vengeance. However, out of nowhere things change. Suddenly God starts talking about the woman and her seed or offspring. *Where is this going? What happened to wrath? This isn't the powerful response we anticipated!*

Although verse 15 might not outline immediate destruction, we do discover that God's response is far more powerful than any angry retort.

Through His words in verse 15, God snatched creation from the hopeless state sin threatened to leave it in. Rather than condemning it for its actions, He ignited it with hope. With words directed at the serpent but meant for all to hear, God delivered a calculated promise, and in doing so, He left the world wondering *"Could this be true?!"*

For Adam and his wife, God's words would have left them in disbelief. Satan would have recoiled in wondrous rage, thinking, *What does He mean, the woman's offspring will crush me? Why is He not throwing out these vermin as He did me?!* But Satan already knew the answer, and its truth began to terrorize him. **He had horribly underestimated God's love for mankind.**

The words God spoke in verse 15 were not just words; they were prophecy, dripping with unrelenting love for mankind and declaring what would come. God was pronouncing victory over Satan, proclaiming that although others (the serpent's seed or offspring) would wage war against the welfare of mankind and the will of God, God would supply a descendant who would come from mankind (woman's offspring or seed). This seed of the woman would fight the serpent's influence, causing hostility and enmity between the two, and would ultimately claim victory, not just over Satan but over Satan, sin, and death, resulting in the crushing and bruising of the serpent's skull.

Inside that moment, through those words, as only He could, God created again—this time creating hope inside a situation that had none. God spoke life when sin threatened to choke it out, and He declared the renewal of all that was broken. There would be a way to shatter the chains of sin that wrapped around earth!

> **" ...words that were spoken with such authority, as a punishment to the serpent, met their ears with the intimacy of a whisper and the intent of a wedding vow... "**

As Adam and his wife heard this proclamation, they found themselves speechless as they tried to understand what was happening. Slowly, as the truth of this promise was illuminated in their minds, a new spark ignited in their hearts.

After all God had given them and the way they had rejected Him, they knew He had every right to leave them to suffer, but He was refusing! He was not done with them. He was going to correct their error. He was pursuing them! He was giving them life, again! ***What kind of love was this? How could they deserve a God so faithful?*** His promise to redeem gave them strength for today and hope for tomorrow. Instantly His words became central to their lives.

Those words that were spoken with such authority, as a punishment to the serpent, met their ears with the intimacy of a whisper and the intent of a wedding vow, as they heard God assure them, **"You are my creation. I will never abandon you. I created you for Myself, and I will fix what you have done. In My time I will provide the one who will make right all that has gone wrong. I will never leave you nor forsake you. I love you, My children."**

God's declaration was far greater than retaliation, His love deeper than retribution! He took control of mankind's ignorance and foreshadowed things to come—announcing the provision of a cure for the sin and guilt that would plague the world.

Understanding God's desire to pursue His creation and restore the broken relationship brings such passion to the story. We wouldn't want to read it any other way. The power in His words was immense, revealing that He had a plan.

As astounding as the moment was, it did not excuse Adam and his wife.

SUDDENLY, THEY DETECTED A CHANGE IN ATMOSPHERE AS GOD SHIFTED HIS ATTENTION IN THEIR DIRECTION.

CHAPTER 9

AS GOD'S WORDS SENT AN UNANTICIPATED SHOCKWAVE THROUGH all of creation, the serpent made his exit in anger, leaving Adam and his wife to process what had happened.

As they searched one another for an explanation, their gaze was suddenly interrupted by the realization that they were no longer mere witnesses to God's response. His focus was now on them. Standing before their Creator, they were left to face the consequences of their decision. Everything was about to change.

A new and nauseating emotion grew inside them, an emotion that consumed them. Struggling to understand the power of what they felt, Adam and his wife wanted nothing more than to escape it, but standing in God's perfect presence, the misery they felt only grew more pronounced.

THEY FELT HOPELESS.

With His eyes fixed on them, they realized it was impossible not to feel this way. God's presence stirred their emotions, and against the backdrop of His perfection, every fibre of their being had been exposed. Next to their flawless Creator, their denial of His commandment was black ink on white paper—a burden too heavy to carry. There was no way to deny the truth. They were at fault. Guilty as charged. What came next would not be good.

 Genesis 3:16-24

Banished! Adam and Eve were torn from the home they had been made for, never to return.

As they walked away from the garden, it transformed from a beautifully inhabited sanctuary to a desolate fortress.

As painful as it was, their removal further revealed God's provision. By banishing them, He ensured they could never eat from the Tree of Life and secure eternal life. At this point, eternal life would only trap them in a state of sin and separation forever.

A flaming sword and mighty angels, known as cherubim, then defended the garden. Commonly associated with the throne of God or the presence of God (**Isaiah 37:16; Ezekiel 10:4; 2 Chronicles 3:10; 2 Kings 19:15**), cherubim were visually overwhelming entities, depicted as colossal figures endowed with magnificent wings, human arms, a quartet of faces, and bodies covered with eyes (**Ezekiel 10:12–14**). There would be no return to the Garden of Eden.

Adam and Eve's first steps *away* from their home were their first steps *towards* God's promise to redeem, though it did not feel like it. As they walked together, hand in hand, away from the garden and all its beauty, they trudged woefully towards a new life filled with uncertainty.

Reflecting on how quickly things had changed, they realized that their new life would be far more complicated than what they had known. Sin had affected every detail of their existence. It was hauntingly clear that sin had the ability to destroy what was meant for good—and quickly.

Not only had sin brought destruction to their own lives, they now realized it had infected all of creation. Seeping out from one tree in the centre of the garden, it poured over the earth like oil, covering everything in a thick, lifeless coat and sinking into the core of all that was. Feeling sin's influence, all of creation would now protest its effects. The oceans would surge in anger, mountains would erupt in disapproval, fields would withhold crops for the hungry, and the ground would quake and shift like muscles held tight with rage. The whole earth would now groan like a woman in childbirth (**Romans 8:22**).

Shocked by such a drastic fall from glory, Adam and Eve fell silent. As they tried to process all the ways sin had twisted the garden's innocents—twisted their innocence—their imaginations ran wild.

Walking beside her husband, Eve reflected on the original purpose of her relationship with him. Adam had been a gift to her, and she was to him. He was someone to share passion with, to laugh with and love. But now, sin would alter this great treasure. With sin's presence, Eve, and every woman after her, would endure a strain in her relationship with her husband—desiring to be over him, to lead him and to be in control (**Genesis 3:16**). Eve sensed immediate tension in her once-perfect relationship. She began to fear that, over time, she might come to despise Adam and reject his protection and guidance entirely. *What would that look like?*

Thinking through such a scenario, Eve wondered how Adam would respond. What if he retaliated through force? What if he belittled her in a skewed attempt at being her protector? Such a situation would leave both parties guilty of abusing their gift of companionship. Their relationship now faced threats from both sides. Relationships had been impacted by sin—forever.

As Eve's mind wrestled with this new dynamic, her thoughts progressed to another dreadful reality. Sin would now play a horrible role in childbearing. Now birth would come with excruciating pain. Bearing a child would undoubtably leave its mark on the female body. Would this scare women away? The beautiful celebration of life that it was might be lost on them. Robbed of its pure joy, the gift and miracle of bringing forth life had been altered—horribly warped by sin—forever.

These new pains of birth reminded Eve how sin now threatened sexuality. No longer would sex be the invigorating celebration of a married couple's uncontainable and intensifying love for one another. Rather, sin threatened to turn sex into little more than a pursuit for personal pleasure, a tool used for gain and even punishment. Sin threatened relational intimacy, and, if misused, sex would bring with it the baggage of guilt, shame, regret, and a distorted concept of intimacy. Something intended for such intimacy and fearless enjoyment would now break the hearts of many. Undoubtedly, sin had distorted sex and its original purpose—forever.

As these thoughts slowly poured through Eve's mind like concrete, Adam trod sombrely beside her, no less weighed down by his own discoveries.

Adam recalled the way he and Eve had somewhat effortlessly enjoyed the bounty of the garden. Sin would now make reaping and harvesting a laborious task. Despairingly, he knew he had waved goodbye to the carefree, naked, frolicking ways of the garden. Work would now be cumbersome. Thorns and toil had changed his task of overseeing creation. The gift of dominion over the earth had been disfigured by sin—forever.

Adam's mind wrestled with the unknown challenges that awaited him, until another memory surfaced in his mind: the warning God had originally given him—of death. Adam had ignored the warning, and now he would return to the dust from which he had been formed. Death for him and Eve was inevitable, unavoidable, and inescapable. *But when?*

And how? In an instant, the frailty of life consumed his every thought, overshadowing all other worries. Death was something he had never considered, never imagined, never understood, but now, incapable of escaping it, it was as real as the ground beneath his feet. All of mankind would taste death, an unnecessary consequence they had chosen. Life as they had known had been pillaged by sin—forever.

Overwhelmed by their thoughts and startling new emotions, Adam and Eve reluctantly moved farther and farther from the garden. Beneath their feet, the soft garden floor that had once cushioned their soles began to break apart, replaced by hot desert sand.

Without speaking a single word, Adam and Eve knew that they both understood their desperate state. Moving forward with an overwhelming sense of emptiness, it was as if the air they breathed lacked something it once had. Something they began to crave.

How can we continue like this? What is our purpose? The very one they needed, the one who filled the earth with its spark and spoke them into existence—they had rejected Him.

> **"They had rejected a relationship with God and ignored His counsel in exchange for what they now felt —a longing and desperate need for Him. "**

Thus marked the beginning of Day 1 outside of the garden, with the earth so twisted, its original beauty seemed hard to recognize. Clouds of worry settled over their hearts. Fear and anxiety told them they should just give up. Yet somehow, strength was renewed, as long as they remembered God had promised to fix this.

With flowers less vibrant, tree branches sagging, and a grey hue washing over everything, Adam and Eve marched on. The garden shrank into nothing but a faint mark on the horizon, a distant memory and a reminder of what life was supposed to be like. Unable to fight it any longer, they couldn't ignore how desperately their hearts longed to be back there. They wanted nothing but to experience life as they had been made to.

No longer able to move, in light of their helplessness, they broke down. Heavy sobs burst from their lips as they sank to their knees. They had never shed tears of pain before, only joy. Though their weeping had no words, the cry that rose from their hearts proclaimed, *"This is wrong! I need help! Can't someone take me home?"*

And as sin aimed to eradicate them entirely...

**THIS CRY WOULD
ONLY GROW LOUDER WITH TIME.**

CHAPTER 10

IT'S HARD TO KNOW FOR CERTAIN WHERE ADAM AND EVE SETTLED. Tradition places them somewhere inside the borders of modern-day Iran, Iraq, Saudi Arabia, or Syria.

POTENTIAL VICINITY THEY MADE THEIR NEW HOME IN.

TURKEY

NICOSIA

SYRIA

TEHRAN

BAGHDAD

LEBANON   DAMASCUS

IRAQ

JERUSALEM   AMMAN

PALESTINE

IRAN

JORDAN   KUWAIT

ISRAEL

KUWAIT

CAIRO

EGYPT

MANAMA

RIYADH   BAHRAIN

ABU DHABI

QATAR

MUSC

UAE

SAUDI ARABIA

OMAN

MODERN DAY LOCATIONS

GENERAL AREA

POTENTIAL TRAVEL ROUTES

BIBLICAL LOCATIONS

Locations not exact. Not for navigational purposes.

SANAA   YEMEN

As they staggered along for what may have been days, deciding where home would be likely led to the young couple's first disputes. Oftentimes, travel and directions are unstable territory for the best of couples. But after heated discussions over where they should go and whether or not they wanted waterfront property or open pasture, eventually they embraced a new location.

THEY WASTED NO TIME SETTLING IN, AND SOON CHILDREN ARRIVED.

" The first man to die on earth did so at the hands of his brother. "

With the arrival of two boys, the world's first parents were ecstatic. Marvelling over what had just happened, the awe of new life left them wondering, *What kind of miraculous event have we just been part of?* Though the births had surely been painful, sin had not completely removed the joy of bringing forth new life.

Their boys were a gift from God, and Adam and Eve cherished them deeply. As a result, they soon learn that the more you love something, the more susceptible you are to being hurt by it. And as any long-time parent knows, a father and mother are only as happy as their saddest child. With sin on the prowl, this small family would once again feel its impact as it left everyone a victim of its influence.

 **1 Peter 5:8**

 **Genesis 4:1–8**

In a moment of blind rage Adam and Eve's family was ripped apart. The anguish they felt over the loss of their child was immense, especially due to the fashion in which it happened.

Confusion over the painful events plagued husband and wife. The guilt-laden thought that this had all been their fault threatened to consume them and may have led Adam and Eve into a state of frustration with God, wondering, *Where has He been in the midst of all this? If He had only looked upon Cain with more favour, this never would have happened! Has there been a shift in God's character? Why the favouritism?*

As confused as they may have been, Adam and Eve eventually learned that God's interaction with Cain had nothing to do with favouritism. Instead, it revealed that God not only looks at a man's actions but, more importantly, He observes the heart behind the actions. It didn't take them long to realize that the offerings their sons had brought God displayed the difference in heart Cain and Abel had towards their Creator.

By bringing God large portions of what he profited from, Abel had revealed thankfulness for God's blessings in his life. In contrast, Cain's miniscule portion showed that his offering was nothing more than an act of duty and responsibility. God had not scorned Cain over the amount. In no way was He insisting that the *more* you bring, the *happier* He is. In fact, at no point had God even asked the brothers to bring Him any offering. Their offerings were prompted by their own desires. God was not disappointed in the amount; He was disappointed in Cain's heart.

Even though sin had caused a separation between God and mankind, Abel brought large offerings that showed gratitude and thankfulness for God's provision. He gave God the best he had to offer—a complimentary present out of love. Cain, however, came to God without sincerity and thankfulness. It was as if he believed God demanded sacrifice and heartless submission, though He had not asked for anything so grotesque. Worse yet, Cain appeared to view God as a genie in a lamp, believing that if he appeased God with gifts, God would bless him.

Such a view of God showed that Cain was confused. His view of God had been affected by sin. God did not desire a "you scratch my back, I'll scratch yours" arrangement; He wanted relationship. He had already shown that even when they turned their backs on Him, He would lay His hand on their shoulder in comfort. Therefore, He desired a heart of gratitude, like Abel's—a heart of thanksgiving (**1 John 3:12**).

Cain's actions were devastating to God, and God's reaction was not one of condemnation but mostly of correction. God's response to Cain was an offering of His own, as if to say, **"Dear Cain, you have missed the point of My love and provision."**

As the story progresses we will continue to see that God desires sincere love and a cheerful giver (**2 Corinthians 9:7**), someone who embraces Him out of gratitude, not duty (**Psalm 50:9–14; Psalm 50:23; Exodus 25:2**). God wanted Cain to choose Him *freely*, the same way He had wanted Adam and Eve to freely choose Him over the tree. But, just like his parents, Cain missed the point.

Quickly, the absence of gratefulness in his life became a snare. Refusing to look at his own heart for error, Cain pointed fingers at his brother. Avoiding self-examination at any cost (another pattern his parents set back in **Genesis 3:12–13**), Cain began to despise Abel. However, God did not leave Cain blind to his own rage. In another display of His grace, God reached out to Cain with a warning in **Genesis 4:6-8**. God knew sin's poison and encouraged Cain to identify what was happening, but it was to no avail.

Like his parents before him, Cain paid no attention to God's warning. Rather, it only fuelled his rage—as he lured his brother into the field.

Cain's rejection of God's warning created an opportunity for sin to make its grip on him even tighter. Suffocated by sin and emboldened by anger, he then set about the task of mimicking a similar chokehold grip on his brother. Creation continued to fall.

 **Genesis 4:9-16**

In a cold, dramatic fashion, Abel's story came to an end.

> **"**The first man
> to die on earth did so
> at the hands of his brother.**"**

The level of resentment that must have boiled inside of Cain would have terrified even him.

Since they were two of the few people on earth, it's no stretch of the imagination to picture these brothers spending lots of time together. With no one else to play with, no one else to rely on, Cain and Abel would have looked to each other. But somewhere in his anger, that no longer mattered to Cain. His hatred towards Abel blinded him to anything they shared. Yet God still refused to withhold His grace and mercy from this broken man. After all he had done, God sought out Cain.

Though Cain faced consequences for his actions, God showed him mercy by giving him a peculiar marking—a sign of mercy, despite his error. Whatever the marking was, whether Cain viewed it as a blessing is unclear. Regardless, God sent him away and ensured he would never endure the same fate he had bestowed on his brother.

As their remaining son disappeared into the distance, Adam and Eve buried the other and mourned the loss of both boys. Launched back to where they had begun, once again they were alone.

Aching and confused, their homesickness for the garden found new depths. Wishing they didn't have to feel the way they did...

THEY WOULD HAVE GIVEN ANYTHING TO BE BACK WHERE THEY BELONGED.

CHAPTER 11

WITH CAIN TRAVELLING EAST, PUTTING DISTANCE BETWEEN HIM and his parents, man's boundaries on earth expanded. With the original family split in two, the story would only get more dynamic.

For Adam and Eve, the loss of their sons hit the reset button on their lives. Thrust back into the same position they had been in after leaving the garden, they were all alone. As for Cain, removed from his family and filled with despair, as he wandered the land he began the task of establishing himself the same way his parents had—and the population increased.

 **Genesis 4:17–24**

WITH POPULATION GROWTH, LIFE ON EARTH BECAME MORE AND MORE DIVERSE.

To showcase this, the story uses genealogies to highlight the changes. Although genealogies are often viewed as boring, they play a central role in storytelling by offering insight into the lives of the people.

Starting with Cain's genealogy, we're able to make many observations and one disturbing discovery. One look at Cain's family tree, combined with the fact that his parents were the only other people mentioned on earth, and we arrive at a question we're almost afraid to ask: *Where did Cain find his wife?*

Fearing the worst, unless events transpired that were not recorded, our nightmares seem to be true. It seems that, most likely, Cain locked down a sister or an *extremely* close relative for a wife. As disturbing as this is, it should be noted that the culture early in the Bible was vastly different from our own.

In the early years of the story, it was not viewed as wrong or abnormal to take a relative in marriage; neither was it forbidden. Although it's disturbing to consider, there's a chance that marriage to relatives was not as risky due to an absence of genetic defects and birth complications. The bottom line is, regardless of how it happened or whether or not we like it, Cain found himself a wife, and his family was on the rise. Displaying growth over six generations, the genealogy leads us to Cain's great-great-great-great grandchild, Lamech.

This may not seem impressive at first, but what we learn about Cain's family is that these six generations, from Cain to Lamech, covered a 1,500-year time frame. In today's culture it would be a stretch for six generations to span more than 200 years. But, by shifting our attention back to Adam and Eve, the numbers start to make more sense.

Back where we left them, outside the garden, aching over Abel's death and the departure of Cain, Adam and Eve were busy rebuilding their lives a second time. Blessed with the arrival of another son, their family was back on the rise and growing tremendously, with some of their offspring surviving well into their *900s*.

 Genesis 4:25–5:32

Without question, the monotony of genealogies can be a real story killer. As cumbersome as they are, they cannot be ignored, because the Bible communicates *a lot* of information through them.

Stepping away from the narrative for a moment, to help grasp how important genealogies are we need to understand their role in storytelling.

Nowadays, when the author of a book wants to jump ahead in a story he's writing, he only needs to make a statement like "fifteen years later." From this statement, readers know that there's been a time change, which usually includes a change in society, culture, technology, fads, and so on. A lot can be communicated through a jump on the calendar. Similarly, if an author ever needs to highlight a family's lineage, he could use a family tree to do so. Although Moses, the writer of Genesis, did not use either of these techniques, the information provided in the genealogies helps us build family trees and arrive at an understanding that the next part in the story happened "however many years later." Here's how it works.

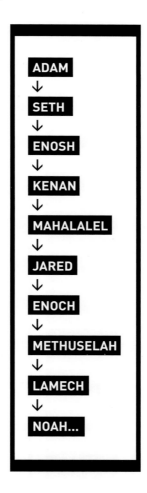

ADAM
↓
SETH
↓
ENOSH
↓
KENAN
↓
MAHALALEL
↓
JARED
↓
ENOCH
↓
METHUSELAH
↓
LAMECH
↓
NOAH...

By using the names listed in Genesis chapter 5, we can develop a family tree of the men who succeeded Adam, right down to the tenth generation. Ending with a man named Noah, the genealogy in Genesis 5 takes us to the *next* great figure in the story (Adam's great-great-great-great-great-great-great grandchild). However, before the story picks up again with Noah, the genealogy tells us more, as a way of helping us fill in the gaps.

Though many generations separated Adam and Noah, the numbers in the genealogy can help us to develop a context of what life on earth was like at Noah's arrival.

Through the genealogy in Genesis 5 we can take each man's age when he died (Seth: 912), and add it to the age his father was when he was born (912+130=1,042). In doing so, the numbers we arrive at help us establish a timeline for the story. We quickly discover that the genealogies aren't included to test our commitment to reading the Bible; rather, they are leading us to a new moment in time, showing us there had been cultural changes, and communicating how long it had been *since* Adam's birth and the beginning of the story.

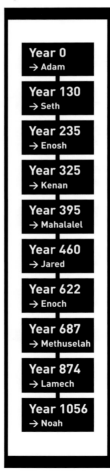

Year 0
→ Adam

Year 130
→ Seth

Year 235
→ Enosh

Year 325
→ Kenan

Year 395
→ Mahalalel

Year 460
→ Jared

Year 622
→ Enoch

Year 687
→ Methuselah

Year 874
→ Lamech

Year 1056
→ Noah

Through these numbers we discover that Adam's genealogy covers an incredible length of time. From the birth of Seth to the birth of Noah, the story jumps 926 years. If this were a movie, the screen would fade to black at the birth of Seth, and before opening the next scene with Noah, the words "926 years later" would flash across the screen. Given these numbers from Adam's family, we now learn a few things about Cain's lineage.

If Cain's genealogy remotely reflected Adam's, his son Lamech would have been born around 400 years *after* our story began (around the same time as Jared was born). These "boring" family histories then reveal to us that there has been a 1,000 to 1,500-year gap *since* creation, which raises the questions, *What was life like for Noah compared to Adam? What did the world look like 1,056 years after our story began in the garden?*

WHAT WAS LIFE LIKE FOR YOUNG NOAH AS OUR STORY FOCUSES ON HIM AND HIS FAMILY?

CHAPTER 12

THROUGH SEEMINGLY UNNECESSARY GENEALOGIES, OUR STORY jumps over 1,000 years, from the birth of Adam to a man named Noah. That's roughly 1,000 years since man was first placed in the garden, roughly 1,000 years since creation fell from what it was meant to be, and roughly 1,000 years since God had promised the earth "I will fix this."

Before we pick up the narrative with Noah and his family, it's important to try to establish what society looked like in our quickly advancing story. The timeline and genealogy can also help us develop a picture of what society looked like for Noah and his family, although it may be somewhat inconclusive.

By taking information from Genesis 5 and applying a few modern-day statistics, we can note a drastic spike in the population, which will help explain the cultural advances made since the time of Adam and Eve.

Even though the genealogies in the Bible usually only list male descendants, each family undoubtedly had other children. The question is, how many? This is where numbers get inconclusive.

Using today's standard of living, let's assume that the average family has roughly 2.5 kids. For simplicity's sake, we're going to round that number up to three children per family (cpf).

Embracing a three-cpf demographic, let's assume that this was the pattern for Adam and all his succeeding generations. If this were true, by the time Noah was born, the population increase would have been considerable. With growth at this pace, there would have been an estimated population of 19,683 when Noah was born. Not exactly earth-shattering numbers. Today, a city this size has trouble earning a spot on a map; however, it does reveal that Noah was far from alone.

To develop this number further, we need to take a few variables into consideration since society has changed drastically. Unlike today, people in our story didn't have access to birth control. Combine this with the instructions God had given to *"multiply and fill the earth"* (**Genesis 1:28**), and without being drastic, let's raise the average cpf number by one, bringing it to four.

Another detail to consider as we contemplate population growth is life expectancy. Today's life expectancy leaves parents roughly a fifty-year window to have children. However, at the time of our story, people were having children well into their 100s and even 200s. This large time frame then *doubles* the window of opportunity for family growth, and perhaps a few "oopsy-daisy" babies. Applying this to our current average of four cpf, we now sit at eight—sometimes more, sometimes less.

ADAM	TODAY	THEN
	3	8
	9	64
	27	512
	81	4096
	243	32 768
	729	262 144
	2,187	2 097 152
	6,561	16 777 216
NOAH	19,683	134 217 728

Restructuring our population chart with these numbers, it now looks like this: 134 million people on earth at the time Noah was born! All extending from one couple! These numbers are astounding and still have room for growth, as they do not include the descendants of Cain (who were potentially increasing at a similar rate). They also do not take into account men like Lamech, who was pumping out families from two wives.

Obviously, there were deaths, barren women, and other variables that would cause a decrease in this number, but regardless, the point that we need to recognize is that upon Noah's arrival, the world was well populated.

With such a great stretch of time interrupting the storyline and so many people walking the earth, it's now easy to understand how men and women had developed to the point of making instruments and forming iron (**Genesis 4:21–22**).

With numbers rising and the calendar flipped past the first millennia, the stage was set for Noah. In a culture that had cities, developing architecture, men and women known for their traits, and a whole new social structure, Noah and his family faced a significantly different world than Adam and Eve had. The arrival of Noah's sons added a whole new generation to the earth, one that potentially tipped the scales at over one billion people.

As Genesis 5 ends and the scene fades to black, Genesis 6 now begins, but not before the words "1,556 years *since* Adam's birth" float across the screen.

...A WHOLE NEW GENERATION TO THE EARTH.

CHAPTER 13

THE BIRTH OF NOAH'S SONS MARKED A 1,500-YEAR GAP IN OUR quickly developing story. At a time where the earth's population catapulted from two people to potentially over one billion, it was apparent that mankind had greatly evolved (and I don't mean from monkeys to humans).

Mankind had progressed from simpler ways of life to more advanced technology, acquiring skills in trades and the arts. Yet, amidst the advances, one situation was not improving.

Having embedded itself into the heart of mankind back in the garden, sin's influence was strong. It worked like an incurable virus that set in at birth and saw every man, woman, and child as a suitable host. The ballooning population was a petri dish that cultivated sin. It was an epidemic.

NO ONE WAS EXEMPT.

Everyone on earth was exposed, oblivious to the fact that they were made for something different. Naively believing they were living life freely, they couldn't have been more wrong. The only thing scarier than having a fatal disease is having one and thinking you don't. Society was about to realize they were running frantically towards destruction— incapable of gaining control.

 Genesis 6:1–3

If the genealogy didn't give us enough detail about what life was like at the time of Noah, the opening record of Genesis 6 tells us what we need to know. Things had gone from bad to worse, a point made abundantly clear through the actions of the "sons of God."

" The only thing scarier
than having a fatal disease
is having one and thinking you don't "

Though the referral to the "sons of God" may be confusing, this term is used on numerous occasions in the Bible's story (Job 2:1, Matthew 5:9; Romans 8:14; Galatians 3:26 ESV). Most commonly the biblical use of this term is for referring to humans who followed God, trusted God, and obeyed Him. However, it's used to reference men, women, and angels. Anyone who was created by God and followed Him is considered a Son of God. Something similar can be seen in our country. It is filled with varying ethnicities, yet we are all referred to as Canadians.

A second meaning for the peculiar wording "sons of God" and "daughters of men" is found in Genesis. At the time of creation, although both men and women were created in God's image, Genesis highlights man's formation from the breath of God (son of God, Luke 3:38), and woman's creation from the side of man (daughter of man).

Understanding this terminology helps us discover that, at this point in the story, men who had been designed by God, designed for God, and possibly even served Him, no longer cared for Him. Mankind had turned from their Creator and were consumed with a lust for what He'd created. They had no interest in God's presence. God's promises and provisions had fallen off their radar. The result of their actions reveals that society had entered a deplorable state of moral decay.

For men, their overwhelming desire for women began to consume them. Women became nothing more than tools for sexual fulfillment. Filled with a desire for flesh, men did as they saw fit. Men everywhere abandoned God to worship the gifts He had given.

Destroying the beauty inside male and female relationships, just as Eve had feared, they took whomever they wanted whenever they wanted however they wanted. Forced marriages and sexual assault became a lifestyle norm. Society was barbaric.

God saw the terror in this way of life. Despite how far His creation had fallen, He never abandoned them. Watching the ones He loved become blinded by sin grieved His heart.

Amidst this time of darkness, the story takes time to note a people of distinction.

Genesis 6:4

A powerful people still talked about as Moses wrote Genesis, the Nephilim are the stuff of legends. For people familiar with the Bible's story, the Nephilim have long been a topic of confusion. The notes in some Bible translations present them as the offspring of an unholy union between angels ("sons of God") and humans ("women of men"). Others believe the Nephilim were purely human in nature.* In either case, it's always agreed that they were tall, large, and powerful—a lineage of warriors, leaders, rebels, villains, and nobility. It would be like looking at a family tree filled with men like William Wallace, Achilles, King Leonidas, Thor, Hercules, Maximus, Aragorn, Rambo, and Lancelot. This was a family of renown. Their impact had been legendary, leading people to believe there might be truth behind mythological stories of powerful godlike warriors.

Despite how great the Nephilim had been, they clearly didn't help point mankind back to their Creator. God was burdened over society. No longer able to watch men and women run confused, further from their design, He had to do something. Things needed to change. A timeline would be set. A countdown would begin, and 120 years from this point,

THE DARKNESS WOULD END.

*To learn more about the Nephilim go to www.Q830.com/more

CHAPTER 14

AS CREATION FRANTICALLY TORE ITSELF APART, GOD SEARCHED the intentions of those He loved and found only wickedness. *Surely someone remained whose motives were pure? Had everyone failed to understand the life they had been given? Had the cancer of sin grown too large? Had they all gone blind?*

 **Genesis 6:5–8**

Heartbroken. How agonizing it would have been for God to arrive at such a verdict! Distraught over the creation that *He* had breathed to life, moulded with *His* hands, and placed *His* image inside, their rejection after all He had done and everything He had offered led Him to ache over their existence.

God's heartache for His creation had reached a breaking point. Pained by His passionate desire for men and women to return His love and trust Him, He only wanted them to recognize the destruction they heaped on themselves and the beautiful life He had to offer. He knew they were not designed for this. Like a prince consumed with the purest love for his princess yet left to watch his beloved run into the arms of another who would belittle her, beat her, and enslave her, God could not bear to watch any longer.

Meanwhile, mankind paid no attention. Running from their original design, they had created a lifestyle that was a dark contrast to the garden they were meant for. Caught up in the mayhem, at no point were they contemplating a return to God.

THEIR END WAS NEAR.

At this point in the story it's difficult not to ask, *How can this be true? What about God's promise to redeem? How would wiping out mankind accomplish His goal of removing sin's cancerous grip on creation?* As valid as these questions might be, the real question is, *How could God bring His promise of redemption to a people who desired nothing from Him?* That would only be Him forcing His love upon them when they did not want it, the very thing He set out *not* to do in the garden. So rather than force His love and provision into their lives, He gave them what they thought they wanted. If darkness was the life they chose, darkness they would have.

Like radiation therapy focuses on the cancerous cells inside the suffering body of a human, God decided to focus on the cells on earth that were consumed by sin and made creation suffer. Though it would hurt the collective body, by attacking the cancer God would give creation a fighting chance at survival—before the disease destroyed everything. From this multitude God would show His love and mercy to one man, Noah. Through Noah, God's promise to redeem would continue—transforming Noah into the last "healthy" cell on earth...

RESPONSIBLE FOR REBUILDING LIFE.

CHAPTER 15

IT HAD BEEN 1,556 YEARS SINCE ADAM'S BIRTH (TWENTY YEARS since God had numbered man's days), and now our attention shifts to Noah, a 500-year-old man.

Noah found himself in the centre of the world's moral decay. As corruption ran mercilessly through the streets—like in a city filled with criminals and no authorities—sin bullied society and affected everyone. No one could be trusted. Yet, inside this dark world, God's grace shone on Noah like a lighthouse, guiding him into one of the most often-told stories of all time.

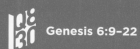 **Genesis 6:9–22**

When hearing stories as astounding as Noah's, we can have a tendency to dehumanize the people involved. There is a temptation to view Noah as nothing more than a character, perhaps fictitious in nature. Whenever we do this, we instantly drain the story of its meaning. It is a necessary reminder to pause and remember that Noah was just like us; he was human. This makes the magnitude of the task set before him overwhelming.

Today, there is no doubt that many of us have lofty goals we hope to accomplish. Perhaps it's to become a doctor, get accepted to an Ivy League school, become an astronaut, or win the presidential election. As lofty as these goals are, none of them compares to the task God had set before Noah.

Considering the ark's dimensions as given in the Bible, we know it was one massive structure. To try to wrap our minds around its magnitude, we could break it down like this: The ark would have been roughly half as wide as an NFL football field. It would have been thirty yards longer, including the end zones, and higher than the highest point of the goalposts. Building such a monstrous structure would be daunting for anyone. But the magnitude of Noah's preparation went *far* beyond swinging a hammer.

"Noah's preparation went far beyond swinging a hammer."

Reflecting on life today, if we discovered that it would be up to us and our immediate family to rebuild society from the ground up, wouldn't our to-do list have a lot more written on it than "Build a boat"?

With the amount of time we had been afforded, we would be wise to prepare as throughly as we could. There would be no one else to blame if we came stumbling out on the other side only to twiddle our thumbs and wonder "Okay, what now?" If we didn't ask a lot of questions in preparation, we would have to try to answer them later, by ourselves, without resources or Google.

Not oblivious to this, Noah would have asked as many questions as he could in preparation for post-flood life. Since society had developed greatly over 1,500 years, it's probable that he wanted to maintain as many cultural advances as he could. He wanted to make sure he dedicated time to learning how to create instruments and preserve music, information, knowledge, and technology, so that once the flood ended he wouldn't be stuck sitting on his porch playing spoons and blowing in an empty jug just to conjure up a rhythm. At the same time, Noah would have learned all that he could about building, manufacturing, and agriculture. He did everything he could to avoid years of trial and error so that when the flood ended, society didn't have to start all over again. This mental preparation resulted in countless hours dedicated to work beyond the ark. Noah wasn't just labouring like a coal miner, he was studying like a med student, building an ark *and* an education, all in hopes of becoming the best farmer, sailor, musician, animal trainer, tradesman, cook—you name it—that he could be.

As for the construction itself, there was another daunting task. With physically demanding hours packed full of missed nails, smashed thumbs, pinched fingers, pitch-covered hands, hair with tar in it, incorrectly measured cuts, unanticipated setbacks and a few good temper tantrums, Noah and his sons were about to endure more work related frustrations then we want to imagine. As anyone who's assembled anything (be it cheap furniture or a skyscraper) can attest, building projects never come together flawlessly.

If the mental and the physical demands were not enough, there was also the spiritual exhaustion he faced, as the Bible tells us Noah was also a preacher of righteousness (**2 Peter 2:5**). Noah knew God could have wiped out creation at any time, but since He hadn't, Noah knew that the 120-year time frame was not a countdown to destruction; rather, it was an opportunity graciously afforded mankind so they could turn back to God. This means Noah didn't work in silent disregard to the coming doom of the population, but he ached to get the message out! Noah understood that God wasn't sitting back anxiously awaiting the annihilation of His creation like the villain in a Bond movie. After everything the story revealed about God's character and love, there couldn't be a more error-filled thought. God desired that *everyone* would seek Him, that He might bless them. Their deaths were not for enjoyment but preservation. The flood was shattering His heart, and He mourned the fall of His creation. God wanted them to turn to Him, repent, and live, that He might bless them (**Ezekiel 18:23**).

God waited patiently over those years (**1 Peter 3:20**) as Noah preached a message that encouraged the people to seek God, pleading with them to forsake their evil ways and unrighteous thoughts so the Lord could have mercy on them (**Isaiah 55:6-7**). But the hearts of the people had grown cold, their minds were twisted, and their ears were deaf to Noah's warning. Noah saw hostility, not repentance. In light of all this, barely a day passed when Noah did not feel crushed by the weight of what was asked of him. His work demanded *all* of him, leading to exhausting days that drained him mentally, physically, and spiritually. These were far from the easiest 100 years of this 500-year-old man's life. The hard work and persecution weighed heavy on his soul.

Warning people that a flood was coming would be like going to Phoenix and telling everyone they are in danger of being wiped out by an avalanche. Noah's audience was both skeptical and unpleasant. The insults only multiplied due to the fact that there was no such thing as rain at that time. Up to this point in the story, water bubbled up from the ground through springs (**Genesis 2:5-6**). The thought of water suddenly falling from the sky and consuming earth was, well, unbelievable.

> **"**...like going to Phoenix
> and telling everyone they are in danger
> of being wiped out by an avalanche.**"**

Even in light of all this, Noah set out to fulfill what was asked of him—struggling physically and mentally, wrestling as much with himself as he was with others. During the quiet hours of many sleepless nights, it's not hard to imagine that he lay awake wondering, "Am I crazy? Did God really ask me to do this? How will water cover the entire world? Perhaps everyone else is right? What if they are? How am I going to get this all done? I'm not strong enough to do this. I'm 500! What's it going to be like when this is all over? I'm scared, I'm weak, I'm tired, I'm overwhelmed…"

Despite all the emotions and the fear of the unknown, Noah prevailed. He built the ark and remained firm in his faith. He did as God asked because greater than his fears, greater than his doubts, greater than his weaknesses, greater than his lack of understanding, and greater than any temptation to run was…

HIS REVERENT FAITH IN HIS CREATOR.

 **Hebrews 11:7**

CHAPTER 16

WORKING TIRELESSLY FOR THE 100 YEARS HE'D BEEN GIVEN, NOAH eventually accomplished all God instructed him to. As he scrambled through last-minute details and awaited final instructions, the rest of the world mulled about, oblivious to what would soon take place.

 Matthew 24:38

 Genesis 7:1–16

Instructed to enter the ark, Noah, his family, and countless animals crammed into their new home and braced for the floodwaters. They entered the ark seven days before the flood began, so those who watched Noah and his family disappear inside likely jeered and ridiculed all the more.

Their insults and opinions were voiced with great confidence, mocking the crazy faithfuls who cowered inside their desert-locked boat; that was, until the 1,656th year.

Using a calendar that counts *up* from our story's beginning (Adam's birth being year 0), rather than down from Christ's birth like the traditional BC calendar, our story was only 1,656 years old at this point. And on the seventeenth day of the second month of that year (believed to be spring on our calendar)...

THE RIDICULE AIMED AT NOAH AND HIS FAMILY ENDED.

"A cloud...then released an ever-increasing downpour from the heavens"

As water fell from the sky for the very first time and landed on the heads of the most boisterous mockers, mouths began to close. Beads of water then fell gently onto shoulders, hands, heads, and eventually faces as those outside the ark craned their necks and turned their eyes to the heavens in astonishment. Unaware that people would eventually call this form of water "rain," on that day everyone just knew the unanticipated occurrence of water's descent from the sky as their worst nightmare.

Instantly, with the kiss of that first raindrop, the atmosphere shifted—as if the world stood still for a moment. Suddenly everyone was shockingly aware of an ominous cloud that seemed to have crept in and covered the sky, a cloud that then released an ever-increasing downpour from the heavens.

As the rain persisted, it was clear that this was no coincidence. The showers developed into a torrent that flattened crops and exploded on impact. Wonder turned to panic, which gripped the hearts of everyone, everywhere. The scene outside the ark became frantic, and the level of terror rose along with the water.

Inside the ark, it was the first time Noah and his family had experienced weather like this as well. Despite their protection, concern blanketed their thoughts as they wondered if everything had been properly prepared for the first family cruise.

As rain's angry fists beat upon the ark with thunderous tones, Noah and his family grew worried, concerned for those outside the ark and leery about their own safety. Just when they imagined the pounding on the ark could not get louder, the booming swelled to new heights.

This new wave of noise did not hit the ark like rain, however; rather, its boom was far more concentrated, focused on one location. Noah soon realized that what he heard actually wasn't rain. As he pinpointed the source of the new sound, his heart sank…it was the door.

Outside the ark, bombarded with rain that fell like cords, not drops, barely able to stand, a multitude of people had gathered. Desperate for escape, they shouted in terror, willing to do whatever it would take to join Noah and his family.

For 100 years, Noah's voice had fallen on deaf ears, but now, the volume of the rain could not be ignored. Both hearing and seeing every word Noah had ever spoken, now they were listening.

> **"**The rain washed their doubts away
> like chalk on a sidewalk.
> But it was too late.**"**

From inside, Noah could discern muffled cries amidst the banging, and his heart wrenched at the realization that he could not help. God had shut him and his family in. There was no way to escape the ark. No one was getting in or out.

For those outside the ark, the rain continued without relent, overwhelming their senses and plugging their ears. They heard each drop that landed upon their heads with a knock. And although it was loud, louder still were the memories of every word Noah had spoken. He said this day would come.

Over the course of time, the desert terrain that surrounded them slowly turned to mud. Small streams appeared where once there were none. Those streams then became rivers that spread out their arms, cutting swaths through the land in an unforgiving manner.

As the rain continued, some people lost all hope. Wet, cold, unable to find shelter, and overwhelmed, some embraced their doom, while others continued to fight. People tried everything they could to escape the rain, the cold, and the torment of knowing they had chosen this.

As minutes turned to hours and hours to days, the rain remained steady—and the cries outside the ark grew quieter and quieter. Making a conscious effort to try to discern any sign of life on the other side, Noah could not ignore the fact that the pounding on the ark's door had gotten eerily weaker. Until one day, it stopped completely. One day it stopped, forever.

 **Genesis 7:17-24**

CHAPTER 17

SITTING IN THE ARK, NOAH AND HIS FAMILY COULDN'T IGNORE HOW quiet the rain seemed once it was no longer accompanied by the cries of those outside. Numbed by their circumstances and lost in a daze, as the ark shifted for the first time they were suddenly torn from their daydreams and unblinking stares. Their adventure in the rain had only begun.

As the ark lurched without warning, Noah and his family did what they could to steady themselves. As they stared at one another, confused, the ark released a loud moan, as if offering a response to their wonder. Creaking and rumbling, their wooden prison lunged aggressively, knocking everyone to their hands and knees. Searching for something sturdy to cling to, everyone fought for stability as questions, concerns, and fears grew.

As the ark continued to groan and quake, Noah's family thought their end might be near. Adding to the mayhem, the animals joined in the protest, trumpeting, howling, and cawing. The volume inside the ark reached new heights.

The aggressive movements of the boat had snapped stalls and sent animals piling into one another—the scene was chaotic. Like eight-year-olds playing soccer, the animals clustered in a panicked frenzy, a confusing mass of legs, limbs, and screams. The situation was more than Noah and his family could handle. Mentally and physically, they were ready to surrender, until, with one last protest, the mighty ship surged forward, corrected itself, and began to gently rock in the water. It had worked. The ark was now afloat, carried off by the rising waters.

As relieved as they felt, their success could only mean one thing— everything on earth would soon be gone. The realization that no one else on earth would escape this moment of chaos crashed down on Noah.

ONCE AGAIN, THE ARK GREW SILENT.

Overwhelmed and destroyed by the mighty flood, everything outside the ark—plants, animals, homes, and over one billion people—had been wiped from the planet. The devastating number of casualties would be like losing the entire country of India in less than forty days. Today, a tragedy of that magnitude would cause a 17 percent drop in the world's population, but during Noah's time, it was a 99.99 percent drop. The population plummeted from one billion to eight.

> **"**The devastating number of casualties would be like losing the entire country of India in less than forty days.**"**

A heartbreaking reality. No matter how badly we might hope for survivors, it's unreasonable to expect that anyone or anything outside the ark survived. The violence of the rain and mounting water pressure would have guaranteed no one lived.

Even if someone had lived into the latter days of the flood, their fight for survival would have required swimming inside choppy, aggressive water for a twenty-four-hour period, then repeating this process over and over again on a caloric intake of zero. The end result would be precisely what the story implies: no survivors. Beyond the inability of anyone or anything to maintain life on the surface, nothing below would have fared any better, getting crushed by the pressure.

Today, even though the ocean depth exceeds 36,000 feet, there is very little sea life below the first 50 feet due to the absence of sunlight and the increased pressure. By the time the flood reached its highest point and covered every mountaintop on earth, the additional water would have practically doubled the ocean depths. This remarkable amount of water would have placed extreme pressure upon anything beneath the surface, choking out all life.

The story makes it clear that all life had been destroyed. The world had been washed head to toe, and riding atop the devastation, the ark remained afloat, carrying eight people (and animals) whom God had chosen. Eight people, fighting to find their sea legs, with a daunting task ahead of them.

 **Genesis 8—9:17**

On the twenty-seventh day of the second month in the year 1657 (almost exactly one year since the rain began to fall), Noah and his family stepped out of the ark. Once their craft had docked upon the mountain ranges of Ararat, the crew of eight walked onto dry land for the first time in a while.

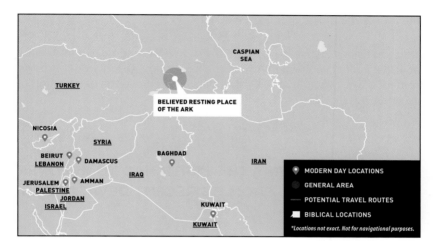

It's believed that the resting location of the ark was along the eastern borders of Turkey, where the mountain ranges still go by the name "Ararat."

Having exited the ark, Noah wasted no time showing God how thankful he was for His mercy and protection. Promptly, Noah offered God a sacrifice to display his gratitude, understanding that sin had caused the flood and he was not immune to its touch. Though he was labelled a righteous man, Noah was not without fault. Yet despite his shortcomings, God had shown him mercy.

God then blessed Noah and his family once more (and ultimately all of mankind). This blessing came by giving them permission to eat *everything*. This meant they were now allowed to eat meat. Prior to the flood, every person on earth had been a vegetarian. It's no wonder society had problems functioning properly, without the gift of bacon! More important than bacon, however, was the covenant God then made with all of humanity, for all time. Never again would He allow water to rise and destroy all that He had made. To guarantee that promise, He then gave the gift of the rainbow, His signature at the bottom of the contract.

As great as receiving bacon and the rainbow had been, or being the first person to eat bacon under a rainbow, there was another promise from God that was even greater. A promise that had not been forgotten by Noah. This covenant had been made 1,600 years before they walked off the ark—it was God's promise to redeem.

God was using Noah to bring about the promised child He had told Adam and Eve about. Somewhere, through Noah's family, God would provide someone who would fix the world's pain and remove the devastation of its sinful ways.

BUT FIRST, THE EARTH HAD TO RECOVER FROM ITS RECENT DEVASTATION.

CHAPTER 18

WITH THE WATER SUBSIDED, NOAH AND HIS FAMILY FOUND themselves wrestling a new flood—one of emotions and loneliness, as they adjusted to new life.

Initially, things were not bad. Noah and his family ran around with thankfulness, basking in their freedom as the sun's long-awaited touch sent pleasant tingles across their skin. Their noses joined in the excitement, celebrating clean air outside the floating barn. But as the days outside the ark progressed, the celebration dwindled. In no time at all they realized how different things were. As the animals bid farewell and spread across the land, an eerie silence followed their departure—a silence that spoke volumes and reminded Noah and his family just how alone they were.

As they worked through the solitude, trying to establish a new kind of normal, though there was a shortage of companions outside the family, one thing they did not take for granted was the privacy they had as couples. No longer confined to the ark, they embraced the extra privacy—and in their alone time, they embraced their spouses. Soon, Noah and his sons began fulfilling God's mandate to repopulate the world.

At the ripe old age of 600, it's probable that Noah wasn't as "inspired" to embrace his wife as his sons were to embrace theirs, so he dedicated his days to something other than building a boat or tending to animals. Even though he did not contribute to the growing numbers, before long (nine to twelve months, I assume), the population was on the rise. And Noah, a man of the soil, celebrated the arrival of grandkids and enjoyed the fruits of his own labour.

 Genesis 9:18-29

The encounter between Noah and Ham can be a peculiar one to read. A quick recount of the events post-flood unravels the scene like this:

Noah got off the ark.
Noah built an altar and sacrificed to God.
Noah planted a vineyard.
Noah harvested what was in the vineyard.
Noah made wine.
Noah drank the wine.
Noah drank more wine.
Noah got drunk.
Noah got naked (at home).
Noah went to sleep, drunk and naked—in his home.

Up to that point in the story, things were fairly straightforward—that is, until Ham came on the scene. Coincidently, Noah's son Ham showed up just in time to witness his father in his drunk-naked-sleeping state. Then Ham left the tent (which was Noah's home) and informed his brothers about what he had seen.

Although Noah's initial response can appear to be an overreaction, we need to understand the extent of what took place.

Even though Noah was in a drunken stupor, he was in the privacy of his own home. Ham's arrival was not a case of "unsuspecting child wanders innocently into Mom and Dad's room without knocking." In fact, Ham wasn't anywhere near childhood. He was well into his 100s. A man of 100 should know when it is and when it is not appropriate to enter someone's private quarters. Yet somehow, Ham "mysteriously" arrived at the foot of his father's bed, where Noah lay naked and unaware.

> **"The image of a 600-year-old body strewn across a bed should have haunted him for weeks!"**

The modern-day equivalent of this story could be a twenty-year-old waltzing knowingly into his father's bedroom. Now, perhaps it's just me, but I like to believe that most twenty-year-old males who think their father might be lying passed out naked on the other side of the door will avoid going into that room at all costs. And if by chance a poor young man still manages to stumble upon such a scene, I imagine it might be something he hesitates to tell his siblings. *Why?* Because his siblings don't want to hear it, and he shouldn't want to relive it! Seeing old naked Dad is not the kind of story you sit around and reminisce about. Rather, situations like this make family gatherings awkward for the next month or so. Ham should have suddenly been cutting conversations with his father short, avoiding eye contact, and waking up in a cold sweat. The image of a 600-year-old body strewn across a bed should have haunted him for weeks! However, sadly, oddly, and disturbingly enough, this was not how Ham reacted. Instead, he came out of the tent and proceeded to inform his brothers.

In contrast to Ham, Shem and Japheth understood the disgrace in this response. Out of love and respect, they took it upon themselves to protect their father. They honoured Noah by covering him up in his vulnerable state, even going so far as to walk backwards to avoid any unnecessary scarring in their own lives.

The next morning, having slept off his stupor, Noah was made aware of what had taken place. In outrage over the detestable actions of Ham, he cursed Ham's son, Canaan. The pain of this for Ham is something any parent can identify with, as few things cause a parent grief like watching their child suffer. This would be the last record of Noah's life.

The rest of Genesis is devoted to informing us of Noah's lineage. Noah died at the ripe age of 950, and his three sons proceeded to fill the earth. As their children grew into great nations, cultures began to develop—

LEADING MANKIND TOWARDS ANOTHER ISSUE THAT REQUIRED SOME *TRANSLATION.*

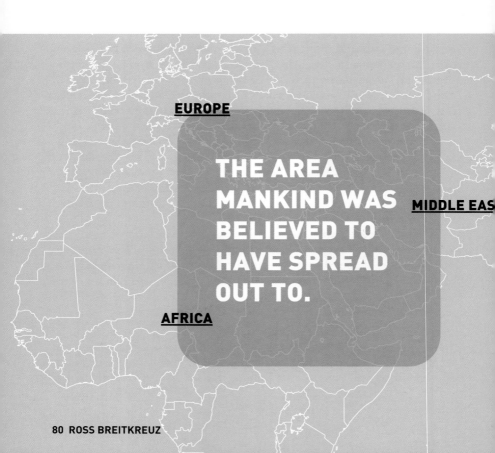

EUROPE

MIDDLE EAS

THE AREA MANKIND WAS BELIEVED TO HAVE SPREAD OUT TO.

AFRICA

CHAPTER 19

WITH THE FOCUS OF THE STORY SHIFTING FROM NOAH TO HIS descendants, we come to our second genealogy, as Genesis 10 reveals the people and nations that grew from Noah and his sons. Combining this genealogy with the one from Genesis 5, we discover that Genesis 10 is a continuation of Adam's family line.

Through the expansion of the genealogy, we see that the earth was once again being repopulated. Genesis 10 serves as our introduction to numerous nations and people groups that will continue to impact the story (for example, Canaanites, Hittites, Jebusites, and Amorites).

"A new dynamic environment was developing on earth."

Over the years this genealogy covers, the descendants of Japheth, Ham, and Shem spread out across the earth. Around this time, it is believed, mankind settled all over the Middle East, northeast Africa, and southeast Europe. A new dynamic environment was developing on earth.

 Genesis 10:1–32

The list of names in Genesis 10 can appear to be daunting to read and easy to forget. But when placed into the format of a family tree, this section of the story starts to have a lot more clarity. A breakdown of Genesis 10 can be seen in the following charts showcasing family growth across five generations. Though the genealogy will continue, before it does, Genesis 11 pauses to tell a story.

In a moment, our story will rewind itself and offer insight into the days mentioned in Genesis 10:25, during the life of Peleg, roughly 1,750 years since the start of the story (93 years after Noah and his family stepped off the ark). Soon we will learn about a moment known as the "division of the earth" that had a monumental impact. The tearing that society was about to experience would not just affect the people back then but would leave an imprint society still feels to this day.

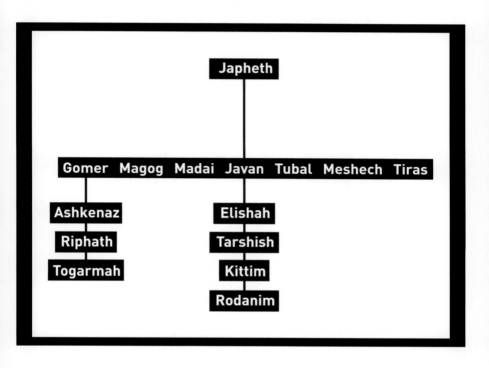

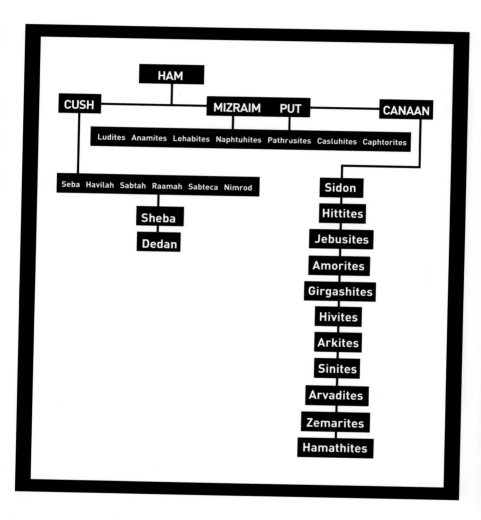

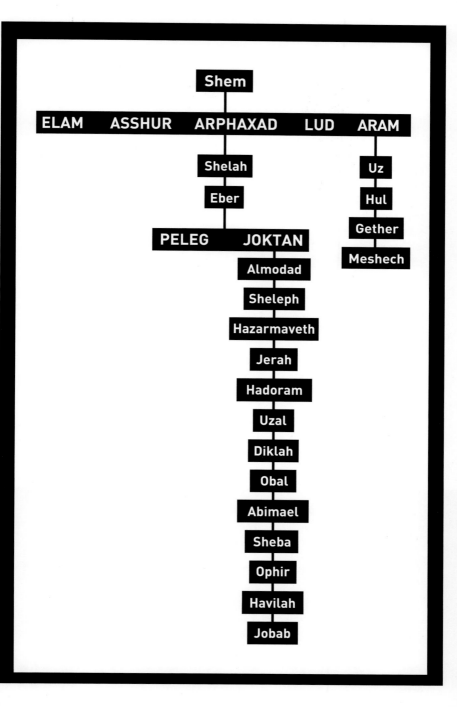

Shem

ELAM   ASSHUR   ARPHAXAD   LUD   ARAM

Shelah

Eber

PELEG   JOKTAN

Almodad

Sheleph

Hazarmaveth

Jerah

Hadoram

Uzal

Diklah

Obal

Abimael

Sheba

Ophir

Havilah

Jobab

Uz

Hul

Gether

Meshech

CHAPTER 20

FIVE GENERATIONS AFTER NOAH, IN THE DAYS OF HIS GREAT-great-great-grandson Peleg, everyone on earth spoke one common language. Man's ability to communicate led to great accomplishments as they worked together with a level of global co-operation unseen since that time. It was a powerful asset. However, as it has been said, whenever great power is available it comes with great responsibility, and these words rang just as true in the time of Peleg as they do today. And we soon discover that great power can also lead to great rebellion.

 **Genesis 11:1-9**

SOCIETY HAD BEEN DISMANTLED AND SENT ON ITS WAY.

As men and women gathered to raise up a monument to human greatness that they would refer to as "the great tower," instead of witnessing its completion they found themselves confused, wondering, "What just happened?"

Numerous events in the Bible can lead us to wonder, *Why did that need to happen? Was that necessary?* And the introduction of the language barrier is no exception. *Had God developed a fear of man and his vast potential? Was He scared of what man could do or accomplish?*

To say that God's decision to introduce a language barrier came as a response to His "fear" of man is both a right *and* wrong assessment of the situation. When God looked at mankind, He did have a degree of *fear*, but not because He was personally threatened by them. No.

As mankind arrived at the location of their great city, their effort to construct a tower was fuelled primarily by pride. Man did not want to build a home; he wanted to build a name for himself. Mankind aspired to be great, set apart and distinguished. Man was trying to achieve separation from God and to display that he was great all on his own. The error found in mankind's thinking wasn't because they were building a tower. There was nothing wrong with building a city. Neither was building large towers inherently wrong. Rather, the error was found in *why* they were building. The heart behind the tower was all wrong. And man's aspiration for greatness was nothing new to God.

Earlier in creation, Satan had tried to achieve a similar goal by making a name for himself. And now, just like Satan, mankind was compelled by sin to think of themselves more highly than they ought, robbing them of humility and keeping them from seeing reality. It's as if the serpent's own desires were influencing society. As a result, man set out to prove that he was the ultimate source of truth and authority.

At this point, God had every right to reach down and slap mankind upside the head. *What were they thinking?!* How simpleminded could they be to so quickly forget where they had come from! Their pride and arrogance was blinding them. They constantly managed to take their eyes off the author of their lives, naively believing they had everything they needed when what they truly needed was Him.

It was as if not a single person in society was capable of recognizing that only through God were they given the ability to live and move and breathe (**Acts 17:28**). Whether they knew this and chose to ignore it or had forgotten completely, their decision to build this tower led God to a point where He finally decided He would come down and see what all their effort was about.

It's important to understand that God's act of "coming down" does not mean that at some point He had removed Himself from the story, leaving the world to spiral out of control. No. In this moment, God *came down* to see this "mighty" tower, in the same way a seven-foot-ten-inch NBA player would *come down* to observe a mud pie teetering in the dirt, sculpted by the proud hands of a three-year-old.

God came down to man's level, because from where He was observing their ignorance, He couldn't quite see the miniscule, dainty, inferior tower they were constructing as a testimony of their greatness. Compared to God, the tower was laughable.

Making it clear that He was far greater than man's greatest efforts or accomplishments, God responded to their wickedness in hopes of getting their attention. Wanting to help set them on the right path, without the force of another flood (since He had graciously promised not to do that again), in verses 6 and 7 God communicated this message to the people:

"Looking at the choices you continue to make, I realize that, since you speak one language, it's easy to communicate. As a result, when one of you has a wicked and rebellious idea, you easily and effectively drag many down with you. Due to your ability to communicate, you are successfully finding no shortage of ways to destroy yourselves, destroy one another, and, in turn, wander farther from Me, My plan, and your purpose. Therefore, to compensate for your limitless ability to lead one another in error, like the blind leading the blind, I am going to confuse your speech and send you away. I do this because I love you and because it is My hope that when one of you falls into temptation, perhaps the rest of you will not be dragged down with them. Maybe you will even learn from one another's mistakes."

With that, new languages were introduced into society.

Though it's difficult to know how the languages were assigned, there is no doubt that their arrival resulted in global confusion. Relationships were torn apart by the inability to communicate.

> **"**...their struggle to communicate probably led to the biggest game of charades ever.**"**

As people tried to overcome this obstacle through the use of actions and hand gestures, their struggle to communicate probably led to the biggest game of charades ever. Waving, shaking, pointing, acting, grunting, and groaning in incoherent dialects, people realized their efforts were futile, and they became irritated. The resulting frustration over one another's inability to understand only further segregated the population as they began to break off and only associate with those who spoke their tongue. With society split, eventually these groups moved to their own lands, established homes, and developed unique individual cultures.

Underneath the calamity, God was busy displaying His unending love and affection. The encounter at the tower had been another showcase of God's continued pursuit of His creation as He worked to save them from themselves.

Though society thought they knew what they were doing, God had walked patiently beside them, reaching out to correct them *before* they lost control and fell over. Graciously offering course correction, God hoped that one day these children would appreciate what He was doing for them. He hoped that one day they would understand that His intervention was purposed not to anger them but to teach them balance. However, despite God's show of mercy, mankind showed little interest in the balance and freedom He offered. Rather than embrace the instructions and appreciate the hand that would help them keep the course, mankind insisted they knew what they were doing. Stubborn, and fighting His aid, they pushed God away and leaned in the opposite direction. Like an arrogant child insisting that he knows how to ride a bike without being taught, it was as if mankind was telling God—the creator of them, the bike, and the laws of physics that make riding a bike possible—that wobbling, falling down, and lying on the sidewalk bleeding is how you *actually* ride a bike. Or at least how *they* would prefer.

GOD CONTINUED TO PURSUE HIS CREATION AS HE WORKED TO SAVE THEM FROM THEMSELVES.

CHAPTER 21

WITH PEOPLE SPEAKING DIFFERENT LANGUAGES AND SCATTERED across the land like seeds, unique and individual cultures began to form, ensuring that society would never function the same way again. Amidst the changes in the world, Genesis 11 leads us back to Noah's son Shem.

After the discussion of Shem's family at the end of Genesis 10, Genesis 11 takes us right back to examining Shem's descendants. At first glance, this second list appears to be copied and pasted from chapter 10; however, closer inspection reveals a few major differences between the two.

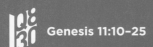 **Genesis 11:10–25**

Though genealogies are less exciting to read than we'd like, their ability to connect times, places, spaces, and people makes them foundational. It's important to keep in mind that they are no less crucial to our story than any other section (**2 Timothy 3:16**). For example, the genealogy in Genesis 11, compared to Genesis 10, provides us with ages and years of life that allow us to further develop a timeline for the story. This shows us the length of time between when the story left off and when it picks up again. Beyond the addition of ages and lifespans, there is also a small variation in the names that are listed.

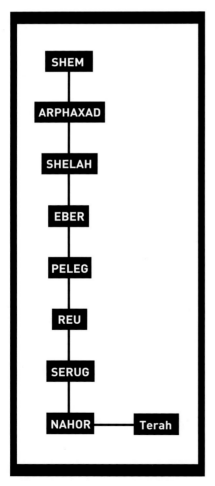

In the Genesis 11 account of Shem's descendants, instead of following the family line through Joktan, the list shifts focus to his brother, Peleg.

The shift from Joktan to Peleg can seem insignificant, but it is leading us towards the next important figure in the story. Through Peleg, the story takes us to a man named Terah, whose arrival came roughly 1,879 years *after* our story began, 222 years *after* the flood ended, and roughly 120 years *after* the tower of Babel. This reveals that the environment on earth had changed drastically since Noah got off the ark.

With cities built and towers erected, society had developed quickly, even though life expectancy had started to decrease. With people no longer living into their 900s (as noted from the genealogy), the earth's population probably hadn't reached pre-flood numbers yet. However, even with a slower increase, it's likely that the population was once again well into the millions.

Inside a changing world filled with diverse people groups and expansion, the genealogy stops at a man named Terah. Already a well-lived individual when we meet him, though his own story won't be long, Terah will play an important part in guiding the story forward, closer to God's promise.

 Genesis 11:26–32

Despite how short our glimpse into the life of Terah is, we learn a lot about this man. Overwhelmed by the loss of his son, he packed up his family and relocated. Moving from his long-time home (suspected to have been located not far from today's borders of southern Iraq and Kuwait), Terah gathered the members of his family who were willing and set off in pursuit of a new home. Taking his son Abram and his nephew Lot, and leaving his son Nahor behind, Terah needed a change of pace, some new scenery, and a fresh start.

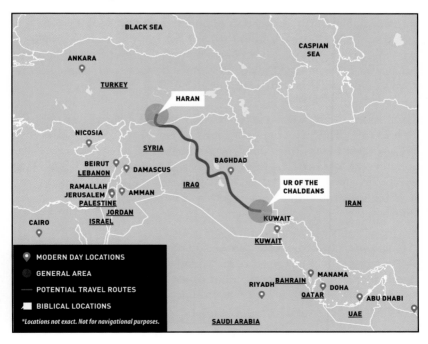

After walking for what we will soon discover was a great length of time, Terah eventually decided that enough was enough. They had reached their new home. Though they were not in the land of the Canaan like

Terah had intended, he chose to establish his new life near the southern border of present-day Turkey.

Though the map provides a guess as to the route Terah travelled, even the most direct approach would have required 1,000 kilometres (600 miles) of travel. This distance would have been especially daunting as it was likely traversed on foot.

The perilousness of this move can be easy for us to overlook. Today, walking great distances isn't common (so uncommon that walking long distances is considered a sport). Travelling 1,000 kilometres (600 miles) is something we do in a day, by car. So we need to establish a modern-day moving equivalent that we can identify with.

To get a feel for Terah's travel, let's start with this: To take a comparable-sized walk today (comparable by distance, not terrain), one would need to travel from New York City to Detroit, Michigan. Though that may not seem overwhelming, this only accounts for distance and does not take into consideration the relocation of an entire family. Today, if we were going to move our family from New York to Detroit, it's highly unlikely we would do it on foot. So, to get a better picture of the modern-day equivalent of Terah's 1,000-kilometre move on foot (with animals and a family), we need to crunch a few numbers.

Let's assume Terah walked at an average pace of 4 kilometres per hour (km/h) (about 2.5 miles per hour, mph) for eight hours a day, seven days a week. That means that Terah and his household would have travelled roughly 224 kilometres a week (140 miles). At this rate, it would have taken him one month to travel 900 kilometres (560 miles). That means it would have taken them one month and three days to reach their new home.

As mentioned before, no one today is going to up and move their family in this fashion, at least not if they love them. And a moving trip that takes over a month is unheard of. So what would the modern-day equivalent be to making a month-long Terah-sized move with a five-person family in a mini-van?

Assuming the average speed of travel by van is 90 km/h (55 mph) and Dad and Mom travel like Terah, eight hours a day, seven days a week, for one whole month, the distance covered would be as follows:

90 kilometres x **8** hours a day = **720** kilometres a day
720 kilometres a day x **7** days a week = **5,040** kilometres a week
5,040 kilometres x **4** weeks **= 20,160** kilometres in a month

Travelling for four weeks at an average pace for eight hours a day, seven days a week, just like Terah, and you're looking at a combined distance of 20,160 kilometres, or 12,320 miles, in a month. That's one month, packed in a van, with no air conditioning, restless companions, numerous pets, a trailer of livestock, and a father who took you on this journey without knowing *exactly* where it was you were going in the first place.

Still tough to picture? To even accomplish a Terah-sized move within the borders of the United States (without driving into the ocean), you would have to come up with a *very* creative route that begins in New York City, New York, and ends in Seattle, Washington. Driving directly between the two locations would be daunting enough, but if we want to know what it was like for Terah, before arriving in Seattle we'd need to spend a month travelling 20,160 kilometres or 12,320 miles. Needless to say, you would be doing a lot of sightseeing on the way.

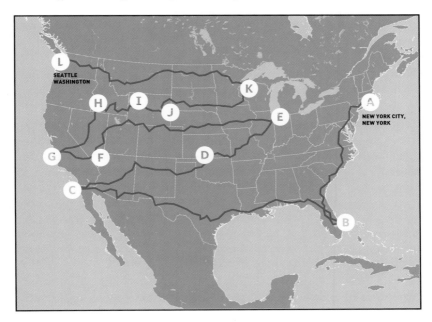

A route similar to the one on the map would take you across, roughly, 19,800 kilometres (12,300 miles), leaving you 300 kilometres shy of having finished a Terah-sized road trip. This is just a glimpse into what a modern-day equivalent of travelling with Terah would be like. Bear in mind, this does not take into account the frustration of tending to animals and the necessity of stopping to keep them fed and watered and allow them to give birth.

What's the point to all this? Simply this: to showcase what a gruelling, long, exhausting task moving was. These people were not vagabonds; they didn't just throw their belongings into a plastic bag and wander off aimlessly. They had homes, families, and numerous belongings. Moving was no less stressful than it is today. It was a major decision for anyone to up and move their family. And, judging from the map, it goes without saying that the journey Terah and his family took was not one any of us anticipate taking the next time we want to *start fresh*. By the time Terah and his family had walked to their new home, I am sure there wasn't anything *fresh* about them.

This may reveal that Terah felt extreme pain after losing his son, a pain that prompted a drastic move. And despite the adversity, Terah arrived at his new home and final resting place. We discover that this home was given the name "Haran," possibly after the son he had loved and lost.

With the closing of this chapter and the end of Terah's story, we receive a brief introduction to the next figure of importance, Terah's son Abram.

God was about to reach out to Terah's son in a way no man had experienced up to that point, and very few would after. Chosen specifically by God as the individual He would pursue His promise through, Abram would be given more details about God's plan to restore His creation than any man previous. He would be a chosen man and his family, a chosen people. God would turn Abram into the instrument through which He would accomplish His will (like Noah); however, it would not be without God's amazing grace, abundant mercy, and plenty of patience. God was about to pursue Abram and his family—and through them, all of mankind.

As readers of the story, we will become more intimately connected with the trials and victories of Abram than those of any other person we've encountered. As the story opens up the life of this man, we discover the monumental call God placed upon him—a call that would never be forgotten, as its promise resonates through the ages.

The impact of Abram's life will be felt for a while as we discover a man of trials, errors, perseverance, and love—

BUT MOST IMPORTANTLY, A MAN OF FAITH.

 **Galatian 3:9**

CHAPTER 22

WITH THE PASSING OF HIS FATHER, ABRAM BECOMES THE FOCUS of our story and, in many ways, the focus of God. Though we are only just meeting him, Abram was already getting on in years. With life expectancy greatly diminished, 75 was no longer young. It had become the new 625. And with Sarai, Abram's wife, incapable of having children, the likelihood of Abram's bloodline extending did not look good.

As dismal as the future seemed, somewhere amidst the move north to Haran and the death of Abram's father, the Lord (i.e., God) had spoken to him. Although we are not given specific details of *how* this message was delivered, that's not as significant as *what* was said. We will soon discover that the message Abram received came with excitement and a promise, but this promise wasn't only for Abram. No. God's promises to Abram were going to impact the whole world.

Genesis 12:1–5

Just like that, our story was on the move again. Reminded of a message God had delivered to him *before* he lived in Haran (**Acts 7:2–4**), Abram packed up and left the place that had become home for him and his family.

As he prepared to make the location change, Abram did so as an individual who fully understood the task that lay ahead of him. All too familiar with the gruelling demands of travelling long distances, having made the journey from Ur of the Chaldeans to Haran, he would not have overlooked the magnitude of God's request.

Abram knew that relocating one's life was not done on a whim. The journey was never easy, no matter how encouraging the prospective location appeared. Yet, despite that fact, Abram acted without hesitation. Having heard the amazing promises God had in store for him and his family, he was anxious to pursue God—

EVEN IF IT MEANT ANOTHER MOVE.

" Abram and Sarai moved off in pursuit of His promises. "

Though Abram was willing to do what God had asked of him, some crucial information regarding the move had been neglected. God had not told Abram *where* he was supposed to move to. He simply told him *to* move. This more-than-minor detail brought a whole new dynamic to the move; however, it never stopped Abram from packing up his family and leading them away from the place they called "home." The simple instruction to "go" was all Abram needed to be on his way. That and the assurance that he would not leave empty-handed. As he moved, Abram did so carrying the promises God had spoken—promises that offered an abundant life he'd only dreamt of. Promises that included a family.

Abram was well aware that he and his wife were incapable of having children (**Romans 4:19**). They'd spent their lives being reminded of this reality. Anytime they saw children playing, saw mothers tending their young, or heard about the arrival of a newborn, they were reminded of their plight. Their inability made the prospect of becoming a great nation that much more amazing. The thought of having *one* child had been a dream. The declaration that they would grow into a people of influence seemed surreal.

Believing that God could overcome their current circumstances, Abram and Sarai moved off in pursuit of His promises. Each step they took was an act of faith. Yet, of all the promises they now chased, the final one was most important.

The final promise God offered Abram was the purpose behind all other blessings. God had told Abram that He would bless him with descendants, yes, but then He told him why: to be a blessing to all people. God was going to use Abram like He did Noah. It would be through Abram's family that God would fulfill His promises from Genesis 3:15—promises that, at that time, were already 2,084 years old.

> **"**At the robust age of seventy-five,
> when all he wanted was a cribbage board,
> a cup of tea, and a slower pace in life,
> Abram began another move.**"**

Having heard and embraced each detail, Abram clung to God's words and set out to fulfill the first requirement asked of him. At the robust age of seventy-five, when all he wanted was a cribbage board, a cup of tea, and a slower pace in life, Abram began another move. Not knowing what to expect of where he was going, he marched on, led by a passionate faith planted in God. In time, we will discover that God was easily as passionate about the future as Abram, as He would reaffirm and allude to His promises no less than eight times throughout Abram's life.

 **Hebrews 11:8**

CHAPTER 23

HAVING EMBARKED ON THE SECOND LENGTHY MOVE OF HIS LIFE, after weeks of travel Abram with his family came to a beautiful land occupied by the Canaanite people (descendants of Noah's son Ham, the Peeping Tom). Abram's arrival had not come easy. At seventy-five, a 600-plus-kilometre (375-mile) journey on foot wasn't as simple as it once was.

If Abram managed to move at the same pace of travel his father had, his journey towards the land God had been calling him to had already lasted roughly two weeks. Hundreds of kilometres from home and still unsure of where he was going, it's probable that Abram wrestled with numerous thoughts during the long days of travel, wondering *Why did I leave my home? How will I ever possess my own land?* and *Why would God choose a simple man like me?*

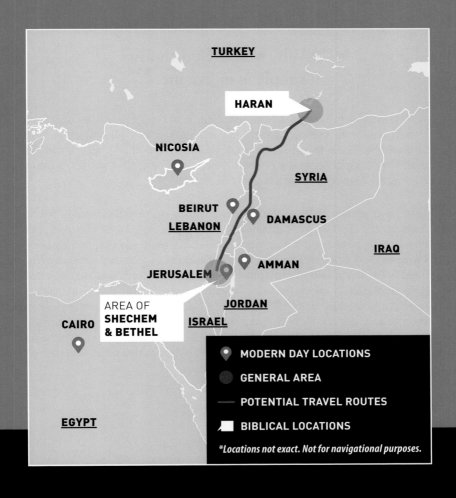

TURKEY

HARAN

NICOSIA

SYRIA

BEIRUT
LEBANON

DAMASCUS

IRAQ

AMMAN

JERUSALEM

JORDAN

AREA OF
SHECHEM
& BETHEL

ISRAEL

CAIRO

MODERN DAY LOCATIONS

GENERAL AREA

POTENTIAL TRAVEL ROUTES

BIBLICAL LOCATIONS

Locations not exact. Not for navigational purposes.

EGYPT

"Abram was not unaware
of the magnitude of God's promises"

"Why would God choose a simple man like me?"

Abram was not unaware of the magnitude of God's promises and how improbable they seemed. And if the wonders of his own mind weren't enough, he likely faced numerous inquiries from those who travelled with him. Undoubtedly they asked, "Are we there yet?" to which Abram could only respond, "That's a good question."

After two weeks of questions without answers, their journey brought them to the land of the Canaanites. Seeing the bounty of the land and how heavily populated it was, Abram may have assumed that this was *not* the spot God was referring to. There was no way that this land, already filled with strong and mighty people who were well established, was the land God had in mind. Perhaps Abram assumed that God was taking him to a secluded, uninhabited slice of paradise. Somewhere peaceful, serene, and less conflicting. A dessert oasis that no one had discovered. Observing that this wasn't the case in Canaan, Abram expected to keep travelling. Until the Lord showed up to tell him that this inhabited plot of land was precisely where He wanted Abram.

Genesis 12:6–9

As exciting as this news was, Abram was not blind to the implications of what he had heard. As he studied the land again, he considered what it would take to displace the current residents and make it his home. Currently without a homeland, separated from most of the little family he had, with a wife who couldn't conceive and with very few belongings— *how would he ever take control of such a sought-after location?* For a moment, Abram's promising future looked anything but.

Despite what he saw with his eyes, Abram clung to God's words with a stout faith. He cherished God's promises and stood firmly on them, trusting that even though the road ahead was not clear, God's words would be his compass. Though it didn't always make sense, Abram trusted that, when the time came, he would see what needed to be done. Though he faced all the realities of how improbable God's promises were, he was fully confident that God had the power to do all that He had promised. Against all hope, Abram believed.

 **Psalm 119:105**

 **Romans 8:18–22**

CHAPTER 24

ENCOURAGED BY GOD'S PROMISE THAT THE LAND THEY HAD COME to would one day be theirs, Abram built an altar of thanks to Him, then proceeded to travel south. Perhaps in search of more space, due to the area's current occupants, Abram moved on, aware that though this land would be his, right now was not the time.

Continuing what had already been a lengthy journey, Abram and his family made their way down to an area known as the Negev. Arriving, their time spent in the Negev was short. Incapable of providing for his family's necessities,

ONCE AGAIN ABRAM MOVED ONWARD.

Genesis 12:8–13:4

Reading about this rather interesting season in Abram's life, we discover that his travels had gone full circle. Travelling away from his location in Genesis 12:8, he returned sometime later in Genesis 13:3.

The confusion and wonder Abram faced during that time would have been immense, starting with the fact that he had travelled in faith only to be met with famine. After numerous days spent moving farther and farther away from family, comfort, and familiarity, all in pursuit of a promise from God, and finally arriving in the land God had picked, Abram was welcomed with a famine. Undoubtedly confused over the way things were unfolding, Abram took his family and went looking for sustenance, which led them to Egypt.

Their time in Egypt, though it turned out to be very beneficial, did not come without more concerns. Abram's strategy for self-preservation when caught in a situation where he feared for his life raises the question, What husband is content with pimping out his wife to another man? Abram's actions suggested that if life were a storm at sea, Sarai might be the first piece of baggage tossed to the waves in hopes of keeping the ship from sinking. When faced with a potential life-threatening trial, Abram responded by abandoning his wife because he valued his own life more.

We can't help but wonder what went through Sarai's mind at the receiving end of his decision. Did she feel completely betrayed by her husband? Did she understand his concern? Or was she so flattered by his confidence in her beauty that she didn't see what actually happened? At any rate, things unfolded exactly as Abram had anticipated, and Sarai was swept away, raising another question: How hot *was* she?

When was the last time someone moved to your neighbourhood and you thought, *That woman is so fine, I think the prime minister or president should be with her! Such an exquisite piece of arm candy should be reserved for a man of distinction*! Though no one may think like that today, apparently Pharaoh had friends who did who were out patrolling the streets for prospects. It wasn't long before Sarai caught someone's attention and was on her way to the palace.

Taken away from her roughly seventy-five-year-old husband-turned-brother, Sarai wasn't young anymore herself. This reveals that, regardless of her age, the years had been kind to Sarai. She responded to aging like a fine cheese or a robust wine.

As odd as all these realizations may be, the most startling fact in the whole scenario is that, amidst his error, Abram was blessed while in Egypt.

Attaining resources for himself and his family, in the end, Abram walked away successful. In the meantime, poor Pharaoh had such a rough go of it that he grew suspicious of the people in his home. Although it's not clear who leaked Abram and Sarai's little secret, Pharaoh wasted no time in making sure things were put right once he realized Sarai was married.

After their dramatic visit to Egypt, Abram and Sarai made their way back through the Negev and towards Bethel, loaded down with cattle and servants. Despite the bounty Abram had acquired, he was still missing the thing he longed for most. Though he had attained money, livestock, and servants, a part of him felt poor and empty,

BECAUSE ALL HE WANTED WAS A FAMILY OF HIS OWN AND A CHANCE TO SETTLE DOWN.

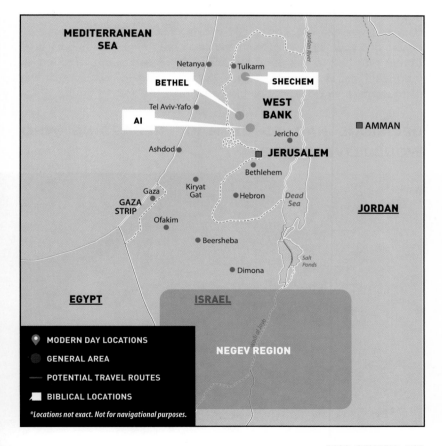

CHAPTER 25

HAVING LEFT EGYPT ALIVE AND WEALTHY, BOTH OF WHICH MAY have come as a shock to him after the stunt he had pulled, Abram found himself back in the same location where he had pitched his tent earlier.

Just north of modern-day Jerusalem, his travelling herd set up camp, and Abram called on the name of the Lord. Having previously built an altar in this same location, perhaps Abram returned as a way of re-establishing himself. This spot, between Bethel and Ai, was the last place the Lord had appeared to him (**Genesis 12:7**), and maybe Abram was back to try to realign himself. Like moving out to do life on your own only to find yourself back in Mom and Dad's basement nine months later, Abram returned to call upon the Lord and receive some direction. In the meantime, as he and Lot surveyed the land and realized that the surrounding area would not be big enough for the both of them,

DECISIONS HAD TO BE MADE REGARDING WHO WOULD LIVE WHERE.

Genesis 13:5–18

Overflowing with riches after a successful journey to Egypt, Abram and Lot were forced by their possessions to go their separate ways. In his generosity, Abram offered Lot the chance to pick the area he most desired.

Abram's decision to handle the dispute with such humility and selflessness suggests that there had been a change in character after his stint in Egypt. Having previously risked the safety of his wife for the sake of personal benefit, suddenly Abram forfeited his right as the elder and offered Lot whatever he wanted. The days of travel, famine, hardship, and longing were shaping him.

For Lot, however, selflessness was something still to be learned, and after a quick overview of the surrounding area, he settled on the land near the Jordan River. Seeing how rich and well-irrigated the land was, Lot couldn't pass up the opportunity to place himself near such prosperity and wealth. *But at what cost?* Lot had likely heard reports about the cities he would be neighbouring, Sodom and Gomorrah. Despite the news of their wicked acts and lewd behaviour, the location was too nice to pass up. Their close proximity never hindered Lot's decision. He settled east of where he and Abram had been living. Today this piece of real estate can be generally located near the Dead Sea.

With his nephew gone to establish his own life, Abram once again experienced an epic encounter with God. Receiving further instruction and greater detail regarding the covenant he had with God, Abram, despite the absence of a son, was assured that he would have a large family to possess the land he was in. God even outlined the very borders they would inherit. So Abram went on a walkabout, as God had suggested, eventually settling at a new location near the great trees of Mamre.

Although he had previously moved to both the Negev and Egypt without building an altar, when Abram went south to Mamre, he erected an altar right away. Reinvigorated by the covenantal update he had received, Abram likely didn't want to forget the call he had on his life or the God who would provide for him. By building an altar, he created a visual reminder of the future he had. There's no denying that Abram would have stared at the altar on numerous occasions, reminding himself of God's plan, especially when the continued absence of a son served as a roadblock

IN HIS PURSUIT OF A FLOURISHING FUTURE.

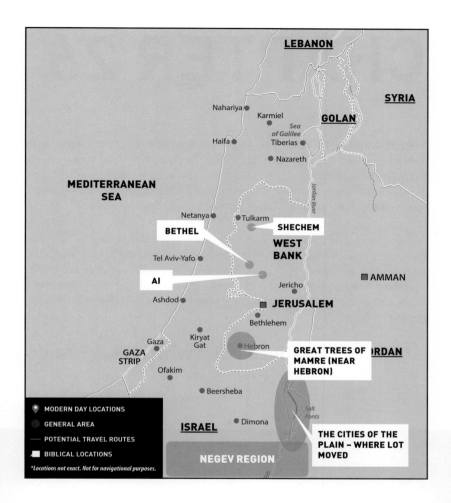

LEBANON

SYRIA

Naharia ●

Karmiel ●

GOLAN

Sea
of Galilee

Haifa ●

Tiberias ●

Nazareth ●

MEDITERRANEAN
SEA

Netanya ●

Tulkarm ●

SHECHEM

BETHEL

WEST
BANK

Tel Aviv-Yafo ●

AI

Jericho ●

Ashdod ●

JERUSALEM

■ AMMAN

Bethlehem ●

Gaza ●

Kiryat
Gat ●

Hebron ●

**GREAT TREES OF
MAMRE (NEAR
HEBRON)**

JORDAN

GAZA
STRIP

Ofakim ●

Beersheba ●

Salt
Ponts

**THE CITIES OF THE
PLAIN – WHERE LOT
MOVED**

Dimona ●

ISRAEL

NEGEV REGION

Jordan River

● MODERN DAY LOCATIONS
○ GENERAL AREA
— POTENTIAL TRAVEL ROUTES
▰ BIBLICAL LOCATIONS
Locations not exact. Not for navigational purposes.

CHAPTER 26

WHILE ABRAM TRAVELLED AROUND SURVEYING THE LAND AND moved to a new location, Lot stayed put and settled into his new home. While he was busy trying to build upon the success he found in Egypt alongside his uncle, the fertile land he had chosen placed him well within reach of the neighbouring cities just east of his home.

Before long, Lot and his family acquainted themselves with their neighbours and "big city living." Immersing themselves in the local culture and adjusting to its way of life, eventually Lot and his family switched from being neighbours to regular residents in the community. What Lot and his family didn't know was that their association with the people of Sodom

WOULD COME WITH A HEAVY PRICE.

ROSS BREITKREUZ

At the time of their move, a man named Kedorlaomer (Key-do-lay-oh-mar) ruled the area Lot chose as his home. Ruling from another city, Kedorlaomer had conquered Sodom and Gomorrah in an effort to expand his own territory. For twelve long years, Sodom and Gomorrah had been under his rule, and around the time of Lot's arrival, the people decided they had had enough—the time had come to end the oppression of the foreign king.

Sodom and Gomorrah rallied together with other cities under the jurisdiction of Kedorlaomer, drew up battle lines, and took a stand. Regardless of how Lot felt about the decision, he was swept up in the rebellion, guilty by association. The battle raged.

 **Genesis 14:1–24**

"The battle raged."

CHAPTER 27

DRAGGED OFF INTO CAPTIVITY ALONGSIDE THE RESIDENTS OF Sodom, Lot and his family were left to deal with the consequences of their relocation. The bright future he had envisioned when moving to the area had been snatched away faster than he could have imagined. With his home in shambles and his possessions removed, Lot appeared to have lost the very thing he cherished most—his wealth. Having picked the most bountiful land in the area without hesitation, Lot had hoped to see his riches grow and flourish, but now he lost both his wealth and freedom. Devastated, he was dragged towards a new home and a dark future.

LOT WAS DESPERATE TO ESCAPE THIS NEW LIFE.

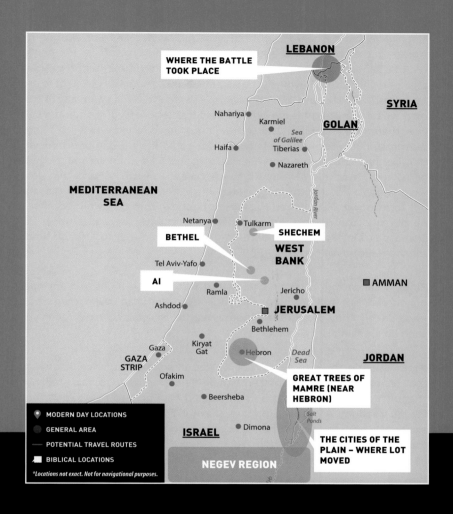

LEBANON

WHERE THE BATTLE TOOK PLACE

SYRIA

Nahariya

Karmiel

Sea of Galilee

GOLAN

Haifa

Tiberias

Nazareth

MEDITERRANEAN SEA

Jordan River

Netanya

Tulkarm

SHECHEM

BETHEL

WEST BANK

Tel Aviv-Yafo

AI

■ **AMMAN**

Ramla

Jericho

Ashdod

■ **JERUSALEM**

Bethlehem

Kiryat Gat

Gaza

Hebron

Dead Sea

JORDAN

GAZA STRIP

Ofakim

GREAT TREES OF MAMRE (NEAR HEBRON)

Beersheba

Salt Ponds

ISRAEL

Dimona

THE CITIES OF THE PLAIN – WHERE LOT MOVED

NEGEV REGION

- ● MODERN DAY LOCATIONS
- ○ GENERAL AREA
- — POTENTIAL TRAVEL ROUTES
- ◻ BIBLICAL LOCATIONS

Locations not exact. Not for navigational purposes.

"The battle raged, as Abram risked life and limb for the freedom of his family."

Meanwhile, having heard about the situation his nephew was caught in, Abram gathered 318 men, all trained in battle, and set off on the heels of Lot's captors. Once again, Abram's response in this moment reveals a changed character. Previously, he had cowered behind lies in Egypt in an attempt to avoid death, but now he didn't seem to think twice about his own welfare, putting his life on the line for the benefit of his nephew. If ever there was a situation that Abram could have found a self-justifying reason to not respond to, this was it. He could have easily told himself that Lot had chosen the land near Sodom and was simply reaping what he sowed. He had known about the people's wickedness, and this was what he got. But Abram didn't waste a moment dreaming up a reason not to respond. Determined to save his nephew from his own ignorance, he pursued the raiding army and caught up with them just north of Damascus. Once again, the battle raged, as Abram risked life and limb for the freedom of his family.

Finding success in a battle that lasted through the night, Abram not only freed Lot but rescued everyone else who had been captured. Immediately they began their journey home, relieved to have received such an amazing deliverance.

As they made the return trip, Lot walked in shameful silence, knowing that his own choices had placed him in his current position and feeling sheepish over the fact that he had caused his uncle to risk everything for his freedom. A peculiar mixture of emotions surfaced. Lot was both excited to be free and, at the same time, ridden with guilt over the risk that had been taken to save him from slavery. Confused by his excitement and his guilt, Lot was humbled by his uncle's love.

As they continued their journey home, the success of Abram's military campaign went before him, resulting in an encounter with a rather peculiar figure: a king from the city of Salem. This king, Melchizedek (Mel-kizz-a-deck or Mel-chizz-a-deck), was unique. In his introduction, Abram discovered that Melchizedek held the titles of both king *and* priest of God—a rare combination. The responsibilities and expectations these offices demanded were *never* shared by one person, at least, not at that point in the story. Therefore, Abram's encounter with the king of Salem made for a very interesting experience. Identifying the unique priestly character of the king, Abram respected Melchizedek and responded by giving him a tenth of everything he had gained in victory.

Along with Melchizedek, Abram also met with the king of Sodom. Feeling indebted to Abram for saving his people from slavery, the king of Sodom attempted to pay him for all he had done. Abram, however, did not accept a single penny from the king, wanting to give no man the opportunity to say he had provided Abram with the blessings in his life. God, not man, was Abram's reward *and* his rewarder. After handing the attempted payment back to the king of Sodom, Abram returned home, content with the safety of his family—a gift he knew God had delivered. Blessed by Melchizedek and refreshed by their meeting, Abram rejoiced in Lot's safety.

Despite the celebration of his recent military conquest, there still remained a sense of discontent in Abram's life. Unwinding at home after the trouble of recent days, once again he heard from God. Aware of his worries, God assured Abram that He had a plan and encouraged him to realize that, although it felt like something was missing, He was all the reward Abram needed right then. God would provide.

 Genesis 15:1–21

Appearing to Abram and putting his worried mind to rest, God knew that His loyal servant was troubled by circumstances that made His promises seem unattainable. God assured Abram that he *would* have his own descendants, who *would* live in a prosperous land. The reminder seemed overwhelming, given the fact that the land currently housed ten separate tribes (**Genesis 15:18–20**). But God, not being a respecter of numbers or statistics, assured Abram that He had never forgotten the promises He had made. The time would come.

This honest dialogue between Abram and God should not be overlooked. This man of faith did not mask his concerns or downplay his worries; rather, Abram spoke openly with God. All he desired was an heir to his fortune and God's promises. He wanted a son passionately, and the absence of offspring caused every other blessing to lose its lustre. What good was wealth if it would only be given to a member of his household? What good would prosperity be if his family and his name would die with him? What good were all the things God had done if they hinged on the one thing He had yet to provide? Abram was concerned.

As God listened to each word His servant spoke, He comforted him. Working to ease Abram's concerns and bring peace, God assured Abram that he was precisely where he needed to be. God took Abram back to the beginning and reminded him that He had pursued him for a long time. God had been leading Abram to this moment for many years (**Genesis 15:7**).

What an encouragement for Abram! As he reflected on the fact that, even in times when he had little to no awareness of God, God had been strategically involved in his life, Abram became overwhelmed. What a thought! Abram heard God's words speak louder than the worries in his mind. He trusted with absolute confidence that God could do all that He said, and he simply believed God (**Genesis 15:6**).

> **"**Even in times when he had little to no awareness of God, God had been strategically involved in his life.**"**

CHAPTER 28

REFRESHED BY THE REMINDER THAT GOD WAS WORKING IN HIS life, Abram carried on, affirmed and encouraged. Life progressed for Abram and Sarai. But as days turned to weeks, weeks to months, and months to years—all without even the slightest hint of a child—God's reassurance began to fade, and the future held less promise for this "family" than ever before.

Abram's family bounced around Canaan for quite a while—ten years had passed since God called him from the land of Haran (back in **Genesis 12:4–5**). Reflecting on the past ten years, Abram couldn't deny that God had brought him through some troublesome situations; however, with little to no tangible evidence of His promises, there was a temptation to view God's words as more of a pipe dream than a promise.

Equally discouraged over what God had yet to do in their lives, Abram's wife, Sarai, grew more and more conscious of her childbearing plight. Having waited a long time for a child of her own, she felt as if her window of opportunity had passed. The time had come to improvise and take matters into her own hands.

 Genesis 16:1–16

How quickly the tables turned in Abram's household! No longer without a child, the woman who encouraged the conception of Ishmael hated the arrival of the child she had asked for. Sarai's distaste for Ishmael was alarming—almost as alarming as the manner in which she and Abram continued to handle stressful situations.

Earlier, during their venture to Egypt, when Abram had feared for his life, he thought the best solution was to abandon his wife to the arms of another man. Now, years later, in response to her frustration of not having children, a scenario she blamed God for (**Genesis 16:2**), Sarai looked to remedy her situation by sending her husband between the sheets with another woman. It seems as if the bedroom was looked to for conflict resolution. As wrong as this was back then, the idea that the mattress is the best way to resolve issues is still believed today. It may seem like an odd scenario, but what's just as unnerving is the fact that Abram was willing to go along with his wife's suggestion. With no sign of hesitation, it's as if he looked at Hagar, looked as his wife, and thought, *Let me get this straight. My wife wants me to do* what *with Hagar? Wow. Just last week she gave me dagger eyes for telling Lot's wife I'd never tasted a more succulent lamb shank, and now she thinks this is a good idea! I'll never figure women out! Oh well, I guess I should do it. Happy wife, happy life.*

Though this is almost certainly not what Abram thought, the fact that he didn't appear to question his wife or insist that they wait patiently for what God had promised suggests that he didn't think it was the worst idea he'd heard. Using Hagar to take a shot at producing a family didn't sound as absurd as it should have. So, as Abram went about fulfilling his wife's wishes, a little love triangle formed, and the situation became dynamic.

Unfortunately for the three of them, the plan went off without a hitch. The realization that everything worked the way she thought it might haunted Sarai. As Hagar's stomach grew with child, so did her arrogance as she paraded her mothering abilities before Sarai. Hagar no longer responded to Sarai as she once had, lording her pregnancy over Sarai. The situation inside Abram's household became poisonous.

As the friction between the two women grew, Sarai's disdain for Hagar finally reached a point where she could no longer stand to have her around. Treating her horribly, Sarai set to the task of removing Hagar, her attitude, and, ultimately, her child. But chasing Hagar into the desert didn't bring Sarai the relief she hoped it would. Having chased away a woman she was close with—a woman she, at one time, thought so highly of that she offered her to her husband—Sarai sat alone and contemplated her choices. She was tormented over her treatment of Hagar, the loss of her friend, and the fact that she was still without a child.

As Sarai mulled over everything that had transpired, Hagar sat down, distraught and overwhelmed. Confused over how things had progressed, she knew she shouldn't have been so conceited over her pregnancy. Ashamed, guilty, scared, sad, and alone, Hagar sat by the springs, a broken spirit. What would she do now?

Despite the debacle that it was and the poor decisions that were made, God intervened and mended broken hearts. Even though all three people involved were responsible for allowing their lives to turn into a midday talk show, God went to Hagar and comforted her. Assuring her that all would be well for both her and her child, He encouraged Hagar to return to Sarai and serve her well. Upon her return, she gave birth to Ishmael.

With a promise from God that Ishmael would grow into a large people group, it looked as if things had worked out after all. This son would also lead to many people. However, despite what God had spoken to Hagar regarding Ishmael, somehow it was clear to Abram that Ishmael was not the son God had promised. Abram would have to wait for the arrival of God's promised descendant. And at the age of eighty-six, he had no choice but to trust that God's timing was perfect and

THAT MIRACLES COULD HAPPEN.

CHAPTER 29

ANYONE WHO WAS AROUND TO EXPERIENCE THE '80S OR THE '90S can testify to the dramatic shift between decades. Ten years can be a long time, and a lot can change. With that in mind, our story moves into Genesis 17 with another decade gone by. To be exact, thirteen years had come and gone, and Abram was just shy of breaking the century mark—

STILL WITHOUT THE PROMISED SON.

As we catch up with Abram at the healthy age of ninety-nine, we look back and realize it has been almost twenty-five years since God had called him away from his home in pursuit of promises he had yet to fully receive. The last twenty-five years had involved serious mental battles. With unanswered questions, concerns, and wonders that tested his faith—and his sanity—Abram had to possess amazing faith to still trust God with his future. Still awaiting the things God promised, he was less settled now than when God first called him. Sure, he'd acquired assets, but the fact that he had so many possessions and no permanent place to keep them only fuelled his longing for a home.

For twenty-five years, he had been chasing after God's promises, feeling like he had little to show for it. Without question, this resulted in ridicule from family, friends, and his own conscience. Others wondered *why* he kept pursuing God the way he did and questioned his rationality when he insisted that God was leading during the difficult seasons. Even Abram occasionally wondered if the promises he clung to were God inspired, and not birthed out of his own longing. Sometimes he felt the urge to downplay God's presence by believing his success had come through luck or being in the right place at the right time. In the hard times, it was a mental wrestling match, but he remained firm in his faith. He was not going to let fear and doubt toss him around like a wave in the ocean (**James 1:6**). He knew that allowing room for them only made room for *greater* fear and *greater* doubt.

What were his options? Was he going to chase after an unpredictable future in his own strength? Was he going to exchange his faith and trust for doubt and uncertainty? Was he going to forfeit a life of rich purpose and love and forgo his trust in a God who would work all things out for his good? Was he going to surrender to the threats of sin and pain and refuse to believe he was made for more? Was he going to walk away from an existence that challenged him to look and live beyond himself, beyond his circumstances, and beyond his pain, believing that he would simply live and die and merely fill time and space in between?

Abram knew it would take just as much effort to reject God and embrace his doubts and fears as it would to trust God with his life. Despite being attacked by doubts, he refused to surrender his future to anything other than the promises of God, and he saw nothing crippling about accepting the fact that he didn't have all the answers. He didn't find it impossible for something to be true, even if he couldn't fully comprehend it. And he knew that if he had been fabricating a call from God, he probably wouldn't have led himself down the road he was now on. He wouldn't have chased after having a son for twenty-five years or placed himself in the situations he had. Despite the inquiries from others and his own mental pressures, Abram knew God was real, He was active, and He was the only one worth trusting his future with. Firmly he stood, staring headlong into the unknowns of his future, not scared, as doubts and questions flew towards him like snow to a windshield. Amidst the flurry, his vision remained firm, not focusing on each doubt-filled speck and becoming so overwhelmed that they appeared before him as one giant wall. Abram looked beyond the doubts and in faith believed his footsteps would be laid out to guide him, like road lines in a snowstorm. Because of this, amidst each flurry of doubt that he faced he continually found an uncommon peace, by looking beyond the fear, doubt, worry, and self-reliance. A peace found only in great trust (**Philippians 4:6**). A peace that came only from God. Abram knew that his life had been no pipe dream.

If Abram's faith in God's ability to do what He said He would was not evident already, the test Abram faced next revealed just how greatly he trusted God, as he took part in what most men would consider one of the greatest acts of faith in the entire Bible.

Genesis 17:1–27

Abram was, without question, a man who followed God *no matter what* the cost. It's apparent that he was committed to doing *whatever* God asked of him. If you know what circumcision entails, you likely agree. Abram had to have been 100 percent committed to God to agree to this, because circumcising an infant is one thing, but having it done as a ninety-nine-year-old is entirely different.

Though the request for circumcision seems more than odd, it could be said that, since it was such a sensitive undertaking, it had to have been divinely inspired. The reasoning behind this is simple: No man in his right mind, on his own volition, would *ever* take a knife *anywhere* near his "manhood" thinking it was a fantastic idea. This was not something done on a whim or a passing notion. No. This was not a point in the story where Abram couldn't decide if he *had* heard God or he had just dreamt up circumcision on his own. The influence behind such a request had to have come from beyond him. It required more than sheer willpower and a can-do attitude to go through with. It would have required conviction and nothing short of a command from God to go through with cosmetic surgery on that particular area. The man pioneering the mission for the rest of the men needed to have complete trust in God.

Abram had to be confident that this was what God required of them; otherwise, he probably wouldn't try to rally all his buddies in an effort to convince them to join in the festivities. The responsibility he carried was immense. He wasn't just required to circumcise himself; he also had to break the news to the other guys. Somehow, he had to stand up in front of a group of men and convince them that God told them they needed to do this. It was a group of men that included his thirteen-year-old son, Ishmael. Since he was undoubtedly going to encounter a few sideways glances, he needed to be certain.

Considering all that Abram had to face, even though Genesis gives us details on his exchange with God about circumcision, it's hard to not stop and wonder if Abram had a question or two about the whole process. There had to have been a few things he wanted to go over, just to make sure he had all the details. This wasn't trimming fingernails or shaving a beard. There wasn't much room for error. This was not a time to learn by doing. Abram wanted to do it once and do it right. All of this raced through his mind as he was caught off guard when God added this peculiar request to the end of a majorly encouraging conversation.

When God and Abram began their exchange, God started off by reaffirming His covenant and adding even more details to it. He changed Abram's name to Abraham (meaning "father of many") and Sarai's name to Sarah. God used the first eight verses to get Abraham excited about his future.

Thrilled that he had not been forgotten and feeling like the best was yet to come, Abraham was electrified by the words God spoke. He felt like a star quarterback about to take the field, getting amped up by his coach before the big game. Anxious about what would lie ahead, he listened to each word intently, his pulse climbing as God's covenant grew. His blood started to boil, and his heart beat with anticipation. Abraham felt like nothing could stop him now; he was ready to attack the future and lay hold of the promises that God had for him. Excitedly listening, all ears, he awaited what other amazing news God had, lost in that moment of rapture, when suddenly God hit him with the fine print. One tiny stipulation on Abraham's end, a small test of his willingness to trust. *Circumcision.*

Hearing that word, Abraham's celebration likely came to a halt. His conquering attitude quickly faded. Processing what he just heard, things got real. And perhaps, in his confusion, Abraham's unrecorded response was "I'm sorry. Come again, Lord? Did I hear You right? Because just moments ago, I was getting excited as You told me about the son I'm supposed to be having. I was all jacked up and ready to embrace tomorrow, and now all of a sudden, You're telling me that before that happens I need to take a knife to my *what*? Forgive my ignorance...

> **"** ...I just can't help but view taking a knife to that specific area as being counterproductive to me producing the children you keep telling me about! **"**

Though any such concerns would have been warranted, it's probably not what Abraham said. Any hesitation he did have did not hinder him from doing exactly what he had been instructed to do. It's abundantly clear why Abraham is known as such a great man of faith. You would need to be a man of faith to carry out such a task. It should also be noted that Abraham wasted no time in setting to the task. Like when pulling off a Band-Aid as quickly as you can, he wasn't about to go to sleep that night, mull things over, and proceed in the morning. There's likely no man in history who would sleep soundly knowing what had to go down first thing in the morning. It was a now-or-never moment.

So in a newly required act of confirmation and identification between man and God (**Genesis 17:11**), Abraham circumcised himself and the rest of the males in his household. (That's one binding contract.) With the deed done, Abraham and his household took time to recover. Perhaps he used the time to contemplate everything God had told him, knowing it was all going to be worth it.

In a twisted way, the symbol that Abraham and the men of his household then carried could be understood somewhat like the rainbow—slightly less publicly viewed, mind you. Like the rainbow, it was a reminder of God's promises, a reminder of what was to come, and a reminder that a year from now, the current discomfort Abraham felt would be nothing compared to the joy of his son's birth.

ISAAC WAS ON HIS WAY.

CHAPTER 30

AFTER TAKING A FEW DAYS TO RECOUP FROM THE PROCEDURE, Abraham and the other men from his household were comfortable enough to get mobile again.

One day, post-circumcision, as Abraham sought refuge from the afternoon heat, he spotted three rather noticeable individuals nearing his home. Somehow discerning that the three men were actually the Lord and two of His angels, excited and anxious, he hurried to meet them.

Upon reaching them, Abraham offered to serve them and supply all their travelling needs. Though he was well enough prepared to assist them on their journey,

HE WAS FAR FROM PREPARED FOR WHAT THEY HAD COME TO ACCOMPLISH.

 **Genesis 18:1-33**

What a shocking end to what would have been a rather pleasant afternoon, spent enjoying lunch together and discovering that his son was no longer a promise but a reality! As Abraham, unsure of how one bids farewell to the Lord, walked with his guests away from his home, the Lord dropped a huge bomb on him, shocking him with His plans for Sodom and Gomorrah.

The news put Abraham back on his heels. He felt blindsided by the revelation. After such an encouraging conversation, full of affirmation about his son-to-be, Abraham realized that, although coming for lunch was very much a trip for pleasure, the Lord had also come for business. As the two angels made their way into Sodom, the reality of what was about to go down gripped Abraham's heart. *Surely this can't be true! What about Lot?* Thoughts of the ensuing devastation burst through Abraham's mind. Lot had been living in Sodom. *Will God truly destroy an entire community?*

"Will God truly destroy an entire community?"

Unsure of what to think, Abraham continued to converse with God, desperate to know where the Lord's mercies lay. People have often viewed this exchange as a moment where Abraham changed God's mind, but in reality, through Abraham's prodding the Lord offered a glimpse into His unending mercy and grace. In their discussion, God revealed to Abraham that even to a community filled with sin and hearts that had rejected their Creator, God would show His mercy for the sake of ten righteous men and women.

Discovering this and content with the answer, Abraham returned home, seemingly satisfied. Encouraged over the magnitude of God's love and grace, surely Abraham had nothing to worry about with cities the size of Sodom and Gomorrah! Of course, they may have been wretched and filled with evil, but were they really *that* bad? No matter how evil things seemed, surely there were at least ten righteous people living among those communities...

...RIGHT?

CHAPTER 31

AFTER ABRAHAM'S CONVERSATION WITH THE LORD FINISHED and he returned home, the two men who had accompanied the Lord arrived in Sodom. We discover then that Abraham's nephew Lot still called Sodom home, as he was seated at the entrance for the city. Clearly, being taken captive by a raiding king hadn't scared him away. For over thirteen years now, Lot and his family had made Sodom their home, and we can't help but wonder why. Had Lot embraced the sinful ways of Sodom?

Though it can seem like Lot's choice of residence must have been influenced by sin, later on in the Bible, as people retell the story of Sodom, we learn that his intentions were not evil. Lot did not get caught up in the ways of his neighbours; in fact, he was rather distressed by the actions of the people of Sodom (**2 Peter 2:7–8**). Despite his concern,

THE PEOPLE OF THE CITY HAD NO INTEREST IN THE WAYS OF LOT OR HIS GOD.

" His two visitors had flipped his world upside down.**"**

As the two angelic visitors arrived at the city gates, the people of Sodom wasted no time revealing why Lot was so distressed and why God had business to attend to in these communities. It didn't take long to realize that things in Sodom were worse than Abraham could have imagined. Far worse. Horrifyingly enough, there were *far* fewer than ten righteous people living in the city, where sin ran rampant.

 ## Genesis 19:1–29

The events of Genesis 19 are nothing short of haunting. The men and women who later travelled past the section of land and laid eyes on the smoldering ashes that once housed Sodom and Gomorrah must have been astounded.

As the events unfolded on that fateful day, the story tells us that, like Abraham, Lot identified the two men coming to his town as unique individuals, taking them in and urging them to stay with him for the night. Lot's insistence may have been a simple act of hospitality, or perhaps it was inspired by his knowledge of what a night in the town square would look like for two strangers. Either way, later that night, with two foreign travellers under Lot's roof, the city of Sodom came unglued.

As all the males of the city crowded at the entrance to Lot's home, the scene grew frantic. The angry mob outside began to pound on the door, shouting at Lot in protest and insisting that they have their way with his guests. As the commotion grew, Lot's houseguests stood near the doorway listening, more aware of the depth of depravity in that city than anyone else.

As the intensity of the moment escalated, everyone in Lot's home cringed as they thought about what might happen if the door failed to hold. Creaking in protest, the door started to bow from the pressure being placed on it. Dust began to fall from the ceiling, and the occupants of Lot's home grew more terrified, shaking and desperate for escape. The family was not naive about the Sodomites. They had lived amongst the people long enough to know that if the men got into their home, it would not end well.

Then, as Lot and his family began to think their fate was sealed, the two guests, who happened to be angels, decided that enough was enough. Aware that the corrupt men of Sodom stood outside the door demanding the opportunity to violate them, the angels exercised their God-given strength and struck the mob with blindness, buying Lot and his family time to escape.

Frantically, Lot and his family grabbed what they could and prepared to leave the city. At the instruction of the angels, Lot exploded from his home and searched for his sons-in-laws-to-be. Upon locating them, in a state of desperation, voice trembling with sincerity, Lot urged both men to quit what they were doing, abandon the city, and escape the coming wrath of God. But they rejected his pleas. His heart twisted with confusion over why they rejected his warning. Lot returned home and faced the task of delivering the news to his daughters. Their fiancés had declined the invitation for freedom. The girls were stunned. Their futures looked dark.

Overwhelmed with fear and feeling like he was trapped in a nightmare, Lot's movements became robotic. The men in the city were more barbaric than ever, staggering around in a blind rage, mauling one another, desperate to feed their lusts. Numbed by the overwhelming scene, he moved in a haze. His two visitors had flipped his world upside down.

In the distance, daylight crept faintly into the darkness—the sun was about to rise. Startled, he found it hard to believe that the battle to protect his guests and his family had lasted throughout the night. The angels then shook Lot from his stupor. With no time to spare, they guided Lot and his family out of the city with the instruction to run and to *never* look back.

As Lot and his family ran in desperation and fear towards the safety of another city, the edge of the sun slipped past the horizon. Lot begged to be asleep at home. At any moment, he would wake up in a cold sweat. But what happened next revealed that this was not a dream.

As they ran with a light breeze in their faces, suddenly, behind them, the heavens discharged an unearthly groan. Covering their ringing ears, Lot and his family released their own muffled cries, which were swallowed by the commotion behind them. Meanwhile, overtop Sodom the sky tore open as if it were a piece of paper that an invisible finger poked through.

Before anyone could discern what lay beyond the pierced covering, the opening filled with blinding tones of white and blue and forced out a torrent of burning sulphur that crashed on the city with the force of a tsunami.

Still running for their lives, oblivious to everything happening behind them, Lot and his family were hit by a shockwave sent out by the events taking place in Sodom. As they were thrust forward, fighting to keep their feet under them, the surge of power was accompanied by a roaring wind and a pungent odour that swept over their shoulders, stunned their nostrils, and made their eyes water. The reality of what just happened wrenched their hearts and sent their minds swimming. Sodom was gone, and they knew it. The smell of sulphur and ash in the air was all the proof they needed. They didn't have to turn around. In fact, they *couldn't* turn around.

Running along, Lot's wife was overtaken with her own emotions, her primary one being resentment. She resented having to leave her home, and she longed to be back in Sodom. How dare God do this to her? What right did He have to pull her from her city?

Burning with the desire to return, ignorant of the grace she had undeservedly received, she only wanted to go back—back to her home and back to a lifestyle she had enjoyed. She didn't want to leave Sodom. She had merely been caught up in the chaos and dragged away by two strangers. She hadn't asked for this. She moved with regret, resenting the opportunity afforded her to live, and then decided that her heart would stay in Sodom. That was where she truly belonged.

When she couldn't resist the urge any longer, too upset to move another step, Lot's wife looked back upon the city she loved. In that moment, the simple act of turning her head revealed the true state of her heart. So the Lord, not wanting to force something upon one who did not desire it, granted her the desire of her heart—the desire to be with her people.

Still in mid-run, holding his wife's hand, out of the corner of his eye Lot caught the twisting motion of her head. He opened his mouth to shout in protest, but before sound could escape, the damage was done. Instantly, the space she had occupied in his peripheral vision became vacant. The sight of his wife's hair bouncing off her shoulders as they ran vanished. Still running, Lot then noticed the empty space inside his palm where her hand had been. As tears built in his eyes and he began to sob, he opened his hand and looked inside. To his horror, grains of salt fell from his palm and landed on the ground. It was his final farewell to his wife.

 **Luke 17:32–34**

Not long after Lot arrived at the small city he had run to, his Uncle Abraham rose to start his day.

Abraham woke with an uncommonly heavy heart, and he made his way out to where he had conversed with the Lord the day before. There, from his vantage point, Abraham looked out over the plains where his nephew had chosen to live. The sight that met his eyes tore the words from his throat and the moisture from his mouth. *It can't be!*

> **❝Mouth open in shock, Abraham could taste death in the air. ❞**

Standing in an early morning silence, Abraham studied the land that had once been considered the most desirable of all. A valley that had boasted abundant crops, abundant water, and abundant life was now a testament to one thing—death. Black and charred, dry and dark, it was almost unrecognizable. If the sight alone wasn't nauseating the smell the valley emitted was, testing the resolve of Abraham's stomach. A heavy scent, filled with traces of smoke, ash, dirt, and sulphur, joined him at his perch. Mouth open in shock, Abraham could taste death in the air. Doing all he could not to heave and trying to understand what had happened, he imagined the manner in which the skies must have opened, like an angry mouth, screaming down wrath upon the cities. With no sign of life or hint of survivors, he had to trust that somehow Lot escaped.

CHAPTER 32

WITH LOT'S MIND SPINNING OVER RECENT EVENTS, WHICH NOW included the tragic death of his wife, he and his daughters moved on after a brief stay in Zoar, perhaps unnerved by the manner in which its way of life mirrored Sodom's.

The family of three sought refuge in the mountains, as they had originally been instructed (**Genesis 19:17**). The destruction of Sodom and Gomorrah was a major setback that relocated Lot to a cave—

A RATHER HUMBLE PLACE.

In the dark seclusion of their new "home," Lot's daughters slowly came to grips with the reality of their situation. Gripped with a deep sense of hopelessness, they felt as if their lives were slipping away. The loss of their fiancés had stripped them of all the future aspirations they had carried only days earlier. With little chance of finding love in the mountains, things looked grim.

Lonely and desperate, the girls eventually decided to take matters into their own hands. Determined to have a life beyond the cave, they would pursue that end no matter what. They were going to write their own fortune. Or, perhaps, their own *mis*-fortune...

 **Genesis 19:30-38**

"What these girls did should repulse us completely."

If you've ever wondered how human genetics obtained defects over the centuries, allow Lot's daughters to offer a potential answer. If the Bible's earlier mention of marriage between cousins and close relatives was not troubling enough, what these girls did should repulse us completely.

The state of desperation the sisters must have experienced in order to even *consider* what they were about to do (and did) must have been a degree of hopelessness few of us can imagine. Though there may be women who, at times, think that their Prince Charming is never going to find them and feel like Lot's daughters, trapped in a desolate cave never to be discovered, this has likely never surfaced as a possible solution—no matter how bleak the future seems. For these sad and lonely girls, stuck inside a cave with Dad, something obviously shut off in their minds.

> **" It was really the caveman equivalent of slipping Dad a roofie. "**

Perhaps the powerful punch of sulphur's scent after Sodom's torching had affected their cognition. Maybe living in close proximity to the sin and corruption of the people in Sodom and Gomorrah had tainted their minds. Regardless, from somewhere deep in the darkest recesses of their consciousness came a voice, an idea, a thought. It began as a subtle, skewed suggestion that presented itself as the "common sense" solution to their loneliness. But it really was the caveman equivalent to slipping Dad a roofie. Get Poppa liquored up beyond comprehension and secure a future through children.

As disturbing as the situation was, that's precisely the point of the story. What the girls did was repulsive, and sadly, as grotesque as it was, the plan worked. In due time, both of them gave birth to sons. And unless Lot had been told about what had happened, he would have been completely oblivious. The next nine months would have raised some *serious* questions.

Assuming that Lot and his daughters continued living the cave life during the duration of the pregnancies, it's possible that they didn't have an overabundance of food or a rich diet. As the months progressed and the girls developed baby bumps, Lot's confusion would have grown, as he asked himself, "I know I can't bring it up because it won't end well, but have the girls put on weight? Are they sneaking food at night? I mean, they've been a bit hungrier than usual lately, but I haven't seen them eat that much! What are those two up to while I'm sleeping?"

As Lot's confusion mounted, it eventually climaxed with the shocking arrival of what could only be known as his grandchildren-sons. Lot had some serious questions that needed immediate answers.

Regardless of what his daughters told him or what he had learned about the conception of the two babies, it was too late. Lot's daughters had succeeded in their plan and had sons. They had secured a family line, just as they had hoped.

Over time, their families would grow beyond what either of them could have imagined. Their descendants would turn out to be nothing short of a thorn in the side of their extended family. Lot's daughters' babies' children and grandchildren were going to cause...

**A LOT OF TROUBLE
FOR THE DESCENDANTS
OF THEIR UNCLE ABRAHAM.**

CHAPTER 33

AS THE STORY SHIFTS ITS ATTENTION FROM LOT AND HIS grandchildren-sons back to Abraham, we find Abraham at his last noted location, the Great Tree of Mamre (**Genesis 18:1**). There in Mamre, Abraham had seen some emotionally charged days. He had talked to God, met with the Lord in person, received affirmation that his promised son was coming, and witnessed the aftermath of Sodom and Gomorrah. After all he had experienced, Abraham had little reason to doubt God's ability.

With such a bright future, surely Abraham would never do something that might jeopardize God's promises. Aware that, within the year, his wife would be able to conceive, he would never make the same mistakes he had in the past,

WOULD HE?

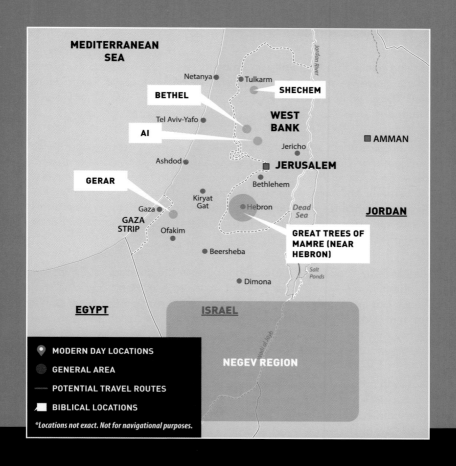

MEDITERRANEAN
SEA

Netanya
Tulkarm
SHECHEM

BETHEL

WEST
BANK

Tel Aviv-Yafo

AI

Jericho

Ashdod

JERUSALEM

Bethlehem

GERAR

Kiryat
Gat

Gaza
Hebron
Dead
Sea
JORDAN

GAZA
STRIP
Ofakim

GREAT TREES OF
MAMRE (NEAR
HEBRON)

Beersheba

Salt
Ponds

Dimona

EGYPT
ISRAEL

NEGEV REGION

AMMAN

Jordan River

⬤ MODERN DAY LOCATIONS
⬤ GENERAL AREA
— POTENTIAL TRAVEL ROUTES
▬ BIBLICAL LOCATIONS
*Locations not exact. Not for navigational purposes.

"[Abraham] reverted to an old way
of handling stressful situations."

 **Genesis 20:1-18**

Having packed up his family and moved, not once, but twice, Abraham found himself in another bad situation near Gerar—located near modern-day Gaza—where he reverted to an old way of handling stressful situations.

The predicaments Abraham found himself in when he travelled almost suggest that God was trying to show him that he should stay close to the Promised Land. Every time he moved from the area, things went bad. Apparently Abraham was a slow learner. It had been just short of twenty-five years since his and Sarah's episode in Egypt, where he abandoned her to the arms of Pharaoh, and now in Gerar, near the Egyptian border, he did it all over again.

As Abraham took familiar footsteps south, in the direction of Egypt, one might think he would have thought, *Note to self: don't pull that stunt again!* But instead, he seemed to think, *Well, it worked last time!* Luckily for him, God was so determined to carry out His plan through their family that He continued to look favourably upon Abraham, even when his repeat offence could have been the most costly of all.

Not long before the move to Gerar, God had told Abraham that he would have a son—*within the next year.* In a display of total belief in this promise, Abraham had circumcised himself. *So we know he trusted what God said!* Obviously aware that the promise of having a child meant his wife would be fertile in the near future, he still let her get taken into the arms of another man. Did he not consider the fact that Abimelech (Ah-bim-ah-lek) could have impregnated Sarah? Or was he so confident in God's grace that he thought, *No matter what happens to Sarah, God promised she would have my child, so it's okay, I can make ignorant mistakes, and He will protect us.*

Regardless of what did or didn't go through his head, the scenario that Abraham put himself in turned out to be just as dangerous as the previous one. Providentially for him, God went to Abimelech in a dream, scared him out of his pj's, and informed him of the situation.

Having received insight regarding his most recent female acquisition, Abimelech scrambled out of bed and wasted no time in telling his servants what had happened. He acted immediately on what he had learned through his dream. He didn't have to try to remember its events. Abimelech knew what he had seen was serious. Once again, through His grace, God saved Abraham from himself, despite himself. Soon we realize that the reason God did this was because Abraham and Sarah had little time to waste scuffling with royalty. Their son was on his way. God's words were not idle.

AND THEY HAD A BABY TO PREPARE FOR.

CHAPTER 34

AFTER THE SHORT BUT ILL-ADVISED SEPARATION FROM ONE another, Abraham and Sarah were reunited. Equipped with roughly twenty-five pounds of Abimelech's silver, they accepted the king's generous offer and stayed in the local area. All things considered, Gerar wasn't such a bad place after all.

With a seemingly stable homestead and some money in his pocket, Abraham felt somewhat settled, and life slowed down a little—just in time. As promised, Sarah and Abraham soon had a child on the way. At the unlikely ages of 100 and 90, the reality of God's promise began to sink in:

ABRAHAM AND SARAH
WERE GOING TO BE PARENTS.

As Sarah's belly grew, so did the excitement over the arrival of their child. There was no denying that God had done something miraculous. Their joy was palpable. Through the arrival of their little bundle, Isaac, they would experience one of God's greatest acts of mercy and love in their lives. Isaac was going to be a constant reminder that God was forever faithful and His timing, perfect.

Genesis 21:1-21

So, 2,109 years after the birth of Adam and over 550 years since the flood, Abraham's son Isaac was born. Like his father, Abraham, and Noah before him, Isaac entered the world with a significant purpose in life. Even before his birth, Isaac was a chosen individual. He would be the vessel through whom God would continue to carry out His promises— promises that, at that time, reached back 2,000 years to Genesis 3. Isaac was going to carry the family one step closer to God's promise to mend creation's brokenness.

> **"** Physical death was one thing, but walking away from the greatest love in your life was a whole other kind of dying. **"**

In his old age, Abraham didn't overlook just how gracious God had been to provide him with a son. Abraham had never doubted God's ability to provide in this manner (**Romans 4:19–20**), but Isaac's arrival still left him in awe. Isaac was received with much celebration, a declaration of God's provision and a testimony of Abraham's devout faith. Despite trials, despite errors, and despite age, Abraham had trusted God and was blessed for his faith (**Hebrews 11:11**).

As exciting as all this was for Abraham and Sarah, not everyone in the family embraced young Isaac with joy. For Ishmael, watching his little half-brother graduate from milk to solid food was nothing but frustrating. Since infancy would have posed many threats for a baby at that time, reaching the solid-food benchmark in development meant Isaac was going to be around for a while. Ishmael knew that the health and survival of Isaac made his small chance at receiving an inheritance from his father disappear entirely. The older Isaac got, the farther Ishmael was pushed from the picture.

At roughly fifteen or sixteen years of age, when Isaac turned two or three, Ishmael's resentment finally resulted in a visible friction between the two boys—a sight that proved to be unbearable for Sarah. Concerned over the threat that Ishmael posed to her son, especially since the young man of fifteen didn't seem to pass up chances to abuse and mock a child far younger than himself, Sarah instructed Abraham to carry out a task that would not have been easy.

At the insistence of Sarah, Abraham sent Ishmael and Hagar into the desert, with eyes that begged for understanding and a look of regret on his face. As painful as it had been to do, he received assurance that God would provide for them. And He did.

The situation that Hagar faced as she was cast into the wild was unbearable. Life as a single mother is never easy, regardless of the time in history. Struggling to survive in the barren desert and running out of water, Hagar eventually reached a point where death seemed inevitable. The maternal instincts that inspired her to care for her son began to torment her. The desert mocked her desire to protect her child and offered her nothing and no way of caring for Ishmael. Her helplessness broke her already aching heart. Having fully embraced the fact that her son would die and there was nothing she could do to save him, she surrendered. Leaving Ishmael under a tree and abandoning her son,

Hagar performed an act that made her feel as if her own death would come as a result of a broken heart.

Young, weak from hunger, and scorched by the desert heat, Ishmael was incapable of moving. Unable to carry on any further, through tear-fogged eyes he watched his mother walk away. No matter how loud his thoughts screamed, he did not have the strength to follow. He would die alone.

As Hagar forced herself away from her son, she knew that hell could be no worse than what she was experiencing. Physical death was one thing, but walking away from the greatest love in your life was a whole other kind of dying. She began to cry.

Hagar wondered how she even had enough water to form tears. She walked until she could no longer hear the cries of her son, and the unwanted silence was her undoing. Raspy moans of pain tore from her coarse, dry throat. Feeling as if her heart had dropped to her stomach, where it was ripped apart by acid, Hagar endured the lowest moment of her life. Arguably, she experienced what could easily be the lowest point of *anyone's* life.

In that moment, God's love shone down on Hagar. In her lowest of lows, He worked in her despair. God resurrected the son she regarded as dead, like only He could. At a time when Hagar thought no one was listening and no one cared, she discovered that God was and did!

As God blessed her and Ishmael and sustained them through His grace, He kept the promise He had made through His angel back in **Genesis 16:10**. Though Ishmael would not be the recipient of His redemptive promise, his family line would still flourish. Through his marriage to an Egyptian, Ishmael's family did grow, and it became a strong and powerful nation. Ultimately, because of God's grace, the impact of Ishmael's descendants was going to be felt throughout the story and throughout all of history. In fact, his people still affect culture today, as Ishmael became the founding father of the great Arab nation.

CHAPTER 35

WITH HAGAR AND ISHMAEL GONE, ONE MORE DYNAMIC HAD BEEN removed from Abraham's life, albeit begrudgingly. As things began to settle down, Abraham had to accept the absence of his first son and trust that God would take care of him.

Abraham remained in Gerar for quite a while, and before long, it was understood that he would be a constant presence in the local area. As his neighbours got to know him better, the depth of his character and his favour with God became impossible to ignore. The local king, Abimelech, along with the commander of his forces, approached Abraham with an offer, hoping that if Abraham was going to be a fixture in the Gerar region, he would at least be a blessing—

AND THEY COULD GET A PIECE OF THE PIE.

Genesis 21:22–34

With oaths sworn and the deal sealed, Abraham took his well and named it Beersheba. Feeling even more settled in the land, he felt it was firmly established that this plot of land was home. In fact, Abraham's presence in the area became so permanent that in modern-day Israel, a city called Be'er Sheva still stands where this well was purchased.

Reviewing where Abraham's life rested at this point, it appears as if things were going well. The son God had promised him almost thirty years earlier had been born, was healthy, and was growing. Abraham had amassed a respectable number of belongings, and now he even had a stable place to live. Although he was still an alien amongst the people he lived near, the Philistines welcomed him.

> **"**...comfortable and secure can sometimes be dangerous— especially if they make you content and complacent.**"**

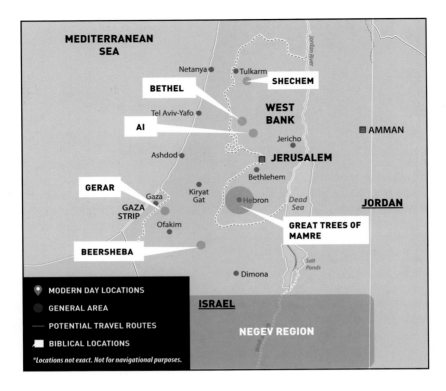

Well into his hundreds at this point, with his own well and a secure home, Abraham began to feel comfortable and safe. Though this is a good thing, feeling comfortable and secure can sometimes be dangerous—especially if they make you *content* and *complacent*. To make sure that wasn't the case, almost inevitably, a new test was coming for Abraham.

With God having great plans for Abraham and his family, it was important that Abraham did *not* grow content and complacent in his life. There was still much to pursue. With all the blessings he had received, though, there might have been a temptation to place his confidence in the *things* he had gained rather than the *One* who had provided them. Having received the son he wanted, *was Abraham still willing to do anything and everything that God asked of him? Did he still hunger to follow God even though he had the son he wanted so badly? Or had Abraham only followed God because of the gifts He had promised? Was God his desire? Or were God's promises all he really wanted?* Abraham was about to answer all of these questions.

Though the following chapters of Abraham's story can seem wrong to us, the further we get into the story, the more we will understand why it was so crucial for Abraham to maintain his faith and depend on God. Abraham had to cling to God as his most prized possession because he was going to be the father of God's people. Chosen as the patriarch of a family that would be called to be faithfully devoted to God, Abraham needed to be a mighty example of what faith in God looked like. He needed to be a pillar that his descendants could look back upon and uphold as a model of faith. As time progressed in the land of the Negev, he would be given the opportunity to do just that. He would showcase, not just for his family but for generations to come, what it looks like to trust God with reckless abandon. Abraham was about to embark on what many believe to be the *ultimate* test of faith,

PLACING HIS TRUST IN NOTHING OTHER THAN GOD'S WORD.

 **Proverbs 3:5–6**

CHAPTER 36

ABRAHAM WAS CHOSEN BY GOD, SELECTED AS THE MAN GOD
would grow a mighty nation through. As such, it was important to ensure
that he fully trusted God with everything he had. His life needed to make
a statement to the generations that God can and should be trusted in
the face of all things. Abraham was going to exhibit a faith that showed
God is in control, God has a plan, and, no matter how dark things look,

GOD NEVER ABANDONS HIS PROMISES.

It's important that we understand what Abraham would soon endure. God was not testing Abraham because He was unaware of the answers Abraham would give. God knew. However, God needed Abraham to learn and to grow through the test, like a grade 3 teacher who gives her class a math quiz. The teacher doesn't hand out a test because she doesn't know the answers and hopes her students will provide her with them. She knows very well what two plus two is. She wrote the test, arranged it, and created the answer key. She tests her students so they can gauge where they are, how well they've been listening, how well they comprehend what they've been told, and, hopefully, so they can make the right decisions on their own. Upon completion of the test, the students will know where they struggle and where they excel. The coming events with Abraham and God would be similar.

"No matter how dark things look, God never abandons His promises."

God was about to test Abraham so that Abraham might discover his own strengths and weaknesses and would never forget that God holds the answer key. Abraham was about to learn that no matter how dark a situation may look, no matter how confusing life may be, God can provide. Even when it seems like God is the one leading you towards the unimaginable.

The war that was about to erupt in Abraham would have been powerful. He would soon find himself standing at a crossroads in his mind, fighting to decide how he should respond, what emotions he should listen to, and what was right or wrong. He was about to face a decision about who he loved most—*God* or *Isaac*.

 Matthew 6:21

Genesis 22:1-8

As Abraham contemplated the horror of God's request, a storm grew inside. Disbelief clouded his mind, and fear threatened to change everything he thought he knew. Like a seismic shift in his worldview, it was if the very foundation of everything he believed was under attack. What was God doing?

Abraham had watched God care for him and Sarah. God had blessed them abundantly, and Isaac was just the beginning of the greatest promises yet. *Now God wants to take him? Was I only given these things to endure the anguish of losing them? How can God make such a request?* Each thought shook Abraham to his core and tested the stability of his faith. The questions, fears, and doubts searched every inch of his faith, looking for weaknesses that could break him. He was forced to decide what was more concrete—death or God's promises.

The friction between his faith and his fears raised a seemingly unscalable mountain as he struggled to maintain a balance amidst the fury. *What will Isaac's death mean for the rest of God's promises?* To say that Abraham faced a test would be an understatement.

Despite the confusion and despite the chaos, Abraham found a way to navigate every question, every fear, and every doubt—by clinging to God's promises more than ever before. Even though it made no sense, he decided that God's promises had to be more reliable than the emotions and fears that threatened him. Despite the fact that the world appeared to be collapsing around him, he needed to trust. God had a plan. Things would work out. Though it was beyond his comprehension, he would choose to make God his refuge.

> **"Abraham knew that God's goodness was not minimized by trials. In fact, he believed it was magnified. "**

Even though it seemed like God was the one allowing it all to happen, Abraham knew that God's goodness is not minimized by trials. In fact, he believed it is magnified. Regardless of everything taking place inside, he knew where to find strength, and he placed his faith in the fact that God held the answer key to this test.

Psalm 46:1–3

Matthew 17:20

Hebrews 11:17–19

CHAPTER 37

THE FAITH ABRAHAM EXEMPLIFIED IN THE FACE OF THIS TRIAL WAS beyond compare. The fact that he rose early the next morning to leave reveals that, having wrestled with his fears and deepest longings, he desired to trust God above all. What a remarkable father of faith! What a testament for generations to come, revealing that you can let go of the things you cherish most and

TRUST THAT GOD HAS A PLAN.

Whether Abraham realized it or not, he was setting an example for all his descendants to look back upon—an outline for what it means to trust God with every part of your life: past, present, and future. Abraham was developing a bold testimony that would be talked about for years. His story would be one of great faith and God's goodness. It was a great beginning for a powerful nation that God would use to bless others. It just didn't come easily.

The journey that Abraham, Isaac, and the servants set out on was a heavy one. With every step they took, questions grew inside the small party of wanderers. Not knowing specifically where it was they were travelling, Abraham moved in faith, trusting that God would show him where to take Isaac. Because Abraham trusted, there was an answer.

Even though the instructions God gave him seemed conflicting, he knew God couldn't lie—God wouldn't lie—and His promise to expand Abraham's family through Isaac would not die.

 **Genesis 22:9–19**

As they parted ways with the servants and set off for the place of sacrifice together, Isaac must have wondered all the more *where* the sacrifice was. Being told that God would provide, he moved forward.

At each phase of the journey, Abraham would have looked for God to intercede, hoping to receive different instructions before the sacrifice took place. However, having received no word other than to offer Isaac as a sacrifice, he and his son moved on.

Arriving together at the place where the sacrifice would be offered, carrying with him the knife and fire while Isaac held the wood, again Abraham hoped and begged for God to move. Constructing the altar a little slower than normal, he uttered prayers for a new direction. "Lord, please! Do not let me go through with this. Take this request away. Lord, if it is at all possible, save me from the suffering I am about to endure. If only there was another way. Yet, not my will but Yours be done."

As he prayed, all Abraham heard was silence.

When the altar was completed, all that was left was to place the sacrifice upon it. Feeling that this would surely be the moment God made sense of his confusion but hearing nothing other than his own fears and the occasional question from his son, Abraham bound Isaac and placed him upon the altar.

> **"** Eyes that held the promise and future of the family... looked up at him and wept. **"**

Back against the wall, the final hour upon him, any tears Abraham had fought over the past number of days came without resistance. As Isaac stared at his father, confused and scared, Abraham felt tormented by the desperation in the eyes of his son. Those were eyes from which he had wiped tears, eyes he had seen sparkle with laughter and joy. They were eyes that held the promise and future of the family, and they looked up at him and wept. Abraham contemplated laying Isaac on his stomach so he didn't have to face his son. Though he trusted God, it didn't make this easy.

Confused and scared, perhaps Isaac understood that his dad still believed God would provide another sacrifice. Bound and lying on his back, with his dad hovering in an ominous position over him, he didn't seem to fight or try to remove himself from the altar. Instead, from deep within his heart, he too yearned for God to come. Together, father and son sent up unspoken prayers for escape.

Discovering a new level of commitment to the call God had placed on him, finally Abraham reached for the knife. Fully succumbing to the fact that this was going to happen without God's objection or intercession, Abraham realized that Isaac would die and, somehow, it would all work out.

With shaking hands wrapped tightly around the knife, he lifted it into the air over Isaac's chest, eyes closed and the words "Forgive me, son" resting on his lips. Abraham exhaled as he tightened his shoulders and prepared to end Isaac's life, determined that if he had to do this, he would strike true and avoid inflicting a slow death.

In that moment of confusion and absolute devotion, a voice suddenly erupted with haste and passion. Hearing the instructions he had longed for since he first received his directions from God, Abraham wasted no time releasing his son and offering the sacrifice that had been provided. He prepared the ram with great praise and adoration, and as he pierced its flesh, tears of celebration rolled down his cheeks. Abraham knew that moments earlier it would have been his son. The father and son duo praised God with shouts of gratitude and thanksgiving few people have matched. Their God is a God who saves (**Psalm 68:20**).

There's little doubt that Abraham and Isaac were physically and emotionally exhausted as they returned home. Both of them had just endured an emotional roller coaster. They settled back into their home in Beersheba. Blessed by the Lord, His promises reaffirmed, and more excited than ever before, as the years stretched on their family saw even more reason to celebrate but also reasons to mourn.

 Genesis 22:20–23:20

As the years progressed, news came to Abraham that his brother Nahor had been blessed with family. Learning of his brother's prosperity would have been encouraging.

Unlike Abraham, Nahor had not left the land they had grown up in; rather, it appears that he stayed in Ur of the Chaldeans when their father, Terah, relocated the family after the death of Haran, their brother (**Genesis 11:31**). It had been over sixty years since Nahor was last mentioned, and now, after all this time, we are told that those years had been good for him. Numbers were clearly on his side, and his household had grown, with twelve sons in total and likely a number of daughters as well.

As exciting as the discovery of his brother's prosperity would have been, it was followed with a jolt of pain. Enduring the loss of the wife he loved dearly, Abraham was faced with the task of burying his beautiful Sarah. She had lived a good, long life of 127 years, filled with many blessings, but the primary blessing had always been her son, Isaac. She had been very fortunate to bear a son in her old age and survive long enough to watch him grow, but the time had come for Sarah's end. As she was younger than her husband Abraham, it suggests that perhaps...

THE END OF HIS STORY WAS NOT FAR AWAY.

CHAPTER 38

THE REALITY THAT TIME WAS RUNNING SHORT FOR ABRAHAM WAS apparent, with the passing of Sarah only making it more obvious. Life's frailty gave him a new intentionality in the days he had left.

Wanting to make sure that the family members who succeeded him continued to follow God, Abraham took special interest in the marriage of his son Isaac. Because Isaac's wife would affect him greatly and would birth more promised descendants, the process of finding Isaac a suitable helpmate became

FAR MORE THAN A MINDLESS VENTURE.

Having witnessed the lifestyle of the people he lived near, Abraham knew that marrying into the surrounding culture could be fatal. After everything God had done for his family, and mindful of the promises that waited, Abraham could not allow Isaac to join with a nation that ignored God.

He decided that the safest way to guarantee that Isaac had a wife who desired to follow the Lord would be to join him in marriage with like-minded people. *And who's more like-minded than family?* So Abraham prepared to send a servant back to the home he left many years before, in search of a wife for Isaac.

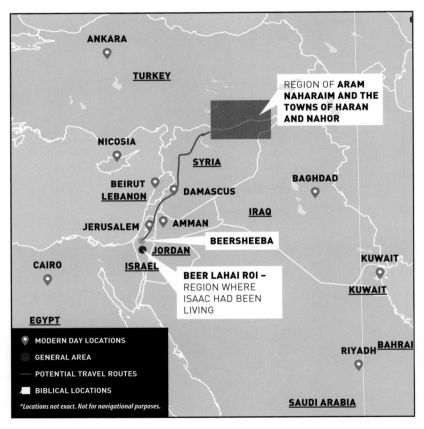

Obedient to his master, the servant set out for Aram Naharaim, where Abraham's former home, Haran, was located. Retracing the steps his master had taken when he came to the Promised Land, the servant came to a town called Nahor (**Genesis 24:10**). The name was probably a dead giveaway that the servant had reached his destination. Apparently, even though Abraham and Lot were the only two males who moved from Ur of the Chaldeans with Terah **(Genesis 11:31)**, eventually Nahor made the trek north as well.

 **Genesis 24:1–67**

God once again revealed that He had a plan for this family, down to the finest detail. Proving that Abraham was wise to send for Isaac's wife among his own people, God made it obvious to the servant that Rebekah was the one to take home.

The scenario appears to have unfolded so flawlessly, it's almost laughable. No sooner had the servant uttered a prayer for direction than God sent him an answer **(Matthew 6:8)**, leaving every reader wishing that prayers were always answered that quickly and finding the right spouse was always that simple.

What transpired after the servant's conversation with Rebekah served as more proof that this was a God-ordained meeting—a fact that did not go unnoticed by either family. When Rebekah was finally asked if she would wait for ten days or leave with Abraham's servant, her decision not to delay her departure revealed that she viewed the events the same way as the servant did. Rebekah knew there was no point in delaying what God had so clearly called her to. God had revealed His will to her, and she would leave at once.

As the servant began his return trip home, he did so with thanksgiving, praising God for His gracious provision. Having travelled a good distance to Nahor and with a lengthy return trip, he was likely gone for over two weeks. Meanwhile, back at home, his masters anxiously awaited his return.

Back in the land of Canaan, Isaac had returned to his father's home in Be'er Sheva, since he had been living further south in Beer Lahai Roi. Together Abraham and Isaac passed the time discussing what Isaac's wife might be like. Assuring his son that northern women were beautiful (which still holds true today), Abraham told Isaac about the customs in the north, the fragrances the women wore, and the colours and the jewellery they often adorned themselves with. With each new piece of information, Isaac's curiosity and excitement grew about the woman he would spend the rest of his life with.

As the two-week window started to close and the time came closer for the servant to return, Isaac found himself spending much of his day casting glances off into the horizon, hoping to catch a glimpse of his soon-to-be wife. Finally one evening, as he was out in the field meditating and contemplating his future, Isaac saw camels approaching. Despite how many times he had played out the moment in his mind, he was still surprised by the excitement that grabbed him the moment he realized *This is it!* He was far more excited than he ever imagined he would be. Studying the veiled figure before him, he longed to learn her name, hear her voice, know her character, catch her scent. He knew he loved her already, and his love for her would continue to grow.

Witnessing Isaac's happiness and contentment was a great source of joy for Abraham in his final days. As he watched his son join in marriage to a good woman, he felt a sense of peace wash over him—a peace that any parent experiences when his or her child happily marries a loving spouse.

Well-advanced in years and feeling like he had his household in order, it seemed to Abraham that it would not be long before he passed on. But as his son found comfort over the death of his mother through his wife, though the years seemed short for Abraham, he decided he wouldn't mind a little female comfort of his own.

CHAPTER 39

WITH SARAH GONE AND ISAAC MARRIED, ABRAHAM DIDN'T know that he'd still have forty years before he would pass away. Undoubtedly, they would have been forty long years without a companion to enjoy them with. It seemed as if Abraham was going to be by himself for a while; at least, that's a generally safe assumption to make for a man who was roughly 140.

As his son Isaac enjoyed a budding relationship, the sting of losing his wife was made all the more real. Abraham missed Sarah dearly. Not wanting to spend his final days without having someone to share the joy of grandparenthood with, like his son he looked to ease the pain of losing Sarah...

THROUGH FINDING ANOTHER WIFE.

The fact that Abraham was even able to secure another wife at such an advanced age is somewhat surprising. However, even more shocking than this is the fact that over his remaining forty years, he managed to stockpile six more sons, before passing away at the robust age of 175.

Genesis 25:1–18

As Genesis prepares to shift its attention away from Abraham, it bookends his story by tying up loose ends. Here we discover that before his departure from earth, Abraham got his house in order, made it clear that Isaac was the *primary* inheritor of his blessing, and sent his other sons away from Isaac to secure a stable future for him. This closing chapter also offers us a quick recap of Abraham's growing family. With the addition of six more sons, plus their descendants and Ishmael and his descendants, we learn that this small family, which started with one man and his barren wife, had grown. Before his story closed, thirty more people were added to the family tree of Abraham.

Despite earlier frustrations in life and complications with conceiving, Abraham's family had grown—and was growing. Though Isaac was set apart, each of his sons was still blessed to some degree, especially Ishmael and his twelve sons. The twelve rulers that came from Ishmael were a testament that God had fulfilled the promise He made to Abraham back in **Genesis 17:20**. Abraham had asked God to bless Ishmael, God had said, *"Yes,"* and He had.

Regardless of the success that the family had seen as a whole, God's promises to Abraham (his own land, a powerful people, innumerable descendants, all nations blessed through him, and a cure for the broken relationship between God and man) were continuing through Isaac alone. Though each son saw *blessings*, no other family line inherited the *covenant* like Isaac did. As Abraham's story closes and our focus moves to the son God had promised, we are left anticipating what the Lord has in store for the next generation

LIVING BENEATH THE ABRAHAMIC COVENANT.

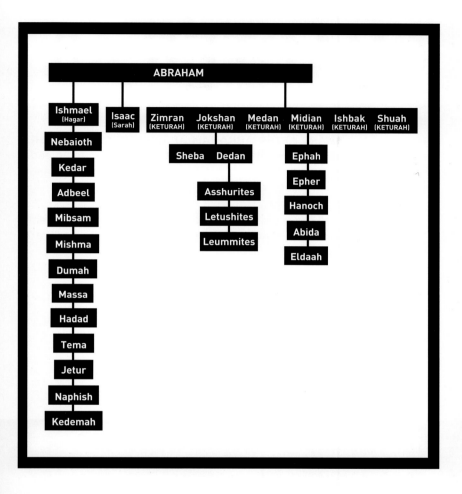

CHAPTER 40

ROUGHLY 100 YEARS AFTER ABRAHAM ARRIVED IN CANAAN, THE land God had called him to, Abraham's dramatic story came to an end. Even though our story now focuses on his son Isaac, it will continually uphold Abraham as the father of faith.

Looking back on all the ways God provided for Abraham, it's apparent that God was passionate about His covenantal promises. And He still had much more to accomplish and many more promises to fulfill.

Though it can seem disheartening that Abraham never got to experience the fullness of some of the promises God gave him, we must remember that the promises had not been given to Abraham as an individual. God had not picked Abraham as a favourite over everyone else who walked the earth. He'd picked Abraham as the starting point He would move forward from. God was not merely in pursuit of blessing Abraham and his family; He was in a desperate pursuit of His broken creation—every aspect of it. Desperate to bring it back into relationship with Himself and to provide creation the peace He offered, God, through Abraham, took some of the first steps towards peace on earth. Abraham had been a stepping stone on a journey towards restoration. His life had been a statement to all, proclaiming that God *can* and *will* work through faith. Through sickness, death, loneliness, fear, doubt, uncertainty, transitions, temptations, family, fire, war, and prayer, God had been chasing after humanity.

NOW THE TORCH WAS PASSED TO ISAAC.

As the story focuses on Isaac we need to keep in mind that it rewinds itself a bit. The Bible has a tendency of telling one person's story up to their death before moving to the next person. In this case, although Abraham's passing has just been recounted, we will discover that he was alive during the early years of Isaac's life.

With God having already done a mighty work in the lives of Isaac and Rebekah, drawing them together in an amazing fashion, the couple didn't wait long before they tried to take God up on His promise to give them a large family—key word, *tried*. As it turned out, they faced the same difficulties in childbearing that Abraham and Sarah had. Just like Sarah, Rebekah was barren. Without question, this would have been a frustrating season for the young couple, and not just for the young couple but for Grandpa Abraham as well.

The fact that Isaac had been clearly and perfectly led to Rebekah, a woman incapable of conceiving, would have been a perplexing scenario for Abraham. With Isaac being the next step towards innumerable descendants, after everything Abraham had gone through personally, the arrival of another childbearing roadblock may have left him thinking, *I thought we were done with all this? I left my home, travelled to a foreign country, took a knife to my privates, and tried to sacrifice my son—all in faith. Despite the trials, I've never stopped believing God would do everything He said He would, and now, this. Just when my son finds a wife and I'm prepared to sit back and watch God multiply my grandkids like rabbits, we find out my daughter-in-law is barren? C'mon!*

After everything God had helped him overcome just to have a child, this new twist in his family's story may have caused some eyebrow raising. But looking back on all the things God had brought him through, what Abraham saw most clearly was God's ability to bring hope to the most hopeless situations. He knew without question that God could and would fulfill His promises. So despite his curiosity about why things happened the way they did, he didn't doubt God's ability. As for Isaac, if he was not fully convinced that God could do miraculous things in his life, he was about to be.

 **Genesis 25:19-34**

Not long after Isaac and Rebekah stepped out from the shadow of Abraham's story and into their own, we discover that God answered their prayers. Turning to God in prayer and trusting Him to provide, Isaac was committed to following in his father's footsteps of faith. As hard as their inability to have a child had been, Isaac and his wife clung to God from the beginning, because Isaac was no stranger to God's ability to provide in the face of trials. It was something he had witnessed firsthand the day his father had placed him on the altar.

Isaac's twin boys arrived when he was sixty years old. Recalling that Abraham was 100 when he had Isaac and 175 when he died, we learn that Grandpa Abraham would have been alive to meet his two grandsons. For the first fifteen years of their lives, Jacob and Esau got to know their amazing grandfather Abraham. At the age of 160, Abraham saw God's promises span another generation. It was exciting, even though the arrival of twins created a new dynamic.

Due to the birth of twins the question could be raised as to who the oldest child was. *Who was going to inherit the covenantal promises next?* Because of this, right from birth, there was a sense of hostility between the brothers—a hostility that followed them for many years. As the brothers got older it became obvious that the inheritance wasn't the only source of friction in their lives, because their personalities didn't mesh either.

" He had a thing for big trucks, big bucks, mud tires, and cheap domestic beer. "

If Esau's red carpet of hair didn't set him apart from Jacob, the brothers' pastimes and vocations did. As the story describes, Esau was a man of open country, the outdoorsy type. He loved watching fishing and hunting videos and spent hours in outdoor recreation stores staring at guns, bows, rods, reels, and anything that came in camo. He had a thing for big trucks, big bucks, mud tires, and cheap domestic beer.

As for Jacob, his personality appeared to be a stark contrast to Esau's. Not so much a man of the open country, Jacob was known to keep to the tents. This likely meant he was the guy who had a lot of friends who were girls, but not necessarily a lot of girlfriends. He probably got bugged by some of the other guys for not being much of an adventure seeker. Jacob's personal bubble was probably larger than most people's, and he was maybe on the shy side. If he ever had something to say, he said it, but only late at night, through a pen, in the safety of his journal. A drastically different personality from his brother, not nearly as rough and tumble, Jacob preferred a more urban lifestyle that involved anything trendy, anything denim, craft beer, a good book, bands no one listened to, and an evening spent manscaping.

That may not be the most accurate depiction of how the two brothers spent their time, but it gives us an idea of how conflicting their personalities were. Their differences were undeniable. It was as if they didn't share much more than a birthdate. Yet there was still one more distinction between them that was even more consequential.

At the time Jacob and Esau entered our story, it was customary for the firstborn male to receive the largest inheritance from the family. In this situation, though it was by only mere seconds, that meant Esau. Esau was not only to inherit larger portions of land and riches when his dad passed, but he was likely going to receive the blessing and responsibility of the family's covenant with God.

Without question, the brothers were not ignorant about the covenant and what it entailed. They had been told all about the promises God had for their family. They would have heard story after story about the things God had done for Grandpa Abraham and their father, Isaac. As youngsters, they would have climbed into their grandpa's lap and listened to stories about their family history with excitement. Childhood play had involved running around and taking turns being Grandpa during his brave rescue of Uncle Lot (**Genesis 14**). Knowing all the details of their heritage and asking to hear a story about their family night after night, Jacob and Esau had probably grown up hearing all about God's covenant. This meant that they should have been excited about their promising future. They should have understood the blessings that were in store.

Since he had been born first, Esau was set to receive the larger inheritance of Isaac's riches, and God's covenant. He would be the one whose family would sprout like weeds. The thought of this should have sent tingles of anticipation up his spine. He would take part in growing a family that would be great and powerful and, most importantly, the one through whom God would send His promised seed to fix creation. If he had been told about the devastation of earth's fall and the passion inside the moment God first uttered His promise (**Genesis 3:15**), Esau should have been honoured to play a role in the resolution of it all, but as it appears, he hardly cared. In fact, Esau despised the rights that he had been given as firstborn so greatly that he sold them for a bowl of soup.

Meanwhile, Jacob revealed that he had a deep desire to be a part of his family's inheritance. He understood what it meant to continue God's covenant, and he longed to follow in the footsteps of his grandpa and dad. Jacob was desperate to share in the work of the Lord, and he wanted to see God's promises grow.

Despite the longing he had, it didn't seem possible that Jacob would ever get to carry the family's covenant onward. But as Esau's attitude towards the inheritance continued to be complacent, eventually an opportunity presented itself. With the help of his mother,

JACOB WOULD GET HIS CHANCE AFTER ALL.

CHAPTER 41

FORFEITING HIS BIRTHRIGHT, ESAU WALKED AWAY, SOUP IN HAND, mistakenly satisfied. We find no sign of regret or remorse for what he had done. But Esau would soon discover that, like any meal, the soup's satisfaction was not lasting. The pleasure he'd found in slurping it down and filling his belly quickly became insufficient. In fact, food for the entire family soon became scarce.

Not long after their exchange in the kitchen, the homeland of Jacob and Esau endured a harsh famine. In a situation similar to the famine in **Genesis 12:10**, which forced their grandfather Abraham to Egypt in search of food, the stress of this famine saw the boys and their family pack up and move. They were ready to go wherever they needed

TO FIND RELIEF.

Genesis 26:1–35

Spurred on by the famine, Isaac packed up his home and started out for Egypt. Though he planned on making Egypt their home until the famine ended, God had other plans. Through an encounter with God, Isaac was instructed to take his family back to Gerar. Included in the discussion was further confirmation regarding the covenant God had made with their family. Hearing God's encouragement to obey Him and pursue His promises, Isaac listened.

Listening to God and staying in Gerar, Isaac had likely avoided trouble by *not* going to Egypt; yet he still felt threatened in the location where he settled. Scared that his wife's beauty would get her pillaged and him killed, Isaac feared for his life. Having apparently inherited his father's problem-solving abilities, he decided to stick to the old family trick and pretend that Rebekah was his sister (**Genesis 20:2**). As it turned out, the lie wasn't necessary, since Rebekah was never taken from him. Regardless, the fib about his sister-wife still caught up with him, as King Abimelech himself watched Isaac get suspiciously *handsy* with his "sister."

We can only imagine the confusion Abimelech experienced the day he discovered the truth about Isaac and Rebekah. The initial shock of uncovering their lie surely disturbed him. It's hard not to wonder how the scene played out when the king witnessed a moment he could never *un*-see.

On the day that it happened, perhaps, while standing on his balcony catching some fresh air, Abimelech spotted Isaac and Rebekah and waved from his perch in a friendly gesture of "hello." Realizing that they were unaware of his presence, Abimelech wasn't concerned until he realized how nervous they appeared. Watching Isaac and his sister look around, like they were trying to escape someone, Abimelech wondered if they were in trouble. Waiting anxiously, he kept an eye on the situation until Isaac's and Rebekah's countenances shifted. Abimelech noticed how relieved they looked to be all alone. Watching as they embraced, he thought, *Such a loving family. I don't know another brother and sister who hug as much as they do.* Before Abimelech turned to go back inside, happy to know everything was all right, something happened. Suddenly he was hit by a mixture of shock and horror. *Wait a minute!* he thought. *Did Isaac and Rebekah just—oh my goodness! I can't believe my eyes! Are they actually—?* **Dude, that's your sister**!

Though that may not be exactly how Isaac and Rebekah's lie caught up to them, their actions clearly disturbed Abimelech enough for him to approach Isaac. Whatever "caressing" he witnessed went far beyond what a brother and sister would ever do. It was obvious that these two were not siblings. At least, that's what Abimelech hoped.

Discovering the truth and not viewing their deception lightly, Abimelech made sure no one would touch Rebekah or Isaac. Then, once again, despite the blunders of man, God provided for Isaac by protecting him and blessing his family greatly—perhaps *too* greatly.

The prosperity Isaac then received as a result of his trickery was so great that his wealth intimidated the people of Gerar. Viewed as a powerful man, Isaac's success scared his neighbours into asking him to move. Graciously, he did as they requested.

After he moved to another location, as time stretched on it became evident to everyone that Isaac's prosperity had nothing to do with *where* he lived. It was because of *who* he lived for. God's presence in his life was so apparent that it was hard for others to ignore. So in a manner reminiscent of what took place in Genesis 21, Abimelech, king of the region, sought a peace treaty with Isaac.

Reaching an agreement with the king, after a journey that began because of a dangerous famine, Isaac ended up with numerous assets while the rest of the local economy seemed to collapse. Meanwhile, his oldest son, Esau, had been acquiring a few assets of his own.

During the years they had been moving around due to the famine, Esau had gone and found himself a couple of wives, choosing women from outside the family line. Esau's wives, Judith and Basemath, were actually descendants of the Hittite clan. And the Hittites had a unique background.

The Hittite people were the descendants of Canaan, the son of Ham. In case we've forgotten, Ham was one of Moses' sons. Ham had been on the ark during the flood and later revealed that he was a bit weird and didn't mind the sight of his drunk and naked old dad (**Genesis 10:6, 10:15**).

With Esau marrying into a family that traced its lineage to a man who got his jollies from watching his father sleep naked, it was almost a guarantee that his wives and in-laws had little interest in the God of his father and grandfather, which suggests, once again, that...

ESAU CARED VERY LITTLE ABOUT FOLLOWING GOD OR HIS BIRTHRIGHT.

CHAPTER 42

AFTER REACHING AN UNDERSTANDING WITH KING ABIMELECH AND agreeing to peace between his family and Abimelech's people, Isaac settled into Beersheba. Here he lived in relative peace, enjoying the land for quite some time, growing old in this location where he found great wealth.

Eventually the time came when Isaac believed his days on earth were ending. As he reflected on his life, all he had seen, the blessings he'd received, and what it would mean to finish strong,

ISAAC'S WANING HEALTH MOVED HIM TO ACTION.

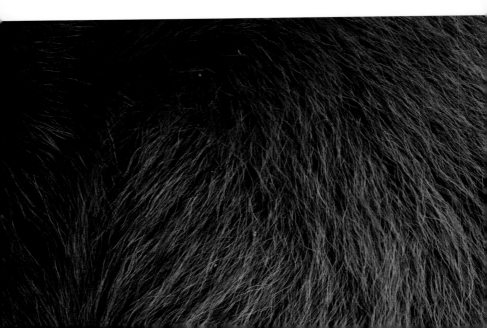

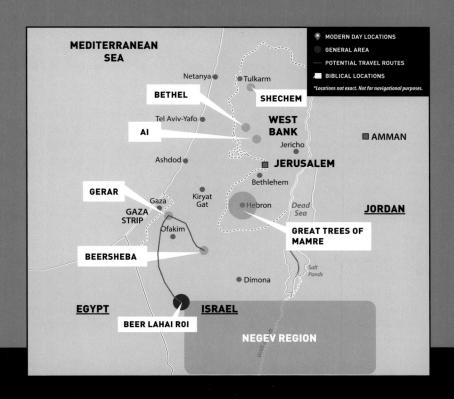

MEDITERRANEAN
SEA

MODERN DAY LOCATIONS
GENERAL AREA
POTENTIAL TRAVEL ROUTES
BIBLICAL LOCATIONS
*Locations not exact. Not for navigational purposes.

Netanya
Tulkarm

BETHEL
SHECHEM

Tel Aviv-Yafo
WEST
BANK

AI
Jericho

AMMAN

Ashdod
JERUSALEM

Bethlehem

GERAR
Kiryat
Gat

Gaza
Hebron
Dead
Sea
JORDAN

GAZA
STRIP
Ofakim

GREAT TREES OF
MAMRE

BEERSHEBA
Salt
Ponds

Dimona

EGYPT
ISRAEL

BEER LAHAI ROI
NEGEV REGION

"The race for the family inheritance was on."

Realizing that it would be a good idea to get his house in order before he passed, Isaac prepared to divide up his inheritance and offer the largest portion of his blessing to the firstborn of his twins, the son he loved most, Esau. Into Esau's hands Isaac was going to pass the torch of blessing that had burned brightly in their family since the time of Abraham. In the meantime, Isaac's wife, Rebekah, decided that she would not sit back and watch Esau take the blessing while the son she loved got overlooked. So Rebekah prepared an inheritance of her own.

The story of this family soon took a drastic turn as the parents pitted their children against one another—Isaac's favourite, Esau, against Rebekah's favourite, Jacob (**Genesis 25:28**). A game of trickery unravelled as Rebekah, determined to land a bright future for her chosen son, pursued a blessing for Jacob. The race for the family inheritance was on. It was a game that neither Isaac nor Esau knew they were playing.

 Genesis 27–28:5

Deceived into blessing his youngest son, Isaac shook with anger over the craftiness he had just seen—or rather, not seen. The words of blessing he had wanted to adorn Esau with had been unknowingly thrust onto the shoulders of Jacob.

Isaac sat in disbelief as he realized that all his earlier suspicions had been true. The son he had blessed had not been Esau. Each carefully selected word and anticipated syllable had been unknowingly offered to his younger son. What deception! As Isaac had sat in his chair, trying to discover truth through the few senses that had yet to fail him, his son had lied and nervously fulfilled each of his requests. The events that led to the blessing had undoubtedly been filled with intense hesitation. Isaac had inquired and tested to the best of his abilities. He had not been content to utter the blessing until his nose had met the familiar scent of Esau. But even with that he found himself deceived.

Covered in fear, doubt, and a layer of sweat beneath the goatskin, Jacob had faced inquiries at every turn as he impersonated his brother. He was questioned about his prompt arrival and why his voice had changed, inspected for hair upon his hands, and blatantly asked, "Are you really my son Esau?" Each time his father probed, Jacob cautiously tried to pacify his father, thinking, *This is it; the jig is up!* Then, to his amazement, as he bent down to kiss his father, thinking for certain their contact would give him up, the words of blessing began to wash over him. Hardly able to hear his father's soft voice through his own mind as it shouted, *I can't believe it worked!* Jacob walked away in joy, excitement, and surely disbelief—making his exit just in time.

As Esau returned to his father, the scene that unfolded was chaotic. Esau was distraught that his dad had not recognized him. As the reality of what had happened set in for both men, so did heartache.

" For Esau, there was *no* understanding. "

The frustration Isaac felt had certainly been immense. How degraded he felt to have such a trick played on him! Knowing he had been taken advantage of in his vulnerable state. Knowing he had been shown little kindness. Knowing he had been lied to. Jacob's actions had been disrespectful and downright offensive. However, despite how he felt about the situation, Isaac maintained his demeanour and responded to the scenario with profound insight, suggesting that, against his own will, this was how things were meant to be. Somehow, Isaac realized that Jacob hadn't stolen something from Esau; rather, he simply received what God had assigned him. At some point during the course of events, Isaac seemed to understand the words God had spoken when Rebekah had been pregnant with the boys; God had told Rebekah that the older brother would serve the younger (**Genesis 25:23**).

For Esau, there was *no* understanding. Jacob had come into his life and taken everything. First, he claimed his birthright as a firstborn, and now, his blessing. What was there left for him? Could his dad offer him anything? As Esau begged for understanding and searched for any blessing crumbs that Jacob may have left, the words that remained sounded less like a blessing and more like a curse.

As Esau's anger increased, the hostility between the brothers found new heights. Esau's rage boiled, flooding his mind and shaking his heart. It was clear that nothing short of Jacob's blood would calm the fury. Under the assumption that their father would soon pass away, Esau immediately gave Jacob a new reason to fear their father's death. Once

Isaac was gone, there would be nothing stopping him from repaying Jacob for what he had done.

The calamity that ensued hadn't been easy for Jacob to bear. Though he had been blessed as ruler over his brother, he felt afflicted. Watching his father ache in frustration while his brother erupted with anger, shortly after acquiring the blessing Jacob didn't feel blessed at all.

News of Esau's anger unnerved both Jacob and Rebekah. Haunted by the fact that Isaac's death would send Esau on a mission to put Jacob into the ground, Rebekah decided she wouldn't let that happen. Jacob couldn't die. Not that easily. There was far too much riding on him now.

As Rebekah contemplated all these things, she realized that the aggressive dissension between the two brothers might be enough to break Isaac's heart. He was already frail enough. Looking for a way to protect Jacob from Esau and protect Isaac from realizing the turmoil in the family, Rebekah attempted to separate the brothers in a manner that looked natural and smart.

Reminding Isaac of the grief that had come through Esau's marriage to Hittite women, Rebekah recounted her frustrations with Judith and Basemath. Though her irritation with her daughters-in-law hardly stretched the truth, Rebekah spoke each word hoping Isaac would realize that Jacob could not be left to make the same mistake. The best solution would be for Jacob to marry within the family. Out of desperation to separate the brothers, Rebekah embellished her fear of Jacob marrying a local woman and encouraged her husband to send Jacob to a better land. Isaac consented.

Equipped with a birthright, a blessing, and plenty of confusion, Jacob fled for his life. Setting off on his journey, he pointed his camel or donkey— or whatever it was he travelled with—in the direction of his mother's homeland. His life had taken a drastic turn. With tears in his eyes, he kissed his mother goodbye and then, his father. Jacob knew it would likely be the last time he saw his dad.

As he travelled off in search of a place of refuge and, hopefully, comfort for his heavy heart, he prayed for guidance on his journey, knowing that the road would not be easy to navigate, especially with misty eyes and a lonely heart.

Though no numbers are mentioned at this time, the story will later inform us that Jacob was roughly eighty years old when he set off for Haran. Not exactly the age we expect someone to leave home to start off on his own,

BUT JACOB HAD NO CHOICE.

CHAPTER 43

SHORTLY AFTER DECEIVING HIS FATHER, CHASED OFF BY ESAU'S rage, Jacob gathered his belongings, left home, and ran north. He was equipped with blessings and a covenant with God, but a life of uncertainty opened up before him.

 **Genesis 28:6–29:14**

Jacob made his way to the city of Haran, located in the land of Paddan Aram. Also known by the name "Aram Naharaim," it was the same area that grandfather Abraham's servant had gone to in search of a wife for his father. It was a search that had brought his dad and mom together (**Genesis 24:10**).

While he was on his journey, once again God affirmed the covenant He had started with Abraham. Although God's words to Jacob were somewhat a repeat of what his father had told him, this may have been the first time that Jacob heard the words directly from God rather than from a family member. If he hadn't been completely convinced that God had a plan, he was now.

AND THE TIMING OF HIS ENCOUNTER WITH GOD COULDN'T HAVE BEEN MORE PERFECT.

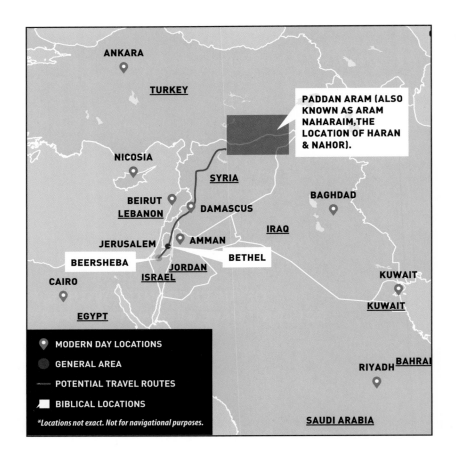

MODERN DAY LOCATIONS

GENERAL AREA

POTENTIAL TRAVEL ROUTES

BIBLICAL LOCATIONS

Locations not exact. Not for navigational purposes.

Having just left his homeland in pursuit of protection, Jacob had abandoned everything he'd known. With unpredictable scenarios and what-ifs clouding his mind, undoubtedly he experienced regret, fear, doubt, worry, wonder, and most definitely loneliness. He'd been plagued with anxiety. Then one night, he curled up with a rock for a pillow, thinking about how lavish his bed had been and feeling more sorry for himself than ever before. As Jacob tossed and turned uncomfortably, thinking he'd reached the lowest of lows, God showed up and comforted him in a way that cushy pillows and a familiar bed never could.

God spoke to Jacob throughout the night, and the words He spoke filled Jacob with a confidence he never knew he had. God was with him, watching over him. He would never leave him, no matter where he went.

All the blessings his dad offered him at his departure (many descendants, prosperous living, and a land that would be his own) received even more emphasis during that late-night encounter.

Coming off an exciting night with God, Jacob rose the next morning with a refreshed intentionality about his journey. Moved by what he saw, the words he heard, and the tangible love of God, he was compelled to rename the location "Bethel," a spot believed to be located just north of modern-day Jerusalem. There at Bethel, though he still had his uncertainties, Jacob knew one thing for sure—God was in control.

In the meantime, back at home, after he learned about his brother's departure and his father's disdain for local women, Esau set out on a search for Uncle Ishmael. Hoping to find a way back into his father's good books, Esau married a cousin: Ishmael's daughter Mahalath. He believed that marrying inside the family, like Jacob planned to, would look good on his resume. So while Esau busied himself with feeble attempts at pleasing his father, Jacob arrived at his destination.

After what would have been an exhausting journey, physically, mentally, and emotionally, the realization that he had made it safely to his family was overwhelming. Consumed with joy and great emotion, Jacob broke down and cried. He found his cousin Rachel and informed her that they were related; he was the son of her Aunt Rebekah. With that news, Jacob was embraced into his uncle's family.

For the first time in a long time, Jacob could relax—he was safe. His journey of fear and trepidation had ended in the safety and comfort of his northern relatives. His acceptance into their home marked the end of a gruelling trip that had been filled with fear and countless glances over his shoulder, hoping not to see his brother on the horizon. Finally in Haran, Jacob hoped for peace. Though many miles separated him from his brother, he soon learned that peace wouldn't come easily up north. He may not have had reason to fear for his life, but Jacob was about to discover that, if you want something,

YOU'RE GOING TO HAVE TO WORK FOR IT.

CHAPTER 44

SAFE AND SECURE UNDER THE WELCOMING ROOF OF FAMILY, Jacob will now be the primary focus of our story. Though his father was still alive at the time, he was now carrying the legacy passed down to him from his father and grandfather—the covenant with God.

As he began his new life up north in the region of Paddan Aram, almost immediately Jacob went to work for his Uncle Laban. Revealing himself to be a man of hard work, he efficiently performed whatever task he was assigned. In fact, he was so productive, he even had the opportunity to choose his own wages. Viewing it as an opportunity he couldn't resist, Jacob made his uncle an offer he hoped he wouldn't refuse, seeking a payment he'd be happy to embrace.

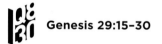 **Genesis 29:15–30**

After seven years of mounting anticipation, Laban put on quite a feast to celebrate his daughter's marriage. For Jacob, it would have been the greatest time of rejoicing he had seen in a while. In fact, as it turned out, the celebration was maybe a little bit too spectacular for Jacob. After completing his seven years of work, placing the last "x" on his calendar, submitting his "bill" to Laban, and waiting for his payment, Jacob celebrated himself into a stupor. Consumed with excitement, he was so caught up in the festivities he couldn't decipher who he ended up taking home. Waking up the next morning and realizing what had happened,

.

HE WAS FURIOUS.

For seven long years he had dreamt of waking up next to Rachel, a woman so beautiful in form. Instead, rather than rolling over after his honeymoon and experiencing a moment he'd spent seven years working towards, Jacob was shocked to discover that it wasn't Rachel lying beside him; rather, it was her weak-eyed sister Leah. Like if awaiting the arrival of a succulent dessert and being served broccoli, Jacob was not impressed. Chances are, he wasn't the only one upset.

Though it's hard to say for sure, there's a good possibility that Rachel was distraught over these events as well. Perhaps she was excited to have Jacob as her husband. For seven years she and Jacob may have discussed their future together. Countless hours had been spent sneaking meaningful glances at one another as they walked around suppressing their intense emotions. They had longed for the day when they could finally let their walls down and cast away their reservations. They had waited for the moment when they would let their growing love escape without reason to restrain it. How they had ached to surrender to the emotions that consumed their minds and intensified their senses! To wait seven years, only to be robbed of that moment, would have been devastating.

Regardless of how passionately Jacob and Rachel may have waited for that day, it had been only a minor detail in the eyes of Laban. Finding a way to do as he saw fit, Laban's twisting of his contract with Jacob revealed him to be a real shady man of business. He was the biblical equivalent to a greasy used car salesman. *(No offence to all non-greasy used car salesmen!)* Not only had Laban secured the marriage of both daughters to a good man, but he guaranteed himself another seven years of service from a great employee. Laban was either underhanded or a genius.

As for Jacob, tasting the sting of another man's deception, perhaps the events ignited a flashback in his memory, reminding him of the deception he had performed on his father—the deception that had led him to Laban. Whether it triggered memories or not, Jacob was disturbed by what Laban had done. Yet, despite his heartache, he was eventually united with Rachel.

He committed to his uncle for another seven years, and as a result of their continued partnership both Laban's and Jacob's households were about to be blessed. Jacob's hard work and God's presence in his life were an equation that led to expanding riches. And with his acquisition of two wives, Jacob's family would soon start to grow—

AND GROW—AND GROW.

CHAPTER 45

UNITED WITH RACHEL AT LAST, AFTER A WEEK-LONG MARRIAGE celebration with wife number two Jacob went back to work for his father-in-law, just as they had agreed.

With Rachel being given as an advance for his work, Jacob happily accepted the contract and got down to business (yes, in both ways). Having already worked seven years for Laban, Jacob now had two wives to show for it and another seven years of stable work. Perhaps Laban's trickery hadn't been such a bad scenario after all?

As time progressed, Jacob discovered what life was like when trying to balance two women. He quickly learned that things would not be as peaceful as he hoped. As he showed blatant favouritism to Rachel over Leah,

MAJOR DISSENSION GREW INSIDE HIS HOME.

Jacob's preference for Rachel resulted in God looking on Leah with pity for the neglect she endured. In response to her pain, God blessed her with a child, revealing that Jacob hadn't been ignoring her entirely. As the family began to grow through Leah, Rachel discovered she was barren, and a war for their husband's affection developed as pressure to birth more sons mounted. Being married to a man who had been promised countless descendants did not help the stress. The situation inside Jacob's home got more and more confusing, and eventually, Leah and Rachel did *whatever* they felt necessary to acquire more children.

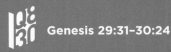 **Genesis 29:31-30:24**

" With children viewed as a sign of favour, a war of the womb broke out in his home "

As Jacob's family began to grow, so did the tension. With children viewed as a sign of favour, a war of the womb broke out in his home.

As Leah and Rachel fought for the affection of their shared husband, a competition arose over who could give Jacob the most children. Throwing themselves at him—and when that failed, throwing other women in for good measure, just like Abraham's wife, Sarah, had—Rachel and Leah believed that having their husband sleep with other women would be a good solution. As a result, both women sent their husband to bed with their maidservants, and the numbers in Jacob's household grew.

Caught in the middle of this domestic dispute, Jacob found himself being traded between four different women. Eventually, his wives became so desperate for his "affection" that they even bought and sold time with him. Reaching a whole new level of odd, when Leah invested in an evening with her husband, Jacob found himself being informed that he had been "hired" for the "job" (wink-wink nudge-nudge).

Jacob must have been exhausted by the antics of his wives. Regardless, when all was said and done, the dust settled, the sheets changed, and the beds made, Jacob had amassed twelve kids. Even barren Rachel gave him a son of her own.

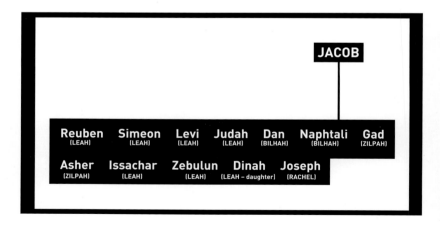

During that time, as Jacob remained living near and working with Laban, his family and possessions grew greatly. Busy starting a family, the years slipped by unnoticed. Before Jacob knew it, twenty years had passed. Twenty years away from his home. Twenty years separated from his family. And even though he had not yet heard from his mother that it was safe to return (**Genesis 27:45**),

HE COULDN'T HELP BUT WONDER IF IT WASN'T TIME TO GO BACK.

CHAPTER 46

ALTHOUGH HE WAS FIRMLY ESTABLISHED IN PADDAN ARAM, JACOB began to play with the idea that he needed to shake things up a bit. *Maybe it's time to return home to see my mother and father.* The thought seemed enticing.

Having found great success alongside Uncle Laban, Jacob wanted to return to his own family to show them how the years of separation had blessed him, to show his mother that her plan to leave home had been a good one, and to show his father that

GOD WAS FULFILLING HIS PLAN FOR THEIR FAMILY.

As enticing as a return to the homeland was, there remained a point of hesitation. Esau. A return trip down south would likely involve an encounter with his brother, who was determined to repay him for his deception. No sooner had Jacob contemplated his return than he also began to wonder, *Maybe twenty years hasn't been long enough?*

 Genesis 30:25–31:21

Jacob's years with Laban, although bountiful, had been filled with trials and frustrations. After twenty years with Uncle Laban, Jacob decided enough was enough. Feeling that it was time for a change, he asked Laban for the blessing to return home. However, aware of how greatly he benefited from Jacob's presence, Laban did everything he could to keep his nephew around.

Not wanting to lose his best employee, in an act of desperation Laban attempted to bribe Jacob, telling him to name his price for staying (**Genesis 30:31**). Laban knew that letting Jacob pick his payment had worked in the past. Though Laban's offer can seem generous, it wasn't inspired by a concern for Jacob's best interest. Laban just wanted to keep prospering off his nephew son-in-law. However, Jacob would not be easily bought this time, so he came up with a counter-offer. An agreement on wages was finally reached, and Laban viewed it as another opportunity to hoodwink his nephew. Old habits die hard.

Having agreed that any spotted or speckled goats or sheep would be Jacob's, Laban quickly removed any goats and lambs that met this description from his flock and sent them on a three-day journey away. He left Jacob without a single marked goat or lamb to use for breeding. Jacob was left to protect a speckleless, spotless, and streakless flock of animals. And Laban walked away confident that he had secured Jacob's presence for a long time. There was no chance he could acquire an inheritance from *these* goats and lambs.

Without any animals that met the description they had agreed on, Jacob's inability to build up his own flock meant he would need to continually rely on his uncle's support. Things did not look good. Once again, Laban revealed himself to be nothing but a greasy goat salesman. Luckily, God had other plans.

As Jacob stood before Laban's flocks, it's likely that he knew *exactly* what his uncle had done. Regardless, being a man of his word, Jacob committed to his duties and tended the freshly rotated stock of goats and lambs. Then he got creative in an attempt to produce a herd for himself.

Picking out the strongest, healthiest, and most vibrant animals from the flock, Jacob began a science experiment built around the age-old adage of "what you see is what you get." Putting the healthiest males and females together, Jacob placed speckled, spotted, and streaked pieces of wood in front of them while they were mating. He was desperate to find a solution to Laban's underhanded dealings, although it was more superstition than fact. But God was on Jacob's side, and He brought to life a healthy and strong herd of animals that was visually distinguishable from Laban's by both colour and pedigree. In time, Jacob stockpiled a large number of his very own speckled, spotted, and streaked goats and sheep, each of them birthed from the strongest and healthiest animals in Laban's speckleless, spotless, and streakless flock.

As Jacob's success continued to rise, so did Laban's frustration. The look of bewilderment that must have crossed Laban's face when he noticed Jacob's growing cluster of marked goats would have been undeniable. Like going home for a high-school reunion and seeing the class nerd turned model, Laban couldn't comprehend the transformation.

Sensing hostility and worried over the anger growing in Laban's sons, Jacob decided it was time to make his exit. Although he was still uncertain about whether or not a return trip home was a good idea, Jacob's frustration with Laban was inspiration enough to finally make the move.

Preparing for the journey in a hurried manner, his family packed up the belongings God had blessed them with and pointed their camels south. They began putting distance between them and shrewd Laban—but not before sticky-fingered Rachel

DECIDED SHE WOULD TREAT HERSELF TO A FEW OF HER FATHER'S PERSONAL EFFECTS.

CHAPTER 47

ON THE WAY TO HIS HOMELAND WITH NO LOOKING BACK, JACOB felt like a free man. His twenty years of service to Uncle Laban had finally ended. The relief he experienced as he took those first steps in the other direction had been nothing short of exhilarating. In that moment, Jacob felt a level of freedom he had nearly forgot existed. Like students getting out of class on the last day of school, Jacob was free to dream over the potential that lay before him. For ten joyful days he enjoyed this newfound life—

UNTIL AN ALARM SOUNDED AND "PRINCIPAL LABAN" CAME IN PURSUIT.

Not impressed with their sudden departure and searching for answers, Laban fuelled up his fastest camel and tore after Jacob in a cops-and-robbers-style pursuit. Though Jacob's three-day head start left him with some ground to cover, Laban had speed and time on his side. It would take Jacob over two weeks to reach his homeland, and that's not accounting for travel with a herd of goats and sheep. Laban's ability to travel light and travel fast would work in his favour. It would only be a matter of time before he caught up to the band of runaways.

Genesis 31:22–54

Laban caught up to Jacob a week after beginning his pursuit, and it's immediately evident that he was enraged by their departure. As if their sneaky exit hadn't been infuriating enough, someone in Jacob's household had had the audacity to pour salt on the wound by taking Laban's idols. In an angry frenzy, he had sped across the land, desperate to catch Jacob, spending each day riding, fuelled by his frustrations and mulling over the choice words he would share with his ungrateful nephew.

Meanwhile, as Jacob travelled between Paddan Aram and his homeland, much like before he found himself continually checking the horizon, anticipating an angry family member in pursuit. Unfortunately for Jacob, unlike his trip north, his escape back home was no clean getaway. On the tenth day of his journey, as he checked the horizon, sure enough, there was Laban.

Laban wasted no time tearing into Jacob, scorning him for his disrespect by leaving unannounced *and* with his belongings. Unbeknownst to Jacob, however, was the truth behind Laban's claims. With Jacob's permission, Laban stormed through tents in a fanatical search for his missing deities. It's worth wondering if Laban ever thought to himself, *How helpful are these gods if someone could so easily take them against their own will?*

With Laban coming up empty-handed after his search, Jacob finally reached a breaking point with his father-in-law. Frustrated over twenty years of shady business deals and the recent accusation that he was a thief, Jacob gave Laban a tongue-lashing of his own, highlighting how mistreated he had been over the years. Jacob made it clear that if Laban wanted to be mad over his success, he would have to be mad at God, because even against Laban's best efforts, God had brought Jacob prosperity.

As he digested the large piece of humble pie Jacob served him, Laban realized that his son-in-law and daughters were indeed moving. The only option he had left was to make peace and return home. With God as their witness, they did just that.

Having reached an understanding and put their relationship in order, the time had come for Laban and Jacob to part ways. After exchanging hugs, kisses, and a sombre goodbye,

**JACOB AND HIS FAMILY
CONTINUED THEIR JOURNEY SOUTH.**

CHAPTER 48

WITH THINGS SETTLED BETWEEN HIM AND LABAN, JACOB FOCUSED on completing his journey. No longer concerned about his possessive father-in-law coming after him, he should have been able to fully enjoy the trip between Paddan Aram and home. However, as good as stepping out of Laban's shadow felt, circumstances did not allow Jacob to enjoy his journey.

Jacob kept thinking about how each step they took brought them closer to the reason he had fled—Esau. Jacob couldn't help but wonder what an encounter with Esau might look like. Had Esau forgiven him for what he had done? Might he still be seeking to kill him, even after all these years? These heavy thoughts darkened Jacob's return home. A journey that should have been full of joy and excitement was accompanied by doubts and uncertainties as Jacob continued to wonder if twenty years had been long enough.

Hauling carts, herding cattle, and moving across the dry landscape at an easy pace, Jacob and his family travelled in a constant cloud of dust that slowly rose into the sky and disappeared. Invigorated by a new sense of liberty and independence, conversations about what their new home might be like, where they might live, and what it would be like to meet other members of the family began to surface. Despite his best efforts, however, Jacob was not able to match everyone else's level of emotion. While they celebrated and looked into the distance with anticipation, he moved in fear—haunted by his knowledge that their future could be significantly less beautiful and exciting than they all hoped.

 Genesis 31:55–32:32

When only a short distance separated him from Esau, Jacob knew it was time to discover the answer he feared. Already filled with concern, the announcement that his brother was drawing nearer, accompanied by an army of 400 men, only heightened his distress. The words from his messenger had

TURNED HIS GREATEST FEAR INTO A REALITY.

In a frantic effort to preserve life, knowing he had no chance against a vengeful brother and 400 men, Jacob divided up his household, hoping to save a remnant from inevitable slaughter. The situation seemed hopeless for him and his family. Twenty years had not been long enough, yet it had seemed as if God had encouraged him to come home. *Why? Simply to lose everything I've gained to the enraged hands of my brother?*

"This time there would be no trickery."

As overwhelming as the moment seemed, we discover that Jacob had not surrendered all hope. In a heartfelt prayer (**Genesis 32:9–12**) he recounted God's blessings and clung to the promises spoken over his life. Encouraged through time in prayer and believing wholeheartedly that his God is a God who saves, Jacob held on to the only hope he had. His God was capable of providing hope even in the darkest hour—an hour in which Jacob now stood.

Leaning desperately on God's grace to save him, Jacob tried to find the point of Esau's mercy. In an attempt to appease his brother's wrath, he sent droves of animals before him as an offering. Five separate clusters were sent, each of them separated to add to the grandeur. As each herd moved forward, they carried a fear-induced message of Jacob's humility. He would let it be known that he was a servant of Esau. The gifts he offered were somewhat a penance for the guilt that he felt for the things he had done.

After a long day of planning, strategizing, dividing, and praying, one last night separated Jacob from Esau. So Jacob parted ways with his family and continued to seek God.

Clearly Jacob's decision to seek God in his trials had been a wise choice, as amazing events transpired in the night. Almost as if the mental wrestling he had been enduring had come to life, that night Jacob found himself wrestling with a man.

Jacob's desperation for God to intervene played out physically as he grappled with a man until daybreak. With many tears and heartfelt pleading (**Hosea 12:4**), Jacob cried out for mercy, begged for a blessing and hoped for a change of heart in his brother. As Jacob writhed and turned, fighting with the man, his body joined in his heart's desperate cry for God to do something in that moment. Then the man spoke.

It seems curious that God would ask Jacob what his name was. One would assume that God knew exactly who He was engaging with. However, the question was not meant for God's clarification; it was more a test of Jacob's character. It was symbolic of the changes that had taken place in Jacob's life, because the last time he wanted a blessing and someone asked him who he was, he responded by saying, *"It's Esau"* (**Genesis 27:19**). This time there would be no trickery.

After his response, the man Jacob had engaged with, who represented God as an angel (**Hosea 12:4**), ended the quarrel with the simple touch of his hand. Instantly it became clear that this man could have done much worse than wrench Jacob's hip.

Equipped with a new name and a swagger in his step, thanks to the wrenched hip, Jacob knew that what had transpired was significant. As he waddled into the sunrise with a whole new level of faith and favour,

THE TIME HAD COME TO MEET WITH ESAU.

CHAPTER 49

AFTER AN INTENSE NIGHT AND LITTLE REST, JACOB, NOW KNOWN as Israel, walked gingerly back to his family. After a nightlong tussle, it's likely that he looked as haggard as he felt, but there was no time for freshening up. Almost instantly Esau and his mob of followers appeared in the distance.

Frantically Jacob rearranged and prepared his family for the encounter. Feeling like he was staring down the barrels of a well-trained infantry, with nowhere to run and nowhere to hide,

JACOB BRACED HIMSELF FOR WHATEVER CAME NEXT.

He trembled with uncertainty, heart racing, sweat pooling on his back, and twenty years of questions dizzying his mind. The reunion that was about to take place would soon put to rest *all* the questions that had plagued him—either affirming or alleviating his greatest fears.

 Genesis 33:1–20

The emotional embrace of Jacob and Esau was nothing short of fantastic. After twenty years of wondering about one another they were brought to tears in each other's arms. Though the story focuses on Jacob and how he spent hours worrying about Esau's reaction, it's obvious that Esau experienced his own myriad of emotions.

Perhaps after he learned about his brother's departure from their homeland because of *his* anger, their separation had eaten away at Esau's fury. Maybe Esau had spent time wondering where his brother was, how he had aged, or if he had a family. Though it's hard to know for certain the thoughts Esau had, the news that this brother was on his way would have ignited a new wave of emotions.

Knowing that Jacob would have just travelled a great distance, Esau may have seen this as an opportunity. Exhausted from his journey, Jacob would be an easy target. *Who does he think he is? Returning home like nothing ever happened.* Perhaps Esau had set off to meet his brother in hopes of catching him far enough from home that their father would not know. Without Mom or Dad there to run interference, Esau and Jacob could have it out—just the two of them—once and for all.

If Esau had begun his trek towards Jacob with vengeance in mind, somehow something changed in the process. For reasons that were beyond even what Esau understood, slowly he began to soften. Esau began thinking about what it would be like to see Jacob after all this time, and rather than getting even with him, he thought about introducing his children to their uncle. His kids were about to meet their uncle, his twin. It was more than likely that Esau himself was about to meet nephews and nieces he'd never heard of. A growing curiosity softened his heart. The closer he moved towards Jacob, the more his countenance shifted.

Moving with a whole new purpose to their meeting, Esau's interest only piqued as he encountered one herd after another, each led by Jacob's servants, each offered as a gift from Jacob, his servant.

As Esau contemplated the meaning behind the offering and the words of Jacob's servants, it struck him that his brother must have still been concerned over their meeting. His anger had scared Jacob that deeply, and now his brother sought understanding and grace through these gifts.

Esau felt horribly misunderstood and wanted nothing more than for his brother to know he had been forgiven. He only wanted to embrace Jacob and celebrate their reunion. At that moment, Esau picked up the pace, anxious to see his brother and longing for him to know that all was well. It was a message that Jacob received loud and clear.

The moment they embraced, every wall Jacob had built around his heart regarding his brother crumbled to the ground. It was obvious that Esau had forgiven him. Their time apart did not matter anymore. What mattered was that they were reunited, healthy, prosperous, and in the presence of one another.

Jacob cried tears of joy and relief in the arms of his brother—thankful for his embrace and grateful that God had heard his prayers. Whether it had been earlier in his life or overnight, God had broken Esau's hunger for vengeance and softened his heart of stone—as only God can.

Jacob had returned to the land he'd called home, and he and his family settled in what would be known as the Promised Land. Stopping near the city of Shechem, Jacob had returned to the very stretch of land God had devoted to his family—first to Abraham, then to Isaac, and now to him.

Free from his father-in-law and reunited with his brother, the blessings in Jacob's life seemed to multiply. It was only fitting that they celebrate their arrival and

THE MIGHTY WORK OF GOD.

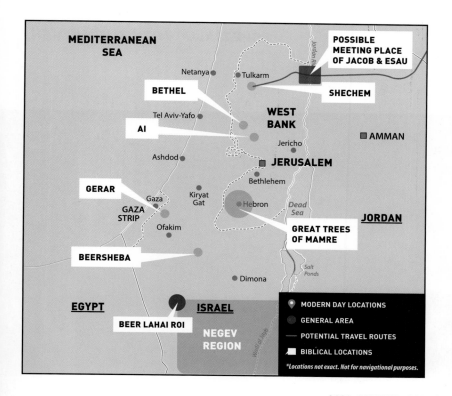

CHAPTER 50

HAVING PURCHASED LAND BEYOND THE CITY OF SHECHEM, JACOB and his family finally settled into their first *real* home, a place of their own.

Interested in the local scene, members of Jacob's household ventured off to introduce themselves to their neighbours—like any new resident of a community might do. As they got acquainted with the local people, it just so happened that the locals wanted to acquaint themselves with Jacob's family as well—

ESPECIALLY WITH THE WOMEN.

Female descendants in Jacob's household seem to have carried a few common characteristics. One, they were often infertile. Two, they were beautiful. With that in mind, perhaps, it was only a matter of time before Jacob's only mentioned daughter, Dinah, captured the attention of local males, who would stop at nothing to have her.

 Genesis 34–35:5

In the aftermath of these events, unexpectedly, Jacob's life started to play out like a mobster film. With Dinah, the youngest of Jacob's first wife, Leah, violated and disgraced, her brothers decided that such actions could not go unpunished.

“ Jacob's life started to play out
like a mobster film. ”

Only a protective older brother can understand the outrage that clung to Simeon and Levi as they learned about the assault that had taken place on their little sister. What Shechem had done to her was unforgivable in their eyes. They would see to it that justice was brought to him for this atrocity, confident that Shechem's distasteful actions gave them every right to respond (**Genesis 34:31**). Through a deceitful promise, the scene escalated in classic gangster I'll-one-up-you fashion. What we are left with as readers is the story's very first man-inflicted mass casualties outside of war.

Until this point in the story, the previous major loss of life had been from the flood, an act done in God's grace and desperation to reach out and provide for His creation. In dark contrast to God's sovereign act, Simeon and Levi took lives out of anger and resentment, as a personal vendetta. The impact their actions would have on the lives of those around them bore no weight in their decision making. This was personal, prideful, and driven by selfishness.

As news about what they had done spread throughout the family, their vendetta did not go overlooked by their father. Jacob was horrified by the actions of his sons. Fully aware of the potential danger that followed their family because of this, he wondered what repercussions there might be. Clearly, Simeon and Levi had never stopped to consider the fact that the people living in Shechem, the Hivites, were descendants of the Canaanites, a powerful people who were great in number. This was a *big* problem.

To make matters worse, the area they had settled in was Canaanite country. Canaan, Noah's grandson, had had eleven kids. His family had grown large and fast. Though Jacob owned a plot of land in the area, he and his family were merely aliens there. Now they were the aliens who had moved to a new country and killed all the men in one small town. This was not going to be viewed lightly by the Canaanite people.

To top it all off, the Canaanites weren't the only threat. This area was also home to the Perizzite people. On their own, the Canaanites or the Perizzites could have easily overwhelmed Jacob's family. The thought that they might join forces to respond to the actions of Simeon and Levi was horrifying. It made Esau and his band of 400 seem like a welcomed threat.

Contemplating all of this and seeing how easily things could go from bad to worse, Jacob prayed for mercy, hoping that the ignorance of his sons had not poked a sleeping bear. Angry over their actions and cautious of his future, he needed to do something, and fast. Thankfully for Jacob, he was not alone in his worries.

In constant provision for Jacob's family and continued pursuit of His promises, God provided a way once again. Guiding Jacob back to Bethel, the location where He had revealed Himself to Jacob earlier (**Genesis 28:10–22**), God led Jacob and his family to their new home and place of respite.

Rushing to relocate and thankful for God's leading, Jacob made sure that all other gods were banished from his family's homes. No manmade statue of wood, gold, bronze, or stone was going to save them at a time like this! *What help could those "gods" provide in their manmade stagnant form?* In fact, only weeks earlier, Rachel had effectively outmuscled one of Laban's gods and hid it under her butt while she bounced around sweating on a camel. Now, in a time of desperation, the sweaty-butt god was supposed to be their comfort? No. Jacob knew dependence on a god like that would be nothing short of laughable. There was only one God who was living and active and

ONE GOD WHO WOULD BE THEIR STRENGTH AND FORTRESS IN A MOMENT LIKE THIS.

 **Jonah 2:8**

CHAPTER 51

ON THE MOVE AGAIN, THANKS TO THE VENGEFUL ACTS OF SIMEON and Levi, Jacob and his family loaded up their household and headed farther south. At the instruction of God, in witness-protection-like manner, they relocated to Bethel,

A DESTINATION JACOB HAD VISITED BEFORE.

Years earlier, as he made his escape from Esau, Jacob had a serious encounter with God in Bethel. It was there that God spoke to Jacob through a dream and affirmed the promises and blessings He'd previously given to Abraham and Isaac. God's covenant with their family had been passed down to Jacob. In response to his encounter with God, Jacob had anointed the place and called it Bethel, meaning "house of God." Offering himself to God, Jacob vowed on that day that if God would bring him back safely to his father's house, God would surely be his God (**Genesis 28:20-22**). Now, as Jacob was led back to that exact location, God was about to remind him of his vow, affirm His own vows, and reveal Himself in a magnificent way.

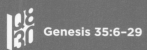 **Genesis 35:6-29**

Living a nomadic lifestyle, Jacob's family travelled from place to place as the drama within their household continued. As they prepared to leave Shechem and head for Bethel, it's apparent that Jacob knew he was moving to a significant location. Reminded of the encounter he had with God twenty years earlier, he commanded his whole household to purge themselves of any other gods they may have had.

It seems that up to this point, Jacob had been somewhat lethargic about making sure everyone in his household followed *one* God. But as he thought about moving to Bethel, a place he heralded as awesome, the house of God and the gate of heaven (**Genesis 28:17**), he knew that needed to change. Jacob had declared that if God brought him home safely, God would be his God—no one else (**Genesis 28:20-22**). And the time had come for him to embrace that declaration and an entirely new level of devotion.

Reaching Bethel, Jacob felt refreshed to have left all the extra baggage buried under the oak tree in Shechem. As he built a new altar upon his arrival, it became evident to the entire family that the God of Bethel was truly amazing.

God appeared to Jacob again, in what was likely a magnificent display, making His promises to the family more specific by informing Jacob that kings would come from his body. That's right, not just *a* king, but *kings* (**Genesis 35:11**).

The news that a king would come from Jacob brought with it numerous implications. A king meant there would likely be a kingdom. A kingdom would likely include a large portion of land. A large portion of land would need to be filled by a large number of people. And a large number of people, settled on a large plot of land, could only mean that Jacob's family would one day have a home. Not merely a piece of land in a foreign country where they had reason to fear their neighbours, but their own domain. God was reiterating His promise of land—*the Promised Land.*

As they had recently travelled from place to place, not knowing what it was like to settle down for an extended period of time, the thought of having a stable home stirred up a deep longing inside Jacob's family. The constant transitions were taxing on everyone. With no permanent roots planted in any location and no peace of mind about the kind of life their kids would inherit, the frustration and unrest of travelling were real. If they weren't aware of the pains of travelling as they moved from Bethel, they soon would be.

As they journeyed down to Ephrath (roughly forty-five kilometres south of Bethel), Rachel found herself going into labour, and things got complicated.

Trapped between locations, with little help outside of his own family, Jacob felt lost. He was desperate to find a remedy for his suffering wife. Despite his deep longing for her survival, the love of Jacob's life died. His heart was torn. Two of his sons were left without a mother. And things got confusing.

Having begun his journey to Ephrath after an exhilarating stay in Bethel, Jacob may have experienced what some people consider a "spiritual high." As he continued his journey south with confidence, believing that God had set his future on cruise control, before he'd gone far Jacob's excitement over God's plans for his future received a major blow.

The loss of Rachel would have been unquestionably difficult to endure, as it painted a dark contrast to the excitement he had been feeling over his future. The contradiction between God's promises and what he felt likely had Jacob asking tough questions.

> **"Why would God allow such pain amidst such promise? Why did this have to happen? How can God claim to have a plan and let this take place?"**

Although, like many of us, Jacob may have never found concrete answers for his tough questions, he remained mindful that God works in our pain. God did not cause it, but He can mend it. In fact, God's work is most blatant in our times of need, when our hearts are broken (**Psalm 34:18**). Jacob knew that God was in the business of healing brokenness because brokenness on earth wasn't a part of His original plan.

The garden God had originally placed man in knew nothing of sickness, heartache, the pains of childbirth, or death. Those all came *after* man rejected God's plan. Jacob knew all this, so rather than getting mad at God over the choices mankind had made, he saw his pain as a reminder of what God was working towards. Pain was a reminder of what God had called his family to, a reminder of the covenant they carried and the things God wanted to accomplish through them.

It took faith and trust for Jacob to respond that way, but he knew what he was called to. So after burying Rachel and saying goodbye, he moved on with his family, further swarmed by confusing emotions as he experienced the heartache of losing his wife and the joy of gaining a son.

As if all this wasn't enough, amidst his heartache and turmoil, another twist was added to Jacob's soap-opera-drama life. Jacob's eldest son, Reuben, slept with Bilhah, the servant Rachel had given Jacob when she was unable to have children. This was the mother of Reuben's two half-brothers Dan and Naphtali (**Genesis 30:1–8**).

Jacob's three oldest sons had now proven themselves to be unfit for leadership, not thinking before they acted. Their self-centred ways would eventually be a snare for the rest of their brothers, influencing future generations through their choices. Sadly, Reuben's foolishness still wasn't the end of Jacob's pain.

To complete the trifecta of his suffering, Jacob also said goodbye to his father. At the healthy age of 180, Isaac's time on earth ended. Since humanity's story began with the birth of Adam, 2,289 years had passed.

Though these were undoubtedly difficult days for Jacob, God was always with him, walking alongside him no matter where the road led. Eventually, the road took him back to Hebron. There, in the place where his wild life journey had begun, Jacob found some stability for the first time.

Though he was still confused by everything that had happened and what God was up to, as Jacob reflected on his past he couldn't ignore that God's promises were true—especially the one regarding lots of descendants. With the arrival of his latest son, Benjamin, Jacob now had twelve boys of his own. A tiny nation was beginning to grow. He had a family with strong numbers, unlike anything his dad or granddad had experienced. Great things were soon to come, although at times it didn't feel that way. God was going to do a mighty work through the lives of his twelve boys. And unbeknownst to all of them, the family was about to include a king-like figure sooner than they imagined.

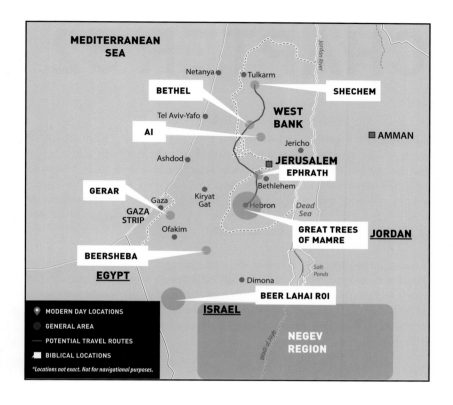

MEDITERRANEAN
SEA

Netanya ● Tulkarm

BETHEL ● SHECHEM

Tel Aviv-Yafo ● WEST BANK

AI ● AMMAN

Jericho

Ashdod ● JERUSALEM

EPHRATH

GERAR Gaza ● Bethlehem

GAZA Kiryat
STRIP Gat Hebron Dead Sea

Ofakim GREAT TREES
OF MAMRE JORDAN

BEERSHEBA

EGYPT Salt
Ponds

Dimona ●

BEER LAHAI ROI

ISRAEL

NEGEV
REGION

Jordan River

Wadi al Jaib

● MODERN DAY LOCATIONS
● GENERAL AREA
— POTENTIAL TRAVEL ROUTES
■ BIBLICAL LOCATIONS
*Locations not exact. Not for navigational purposes.

CHAPTER 52

AS JACOB'S FAMILY GREW, GOD'S PROMISES FOR THEM BECAME more visible than ever. Each new addition brought a fresh anticipation for the things God had foretold, and Jacob was certainly busy trying to keep up with the family God blessed him with. As it turns out, Jacob wasn't the only one busy with family at this time, as we soon discover that brother Esau had a growing family of his own, just like God had said at the time of their birth (**Genesis 25:23**).

Although they would not inherit the same protection and prosperity that Jacob's family did, Esau's family would still have a strong presence in the story. In the future, the descendants of Jacob (Israel) would be known as *Israelites*, and the descendants of Esau would be known as *Edomites*. The Israelites and their not-so-distant relatives the Edomites would face off time and time again.

JACOB

Reuben	Simeon	Levi	Judah	Dan	Naphtali	Gad
(LEAH)	(LEAH)	(LEAH)	(LEAH)	(BILHAH)	(BILHAH)	(ZILPAH)

Asher	Issachar	Zebulun	Dinah	Benjamin	Joseph
(ZILPAH)	(LEAH)	(LEAH)	(LEAH – daughter)	(RACHEL)	(RACHEL)

Genesis 36 portrays the growth of the Edomite people and reveals that the size of these two families would only make Isaac's words ring clearer and clearer (**Genesis 25:23; 27:39-40**). The friction between Jacob and Esau was going to be passed on for generations, long after their days ended.

 Genesis 36:1-43

As displayed through the genealogy, Esau's family grew rapidly. **Genesis 36:1-14** lists his sons and grandsons and the wives or concubines who birthed his children and even mentions those ranked as chiefs. These verses even tell us that Esau's family grew so large, they had to move.

After a fairly straightforward inventory of Esau's family, almost out of nowhere **Genesis 36:20-30** jumps from the family of Esau to a family known as the Horites, not known as direct descendants of Abraham or Isaac. Their mention can seem odd, but the Bible later gives the truth behind them. This was not the start of their story;

RATHER, IT WAS THE END.

Although the Horite people had been around for a long time, dating back to the days of Abraham, Lot, Sodom, and Gomorrah (**Genesis 14:5–6**), when Esau's family arrived in the area, they began to disappear. Unlike Jacob, who made peace with the locals when he moved, Esau overpowered his neighbours. In this case that was the Horites.

Causing the Horites to go the way of the dinosaur, Esau's family removed their neighbours in a number of ways. First it happened through marriage. We see this through Esau's union to Oholibamah. Described as the daughter of Anah and granddaughter of Zibeon, Oholibamah would have been Seir's great-granddaughter. Another act of intermarriage may have come through Esau's son Eliphaz, who is listed as having a concubine named Timna, the name of Seir's daughter. Though it might not sound awful to be blended in with Esau's family, the truth is, the ladies were probably more forced than wooed. This leads us to the second way Esau removed his neighbours, which was by force.

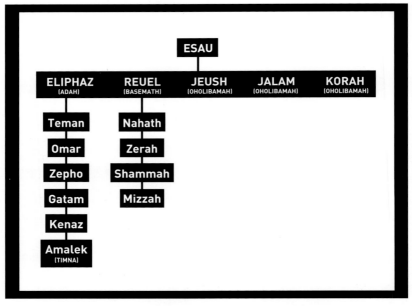

It turns out, Esau never dealt with his violence and aggression and still looked to settle disputes through fighting. Just like his father had spoken over him long before (**Genesis 27:40**), Esau and his family lived by the sword. This was made clear by the given titles of "chief," "leader," and "duke"—all military-type rankings. As a result, it wasn't long before the Horites were wiped out (**Deuteronomy 2:12,22**).

With the Horites cut down or blended into the family through marriage, Esau's descendants multiplied and lived relatively uncontested.

Through two seemingly incompatible boys, Abraham's family tree greatly expanded. For the first time, the development of a powerful nation looked promising. In fact, if Jacob lived long enough, he just might get the chance to see his family's first world changer—

AN UNANTICIPATED SOURCE
OF LEADERSHIP, PROVISION, AND POWER.

CHAPTER 53

ESAU AND JACOB'S RELATIONSHIP HAD FINALLY MENDED, AT LEAST to the point of understanding. So as Esau relocated to the land of Seir and Jacob settled down closer to home, it seemed like Jacob might finally enter a season of rest in his old age. However, with twelve sons who'd been known for their unpredictable behaviour, rest wasn't going to come so easy.

Though his separation from Laban, his move down south, and losing his wife hadn't been easy, Jacob still managed to find a bright spot in his life. He still had something special that put a smile on his face. Something that made him the most proud, and something that he cherished above all other things—and all other people.

IT WAS HIS SON JOSEPH.

In the eyes of Jacob, Joseph was a very special child. Of all twelve sons, Joseph was, without contest, his favourite. Jacob had developed a deep sentiment towards his son due to the fact that he had been the firstborn of his favourite wife, Rachel. Though she was gone, the presence of Rachel seemed to linger through the life of Joseph, and his undeniable representation of his mother gave him great honour in his father's eyes—a fact that was hard to overlook.

Without hesitation—or much secrecy—Jacob favoured Joseph over all his sons. Joseph was the son who always got the best clothes and extra ice cream for dessert. He was never in the wrong when a fight broke out, and he got excused from work whenever he felt like it. Naturally, such favouritism created jealousy and hostility between Joseph and his ten older half-brothers. His father's affection towards him labelled him as an outcast. Try as he might to fit in with the boys, it was only a matter of time before he stepped on the wrong toes. With ten half-brothers unimpressed with his existence, it wasn't long before Joseph squished at least *one* of the 100 toes they offered.

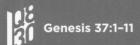 **Genesis 37:1-11**

Young Joseph did himself no favours by complaining about his brothers Dan, Naphtali, Asher, and Gad. If there's one thing that sucks more than being treated unfairly, it's being snitched on. No one enjoys being whined about, especially by someone you already despise. As a result, the brothers made no effort to calm their frustrations with Joseph.

Being younger than all his half-brothers, succeeded only by Benjamin (his only full brother), Joseph was somewhat the baby of the family and continually spoiled by their father. It was infuriating for his older brothers to observe his royal treatment. The extravagant robe proved to be the last straw.

Whether or not Joseph ever boasted about his robe in the presence of his brothers didn't matter—the robe spoke volumes all on its own, broadcasting loud obnoxious messages through its diverse colours. As Joseph strutted around, his brothers glared at him with contempt. Snorting steam from their nostrils, they were taunted by the robe; like the cape of a matador, it encouraged them to charge. Until one day, they did.

With a new depth to their fury, it took the brothers all the control they had not to lash out at their brother the day he nonchalantly recounted the dreams he'd had. Skipping no detail, Joseph made sure they knew what the dream implied—they would bow at his feet.

Maybe Joseph was naive, thinking his brothers would *love* to hear about his degrading dreams. Who wouldn't enjoy being told that someday someone you hated was going to rule over you? As expected, the mere implication of this concept was extremely aggravating.

Though the dreams could seem slightly confusing, to Joseph's brothers the message was clear. He was implying that they would bow down and kiss the dirt at his feet.

Since many of us don't have ten-plus siblings to offend or the opportunity to become kings and queens, in simpler terms what Joseph said to his brothers was the present-day equivalent to telling your older siblings, "Hey guys, I had a dream last night, and guess what? One day, you're gonna kiss my butt!" This may be a bit more forward than Joseph was in the retelling of his dream, but it's probably close to how the brothers heard it. Their younger brother, whom they could not stand, claimed that one day they would be beneath him. No longer would he just be their younger spoiled brother; rather, they were going to bow down to him out of reverence and respect.

As expected, this proclamation infuriated each of them. Joseph had just waved his cape and taunted them for the last time. He'd dug his own grave in his sleep.

Caught within range of ten angry bulls, Joseph had stepped into a bullfighting arena without knowing it. There was no way he would escape the horns of all ten brothers.

NOT WITHOUT BEING GORED.

CHAPTER 54

AS MUCH AS THEY TRIED TO IGNORE JOSEPH'S DREAMS AND WHAT they implied, the brothers grew deeply distressed. The things Joseph had shared haunted them. Regardless of where they went and what they did, Joseph's dreams continued to distract them, entering their thoughts with an unwelcomed whisper. The madness of it all left them anxious to respond to these "fantasies."

THEY HAD TO FIND A WAY TO DEAL WITH THE DREAMER.

Genesis 37:12–36

As the brothers packed up and led their herds to greener pasture, the commotion among them grew. Travelling farther from home, in the privacy of nature the enraged siblings voiced their frustrations with Joseph, adding more and more wood to each other's fire. Eventually, they agreed that the torture of Joseph's presence could not go on any longer. They needed to move beyond his foolishness. Much like the flocks they were leading, they longed for greener pastures, and the only green grass they'd see would be what grew on Joseph's grave. Miles from home, their anger began to subside as they relished the thought of life without the dreamer.

Joseph's dreams had been preposterous, far-fetched, and humiliating. For starters, he had implied that he would rule over them in some powerful manner. *What a ridiculous notion!* The land they lived in was far from being ruled by their family. They had no right to a throne or kingdom where they lived. They were mere aliens in this country. Beyond that, how could Joseph ever believe he would rule ahead of his brothers? He was the second youngest, a half-brother, a runt of the litter. Joseph was eleventh in line to ever being leader of the household. Yet none of these facts stopped Joseph from announcing his dreams with confidence. And none of these facts stopped the brothers from discrediting his dreams as just that—dreams. They would fix him once and for all.

It's likely that very few people can identify with the pain Joseph endured in the events that followed. It's one thing to be attacked by someone who hates you or with whom you have a sharp dispute, but it's a whole other matter when someone you love, should love, or have a familial relationship with beats you. Family is supposed to protect you, be on your side, defend you, and support you. But instead, they beat you, hit you, and harm you? The physical suffering Joseph incurred in that moment would have been insignificant compared to the emotional pain he tasted. As hands and fists battered him externally, internally his heart was torn by their rejection and anger. Inside and out, the savage brutality he experienced at the hands of his own flesh and blood left him distraught, as they worked him over and ignored his pleas (**Genesis 42:21**). In the chaos of their attack, Joseph cried, with tears that landed on the ground unnoticed. His pleas for mercy fell like a tree in the woods—and his brothers never heard a sound. Their rage-filled hearts turned Joseph into a mute. He had lost the ability to have a voice amongst his family.

As desperate and lonely as Joseph felt, his cries did not go ignored by all. God had heard each sob and groan, and He counted the tears the brothers ignored (**Psalm 56:8**). God never ignores those who feel as lost and lonely as Joseph felt. In His boundless wisdom, God knew the wickedness of the brothers and what their hatred would lead to. And in His grace towards Joseph, He used the selfishness of the brothers to open up a door of escape for him.

In the moment of their deepest anger, God orchestrated the passing by of some Ishmaelite travellers—a fairly common sight and never that exciting. But at this moment, the brothers saw the Ishmaelites as a two-for-one coupon. By killing Joseph, they'd gain only his departure. But by trading him, they'd gain his departure *and* some money. They couldn't resist the opportunity to appease their hunger to get rid of Joseph and make a buck or two. Because of their wickedness and greed, God used the brothers. Though they had ignored Joseph's cries for mercy and God's instruction to not do what they were doing, they didn't ignore the opportunity for selfish personal gain through which God spared Joseph.

The transaction between the brothers and the travellers became a twofold "blessing" in their lives. Joseph had been nothing but a splinter under the skin of his brothers, and now they were being paid twenty shekels for his removal.

At the time of the sale, silver likely had a much greater value than it does currently. At the highest market prices in the last ten years (2005-2015), eight ounces of silver wouldn't fetch you $400. Even if the exchange rate was remotely near that, it's clear that Joseph's brothers were far less interested in profit than they were in getting rid of him, but if they could get both, why not?

With the trade done and Joseph on his way, all it took was a slaughtered goat, a ripped robe, a quick stir, and the crime scene was staged. The brothers then used the long trip home to cook up an alibi and perfect their story, as they prepared to deliver the "devastating" news to their father—devastating for their father, not for them.

Shortly after, Jacob was informed that his favourite child had been mauled by a wild beast and torn to shreds—gone forever. The loss of his son would prove to be an incurable heartache in his old age. As for the brothers, life would be nothing but rainbows and butterflies from now on. They were satisfied with the thought that Joseph would end up being nothing more than a dead slave. Eventually, someone else would do their dirty work—

OR SO THEY ASSUMED.

CHAPTER 55

CAST ASIDE, WITHOUT A VOICE, AND SOLD AGAINST HIS WILL, Joseph was picked up, packed off, and labelled as property of the Ishmaelites (or Midianites).

The strange people he travelled with to Egypt were nomadic traders, known for collecting goods and trading them between nations. The buying and selling of humans was common practice back then.

The story shifts back and forth between the titles "Ishmaelite" and "Midianite," which can be confusing, though the reason for the change is quite simple. As it turns out, both the Ishmaelites and the Midianites were descendants of Abraham (Joseph and his brothers' great-grandpa). Not only were the Ishmaelites and Midianites relatives of one another, they lived in the same area, embraced similar lifestyles, and shared similar living conditions. There were so many similarities, Joseph and his brothers used both titles when referring to these people (like calling someone from Canada a "Canadian" or a "Canuck"). Not to mention, the use of interchangeable names for this group of people wasn't restricted to this point in the story (**Judges 8:22–26**).

ODDLY ENOUGH, JOSEPH WAS HAULED OFF BY HIS DISTANT RELATIVES.

During their lengthy journey down to Egypt, Joseph found himself constantly replaying everything that had transpired in the past number of months. Having, not that long ago, been in the safety and comfort of his father's house, lavished with gifts and filled with dreams of the future, he wondered how life had changed so quickly. No doubt bombarded with worries and fears, when Joseph wasn't consumed by the memories of the betrayal he suffered he cringed over what the future might hold. Where would he end up? Who might he be sold to? How would he make his way in such a strange place? He didn't speak the Egyptian language, and he was still so young. As he walked beside the caravan that owned him, scarcely clothed after being stripped of his beautiful coat, he pushed himself on woefully, with streams of sweat gliding down his back, as much from his fear and anxiety as from the heat. He longed to experience rest for his exhausted body and weary mind. But rest did not come.

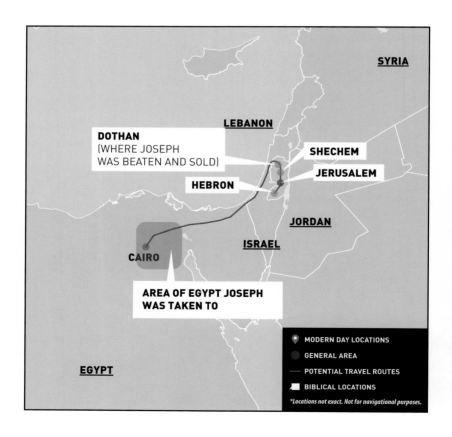

Weeks after his journey began, Joseph arrived in Egypt, exhausted, filthy, and still showing traces of the blood he'd lost at the hands of his brothers. The past few weeks had left him numb to life. He was no longer the boy he was before. Then just like that, he was sold once again.

Meanwhile, back in Canaan, oblivious to the whereabouts of their brother, Joseph's family did its best to carry on with life—a task that was much harder for some than others. Judah, the brother credited with being the mastermind behind Joseph's sale (**Genesis 37:26–27**), found himself moving away from his family after Joseph's departure. Perhaps overwhelmed by the guilt he experienced after what he had done and unable to bear the torment of his father's pain, Judah packed up and left to spend time with a friend.

Judah's time away from his family found him quickly submersed in the local culture, which, as the story has revealed, often isn't a good thing. Adapting to a new way of life, in time Judah married a Canaanite woman—beginning the growth of an entirely new branch on Abraham's family tree.

 Genesis 38:1–30

After having witnessed what he believed was the inevitable death of his brother Joseph and watching his father endure the loss of his child, Judah was subjected to the death of his own sons. The pain of each loss was an all-too-real reminder of what he had done.

With the death of his firstborn, Er, the responsibility that once rested on Er to carry on the family line was passed down to Judah's second son, Onan. It became Onan's responsibility to provide a child for his older brother through his sister-in-law, Tamar. Onan had no interest in providing a child for his brother who would bring him no credit as his or her producer. However, though he was not interested in the arrival of a child, Onan wasn't opposed to the idea of sleeping with his brother's widow—besides, it was his "duty." Happily accepting the responsibility of "comforting" Tamar, Onan then went about fulfilling his responsibilities as younger brother—doing it for the sake of pleasure and avoiding the birth of a child at any cost. As a result, like his brother, Onan found himself in an early grave.

At the end of the tragedies, having buried his two eldest, Judah found himself left with one last son, who was apparently not old enough for procreation. Out of respect, Judah pledged his third son to Tamar. However, Judah sent her to her father's household to wait until his son was ready to fulfill his duty, which was not easy.

Being a childless widow was looked upon with disgrace at that time. Tamar had little choice but to wait patiently for the day when she could become a mother. But when the time eventually came and the third brother was grown, Judah withheld his son, Shelah, from Tamar. Through his attempt to keep his third son from Tamar, Judah tortured his daughter-in-law—as if it had been her fault his sons were wicked and never had children. By keeping Shelah from her, Judah abandoned Tamar to a life of loneliness.

It didn't take her long to realize what had happened. Without a man in her life—or a child—her future seem sealed. Tamar would spend her days living in shame, hiding in her father's house as a disgrace.

Knowing she had been wrongly cheated, Tamar refused to be snubbed by Judah, and she drew up a plan. Full of insight regarding her father-in-law and his "tendencies," Tamar carried out a plan that went off without a hitch. Before long, she was pregnant, carrying her father-in-law's offspring in her belly. There was no way Judah would neglect her now.

As it normally does in a small, close-knit community, news about Tamar's pregnancy spread like wildfire. When Judah heard that his daughter-in-law was "in the family way," he grew outraged. Judah thought to himself, *How dare Tamar go behind my back and turn on my sons and family like that! I will not be disgraced by her actions and inability to control her lustful desires.* According to Judah, she should have stayed devoted to his family the whole time. She was supposed to be true to her word! But now she had brought them disgrace—and Judah would not allow that! The only problem, however, was that, unbeknownst to Judah, he already had "had that" (if ya know what I mean). Now Tamar was pregnant, with not one but two sons on the way. And both of them were his.

The story of these twins, Perez and Zerah, is somewhat a peculiar account, but like everything in the Bible, it serves a purpose. The importance of their lives will actually come out much later in the story, through the birth of a child named David. King David, to be exact. Many years in the story from this point, we'll be introduce to King David, and Perez will turn out to have been David's great-great-great-great-great-great-great-grandpa. Nine generations after Perez, through his family line a mighty king would be born.

While Judah stumbled through life coping with the loss of his sons and cleaning up the mess from his dealings with Tamar, back in Egypt Joseph had been put to work under the authority of a wealthy man named Potiphar. Before long, Joseph proved himself to be a hard-working slave who was trustworthy and had vision. His outstanding character and work ethic did not go unnoticed by Potiphar. Joseph was making the most of every opportunity he was afforded, and Potiphar wasn't the only one taken by Joseph's *giftings*.

As it turns out, Joseph was endowed with some noteworthy characteristics other than his diligence and hard work—characteristics that hadn't gone overlooked by Potiphar's wife. Apparently, Joseph was very easy on the eyes. In time, this desperate housewife hoped to offer Joseph

A FEW "OPPORTUNITIES" OF HER OWN.

CHAPTER 56

AS TIME PROGRESSED, JOSEPH BEGAN TO SEE THAT LIFE AS A slave had some potential. His new master, Potiphar, proved to be a very powerful man.

Serving Egypt as captain of the royal bodyguard, Potiphar was a man of high standing. Since he was likely acquainted with the brass of the country, working in Potiphar's home would have brought Joseph into close proximity with the individuals responsible for running most of Egypt, providing him with the opportunity to learn firsthand *exactly...*

HOW THE MIGHTY EGYPTIAN EMPIRE FUNCTIONED.

Planted firmly in Potiphar's household and determined to be a blessing, by slave standards, Joseph did about as well as anyone could do. There was no denying that, despite the situation he was in, God had been guiding his every step. Though he had faced trials, Joseph persevered. As he persevered, he developed good character. And it was because of his good character that Joseph was able to see a glimmer of hope for a brighter future (**Romans 5:3–4**). Under the ownership of Potiphar, he served diligently in everything he did, leading him to his own position of authority as advisor over the house of Potiphar. It seemed as if God was up to something.

For Potiphar, it was hard to overlook the fact that Joseph seemed to have what one might call "the Midas touch." No matter what task or responsibility he entrusted Joseph with, he succeeded. Realizing the value of a man like Joseph, Potiphar looked to capitalize on Joseph's uncanny ability for success by offering him a position of authority in his home. It was the highest level of trust and responsibility he could bestow on the young man.

Much like her husband, Potiphar's wife also noticed something good in Joseph. Believing she too had something to offer the young worker, as Joseph grew in stature, so did her intrigue.

Taken by his dashing looks and unwilling to control her desires, Potiphar's wife decided it was her responsibility to teach Joseph the meaning of "work hard, play hard." With thoughts of being swept away by their hired hand, her mind ran wild. She was a lonely neglected housewife, and Joseph was the exotic pool-boy-landscaper-carpenter man-child she couldn't be without. She craved him—and this brought a whole new dynamic to Joseph's workplace.

 **Genesis 39:1–20**

Through the advances of his master's wife and his refusal to be seduced, Joseph had proven his character. Incapable of disrespecting Potiphar in such a lewd manner after the way he'd been provided for, Joseph had done all he could not to be overpowered by the empty promises behind the bedroom eyes of his master's wife. He had decided that his life story would not be told in a paperback novel. But never had he anticipated that his life would unravel so quickly—again.

Offended and outraged by the rejection, Potiphar's wife conjured up a story to save face with her husband. Before Joseph knew it, his roller-coaster life story had taken another nosedive.

What happened next would have felt like it unfolded in slow motion in the eyes of Joseph. In disbelief, he stood before his master, shocked, as he was painted with dishonest accusations—unsure how to respond and watching dark storm clouds move in and choke out his future. Maybe Joseph pleaded with his master for mercy and understanding, trembling as he told him what *really* happened. Or perhaps Joseph stood in silent respect for the man who had provided for him, accepting what was being said. Regardless of how Joseph responded, one thing is for certain: as he was hauled off to prison, he once again wondered, *What's happening to me?*

Joseph was thrown into an Egyptian jail with chains around his neck, hands, and feet. The shackles rubbed his flesh raw, chafing burns into his flesh and sinking their bite in deeper with each movement (**Psalm 105:17–18**). Joseph did his best to avoid any kind of movement, hoping that his seeping wounds would heal. He was far worse off than when he had arrived in Egypt—a slave with *no* master, in a foreign country, with no one on his side. The temptation to disappear into a dark corner of the jail, curl up into a fetal position, and wallow in self-pity would have been immense. Had Joseph let that happen, there would have been no end to the bitterness that would have grown out of his "woe is me" and "if only" mindset.

Jail would have been the perfect place for all his frustrations to grow. Inside a warm, damp, stagnant cell, with nothing but time, his anger, self-pity, hatred, and resentment had been given the perfect atmosphere to multiply in—like bacteria. Left to rot, if he had chosen to embrace bitterness there would have been no end to the pain that ravaged him. Self-pity would have told him that his brothers did this to him. They abandoned him! They sold him to the Ishmaelites! They might as well have walked to Egypt and placed him in jail themselves. His hatred for them would have grown. As for Potiphar, Joseph would have looked at him as an ungrateful fool for treating him with such contempt. Joseph had brought abundant prosperity to his home, so much so that Potiphar had nothing to worry about aside from what he was going to stuff his face with, and on a whim, at the word of his harlot wife, he threw Joseph in jail. His hatred for Potiphar would have grown.

Every frustration and every misdeed would have wrought raging emotions that mercilessly attacked Joseph from the inside out. His anger would have burned inside him with flames that licked at his heart. As he looked around at all the things that had gone wrong and the people who had mistreated him, any belief that there was a sovereign God in control could have led Joseph to one conclusion. If God had been there and could have stopped it all and didn't, then God was the source of the fire in his life. God had been blowing on the embers and stoking it to a roar.

Ultimately, thoughts of resentment would have led Joseph to a point of frustration with God. Had Joseph foolishly toiled to honour Him? What kind of plan was this for his life? The dreams from his teen years would have become nothing more than figments of his imagination—fairy tales. Alone, rejected, and enraged, if Joseph had surrendered to his emotions, each blessing in his life would have appeared to be another log on the fire. Any gift he received had only been given to him so he could lose it. It would have caused his blood to run like lava in his veins. Indeed, his placement in jail and the threat of bitterness would have put Joseph in a position that threatened his entire future. But Joseph refused to sit back and play the victim.

Fighting tirelessly and daily to tear out roots of bitterness, Joseph continued to trust God with his future. He did not forget how God had protected him in the past, the way He had delivered him from situations that appeared hopeless. His belief in a sovereign God told him that when there were fires in life, they were sent to refine him, not to burn him (**Psalm 66:10–12**).

So Joseph continued to persevere, learning more about himself and discovering God's presence during struggles (**Psalm 46:1**). Amidst the tragedy, he found comfort, even in the darkest hours. Though it didn't come overnight and some days were harder than others, he refused to surrender to the lies and passion of fickle, fleeting emotions. Joseph resisted all bitterness and continued to live with purpose—even when the purpose seemed unclear.

 Ephesians 4:31

Proverbs 17:3

Job 23:10

Isaiah 43:2

CHAPTER 57

PLACING HIS TRUST IN GOD AND NOT LETTING HIS EMOTIONS dictate his life, Joseph clung to the belief that his time in jail served a purpose beyond what his eyes could see and his mind comprehend—and in that he found peace.

Despite being in jail, Joseph continued to be a blessing to whoever he encountered. As a result, he gained the trust of those around him (or, more accurately, was *given* the trust of those around him by God). Joseph came to realize that life in jail could have some perks. Not even prison removed his belief that God was up to something, until one day, through a conversation with fellow inmates, Joseph didn't just sense God was up to something. He felt as if he could actually see

THE ROAD TO HIS RELEASE.

The two men Joseph encountered would stir up a renewed passion inside of him and bring him a reason for hope—a hope so great that it made all his "farfetched" dreams from days gone by seem not so farfetched after all.

 Genesis 39:20–40:23

Over time, Joseph proved to be a trustworthy assistant to the prison warden and found himself back in a position of authority. This responsibility provided Joseph with the opportunity to chat with fellow inmates. Two such inmates had been thrown into jail after managing to offend Pharaoh (the president of Egypt).

One morning when the two men woke up, they looked quite downcast. As it turned out, they were both disturbed by dreams they didn't understand, dreams that had embedded themselves in their minds and haunted them with a sense of significance. The state of confusion they woke up in did not go overlooked by Joseph, and he asked what had them looking so sad.

Joseph's inquiry can seem like an odd one. Being in jail with no promise of release, exposed public toilets, poor food, and barred windows, reasons for feeling sad would seem obvious and bountiful. But Joseph discerned that there was more behind the downtrodden gazes of the two men. And in fact, he was right.

As Joseph pulled up closer to chat with the men, he learned that they'd both woken with the night sweats. They were perplexed by images they'd seen during the quiet hours of the night, and their confusion and mystery had only grown as they woke up to discover they both had had dreams stamped on their minds. Joseph, no stranger to vivid dreams himself, knew that any accurate interpretation of a dream's meaning could only come from God. Since he was an individual in pursuit of God, Joseph offered to help make sense of the late-night movies that had been projected onto the eyelids of the two distraught jailbirds.

The cupbearer spoke first. Joseph listened intently.

Paying attention to the cupbearer, Joseph also prayed, asking God to grant him insight. Listening to each word, he was captivated by the dream, unaware that his unbroken focus was giving the cupbearer a sense of comfort. He weighed every word the man said, not overlooking a detail, until the telling of the dream was over and the man looked at Joseph, then to the ground, and let out a tight anxious sigh.

> **" He knew Joseph's words would have grave implications on his future. "**

Not afraid of awkward silence, Joseph continued to silently pray as he sought out a response to the man's dream. Meanwhile, the three men sat unmoving in the dark, damp jail cell in quiet anticipation. The occasional drip of water or cough from another inmate far down the unlit hallway was all that was heard.

After what seemed like a lifetime to the cupbearer, Joseph stirred from his position in preparation to speak.

Slowly lifting his head and looking up for the first time since he had finished sharing, the cupbearer looked to Joseph with round, desperate eyes; somehow he knew Joseph's words would have grave implications on his future.

Breaking the silence, Joseph wasted no time in informing the cupbearer of his reinstatement. The atmosphere in the cell began to pulsate. Immediately, the three men grew excited over the inspiring words. The thought that in only three days the cupbearer would return to his old position of honour was almost too good to be true. Tears filled the cupbearer's eyes.

Feeling far less anxious after seeing the relief upon his friend's face, the baker turned to Joseph, excited for the chance to share his dream. Pouring out the events of his dream in half the time it had taken the cupbearer, the baker couldn't help but try to speed to Joseph's announcement of his own favourable forecast. However, the future of the baker didn't look so bright. Sitting in the jail, awaiting Joseph's response, as more and more time passed and no words were spoken, the baker's excitement faded as he discerned that he wasn't going to receive the same hope his friend had. His chest tightened, his breath quickened, and fear crept into his bones as he wondered what his future held.

Across from the baker, Joseph sat in stunned silence. Having already received a clear word on what the dream meant, he searched for a way to tell the man how dark his dream had been. Aching for the baker, and wishing he didn't have to be the one to deliver the news, Joseph broke the long silence with a weighty sigh. Then he spoke.

Joseph's words tore the air from the baker's lungs. His countenance fell. His greatest fear had just been verbalized. Any dreams of being released were gone. All that was left was to lie in fear and hope that Joseph was wrong.

For Joseph, his discussion with the two men had not been easy. It had been an act of faith to offer to interpret their dreams. He knew he had stepped out as a representative of God and that he could only speak truthfully to them. It had been no easy task to tell the baker his time was short. Joseph would never forget the silence that hung in those jail cells as he walked away.

As the next few days passed, they moved all too slowly for the cupbearer and all too quickly for the baker. In the end, their fates lay precisely where Joseph said they would.

A bit taken back by the accuracy of his words, thoughts of the baker left Joseph feeling dismal, while news of the cupbearer gave him refreshed hope for his life. Maybe the cupbearer would be his ticket out of jail.

Joseph had told the cupbearer this was going to happen. He had offered the man comfort in his time of confusion, and he had asked the cupbearer to bring his case before Pharaoh when he was free. Surely the cupbearer would never forget about him, after all he had done. Especially after prophesying about his future!

In the days following the cupbearer's release, Joseph would have woken up with a level of anticipation he hadn't felt for years. Expecting to be freed from his unjust imprisonment at any moment, he would have spent many hours lost in a daydream, wondering how his friend the cupbearer was working for his release. Every sound of jingling keys that echoed down the hall caused hope to rise in Joseph. Every time an Egyptian prison guard requested his presence he thought, *This is it! The time has come for my release!* Daydreams already had Joseph mentally living beyond the confines of the jail. He felt as if he could see God's plan for his liberation. Meanwhile, his ticket to freedom, the cupbearer,

HAD COMPLETELY FORGOTTEN ABOUT HIM.

CHAPTER 58

AS DAYS PASSED, THE HOPE JOSEPH HAD GREW DIMMER. BEFORE he knew it, two more years had slipped by, with no change, no advance, and no renewed hope for release. Left to accept the fact that he had been wrong to trust in the cupbearer for freedom, Joseph was forced to quit dreaming about life beyond jail and to accept that, perhaps, this was God's plan all along.

 **Genesis 41:1-45**

As Joseph sat in jail trying to analyze how God might still deliver him, he did so unaware of the fact that he wasn't the only man in Egypt consumed by his thoughts. As it turned out, not far away, the man at the top of humanity's food chain—Pharaoh—lay awake in bed, overwhelmed by the images his sleep had left him with.

PERPLEXED, PHARAOH DEMANDED ANSWERS FOR THE THINGS HE HAD SEEN.

As the ruler of a *very* religious nation, Pharaoh had numerous gods and deities to look to when he wanted answers. Wise men, magicians, sages, sorcerers, and priests representing the numerous gods of ancient Egypt would have all been called upon to help him with his dream. Considering the details of Pharaoh's dream, he may have looked first to one of the following:

Geb, god of the earth
Hapi, god that brought floods and helped crops grow
Bat, cow goddess
Ma'at, goddess of order and truth
Renenutet, goddess of the harvest
Thoth and Ibis, gods of wisdom

With a multitude of spiritual counsellors at his disposal, it's likely that Pharaoh endured lengthy ceremonies, rituals, sacraments, and other observances as the "wise and learned" tried to explain his dream. Hours of empty conversations, gaudy religious showmanship, and unrewarding liturgy may have left Pharaoh more confused than when he woke up. His frustration likely grew to rage.

Not so far removed from the situation, a witness to his master's confusion, one of Pharaoh's servants was finally shaken from a two-year bout of amnesia. Suddenly Pharaoh's cupbearer remembered a time when he had been in a state similar to his master's. Undoubtedly cautious, the cupbearer explained to Pharaoh that he had encountered a man who interpreted his own bewildering dream. It was a man he had met in jail.

Seeking relief, Pharaoh saw he had nothing to lose by taking a chance on the cupbearer's story. Immediately he sent men to the jail to fetch the Hebrew he had been told of. Within moments, some of Pharaoh's finest guards stood at the foot of Joseph's cell.

Whisked out of his cell with no time to waste, Joseph was marched beyond the confines of the prison. Confusion over his life events reached an all-time high. Even the men in charge of the jail, whom Joseph usually answered to, had no idea what was happening. Had he done something wrong? Had he been framed again? The guards' abrupt arrival at his cell shocked him, especially after he realized they were no ordinary guards;

rather, these were guards who served Pharaoh directly. Joseph grew even more puzzled.

Not so gently pulled from his cell and escorted outside, Joseph's eyes burned as they exited the prison and unfiltered sunlight fell on him. Apart from his eyes, his other senses rejoiced over the change of atmosphere, embracing his surroundings. All the sounds and smells that momentarily overwhelmed him represented one thing: freedom. Vendors yelling, children laughing, parents scolding, dust billowing, sweat dripping, cattle objecting, and food drying in the sun. Most people on the outside took it all for granted, but for Joseph, this was the most living he'd done in a long time. He realized instantly that his life in prison was not living, it was merely existing. And he still didn't know why he was out.

Navigating himself out of his shocked stupor, Joseph realized he still needed an explanation. It was only then that he realized his escorts had been yelling instructions at him the whole time. Trying to get up to speed on where they were going, Joseph recounted what he'd heard in the background of his thoughts. He was being taken to Pharaoh and would stand in his presence. He would need to shower, shave, and change.

The information was more than alarming. A million questions crashed through his mind. Overwhelmed, Joseph failed to pull himself together enough to ask one of the innumerable questions that raced through his head. Instead, he moved ahead dumbfounded, sometimes pushed, sometimes dragged, but always unsure of what exactly was happening. Then came further insight to his plight; not only was he going to see Pharaoh, but Pharaoh was not happy.

As Joseph was hurried to and through a shower and into clothes more suitable for meeting with Pharaoh, he was informed of the deeply troubling dream that Pharaoh had experienced. Joseph was then told that the last thing Pharaoh needed was some *prisoner* playing games with him. If Joseph wanted to live to see the dim light of his cell, he'd better tell Pharaoh what Pharaoh wanted to hear. Joseph had better do something *other* than cause further frustration. Joseph prayed.

Arriving at Pharaoh's palace after a whirlwind trip, Joseph didn't have the time to enjoy the luxuries he had experienced in a shower, a shave, and clean clothes. There was no time for enjoyment when the situation was so daunting. Moments from entering Pharaoh's presence, with his mind racing and sweat starting to mix with the water that still remained after his shower, Joseph asked God one last time to grant him wisdom; then the doors were opened.

Walking down a long elaborate corridor to where Pharaoh was seated at the end, Joseph instantly felt timid in the presence of a man who was clearly the most powerful man in the world. Joseph knew he would have to watch his words carefully. Standing before Pharaoh, Joseph felt less comfortable than he had in his jail cell as Pharaoh looked at him, explained his situation, and asked for help.

His first four words don't seem like a great start to their conversation. Pharaoh was desperate for Joseph's help; however, he was also able to crush Joseph. He had been told that Joseph could interpret dreams, so he went out of his way to bring Joseph into his presence. After all that, when Pharaoh simply asked Joseph if he could do what he was told he could do, Joseph responded with "I can't do it."

If the same guards who had escorted Joseph from the jail were there to hear his response, they must have buried their faces in open palms and thought *Prep the guillotine*—or whatever form of execution the Egyptians were into. As to Pharaoh, his immediate reaction to Joseph must have been a look of condemnation. How could the Hebrew stand before him and offer nothing? Pharaoh must have thought about having Joseph's head for his uselessness. *And* the head of his cupbearer for suggesting he entertain a jailhouse fool.

Aware that he was treading on thin ice with seconds to spare, before Pharaoh could act on his visible frustration Joseph spoke again—this time with an air of confidence that no prisoner ever carried.

Caught off guard, Pharaoh listened as Joseph confidently explained that he could not interpret the dream, but his God could.

> **"** Pharaoh was intrigued.
> Without incense, sacrifices, or religious peacocking,
> it seemed impossible that this prisoner could
> communicate with his God. **"**

And Pharaoh had never heard of Joseph's God before. He was not listed among those worshipped in Egypt. Though Pharaoh was hesitant, Joseph had his undivided attention. Deciding to continue, Pharaoh explained his dreams to Joseph.

Joseph listened intently and prayed for knowledge, for the sake of Pharaoh, for the sake of Egypt, and for the sake of his own future.

After sharing all the details of his dreams Pharaoh sat back relaxed and curious, wondering how the Hebrew prisoner would respond. Would the prayers and petitions to his God start now? Would he need time to go offer a sacrifice in order to receive an answer? Pharaoh's mind had started to wander, as he thought about what religious observance the Hebrew God demanded, when Joseph interrupted his thoughts.

Not wasting any time, Joseph revealed to Pharaoh that his dreams were not just dreams; rather, they were extra-long extended weather forecasts for his nation. God then added to Joseph's interpretation of the dreams by giving him discernment, wisdom, and boldness. Knowing he had the attention of Pharaoh, Joseph took a leap of faith and went well beyond what he had been asked to do. Jumping past the task of interpreting the dreams, Joseph then began telling Pharaoh how he should run his country in preparation for the seven years of famine.

Undoubtedly caught off guard again by the boldness of Joseph, the confidence with which he spoke, and the conviction he had regarding the abilities of his God, Pharaoh knew he was standing in the presence of a unique man. Like his father, grandfather, and great-grandfather before him, Joseph was standing out from the rest in society because God was clearly with him. As a result, Pharaoh raised Joseph to a seat of power.

As astounding as Joseph's explosion into authority was, equally as amazing was the timing of the events. God had placed those dreams in Pharaoh's life to stir him into action. He had sent a warning to the leader of Egypt that a famine would be arriving and his people could be saved. But how would Pharaoh have ever known about the truth behind his dreams if God had not revealed it to him through Joseph? God had brought life to numerous questions, but He also provided the answers.

Through these events, Joseph's life, a life that had looked horrible earlier on, began to look suspiciously perfect in more ways than one. Had the cupbearer remembered Joseph earlier and managed to obtain his freedom, there's no guarantee Pharaoh would have been able to locate Joseph when he had his dreams. Had the cupbearer never been put in jail and then reinstated, who would have told Pharaoh about Joseph's abilities? But God had known what was going to happen, and in His grace, He left Joseph in jail. God had orchestrated Joseph's meeting with the cupbearer and disturbed Pharaoh with visions of the future. Through it all, God was pouring out His grace, not just on Joseph's life but on all the lives in Egypt. He had planted Joseph in that position in order to present him to Pharaoh at the perfect time so he could bring freedom to an entire nation when they would have been slaves to starvation. If Joseph's life was a game of poker, God rigged the deck in his favour. Flawlessly God played the cards to perfection, using Joseph's time in prison like a pair of pocket aces, sitting there, ready to be drawn in a time of desperation. Only God could orchestrate something so perfectly (**Isaiah 48:3; Job 42:2**).

> **"**Launched from zero to hero Joseph became man of the year.**"**

Instantly Joseph went from a place of shame to a position above all others. Taking part in a wardrobe change for the second time in a day, he walked away from his meeting with Pharaoh with the finest clothes money could buy. From unkempt prison clothes to the Burberry, Gucci, Prada, and Louis Vuitton of his day, the transformation left him dumbfounded. While he was still in shock over his new clothes, Pharaoh's officials began sliding rings on his fingers and gold chains around his neck. He was a combination of a GQ model and Mr. T.

Joseph had now become one of the most powerful men on the planet, second only to Pharaoh. Though not the most powerful man, he was undoubtedly the most influential and effective. Launched from zero to hero, Joseph became the undisputed winner of *Time* magazine's man of the year—not just for that year, but for the subsequent fourteen years, as he would lead Egypt through seven years of prosperity and seven years of famine.

Lying down to sleep that very first night, Joseph likely had tears in his eyes as he reflected on the scenarios he had faced in life. The disappointments. The heartaches. Viewing them from his entirely new vantage point, he began to see the grace inside his own pain. He saw there was wisdom being exercised when he was in confusion. And now he knew there were blessings on the other side of affliction. The way God had raised him up to the position he now held was overwhelming. Such a blessing was undeserved. All Joseph had wanted, all he had hoped for, was to be set free from prison, maybe even restored to the life of favour he had in the house of Potiphar. But God had given him something beyond what he dared hoped for or imagined (**Ephesians 3:20**). Joseph would even be able to have a wife. He had never dreamt of having a family of his own. It would have been highly improbable as a slave. But now, an entirely new future filled with limitless potential lay before him.

As he lay in bed in disbelief, he drifted off to sleep. Lost in an attitude of honour and praise, he gave glory to God for accomplishing something he never could have achieved on his own.

CHAPTER 59

TRANSFORMED INTO AN ENTIRELY NEW MAN SOCIALLY, JOSEPH committed to his tasks as second in command with purpose and intentionality. As he travelled throughout the land of Egypt, his fame went before him. Renowned for his wisdom and authority, the voice he had lost many years ago, after being sold by his brothers, was now being heard loud and clear.

Joseph's work throughout those first seven years was like an ancient way of planning out long-term investments. Having received an insider-trading tip from God via Pharaoh's dream, Joseph knew the forecast did not look good. The economy of Egypt and all surrounding countries was going to crash, and crash hard. With that in mind, Joseph began to prepare the entire country for seven years of famine, advising everyone to place one-fifth of their earnings into a trust fund that he would oversee. He was going to make sure that the seven years of abundance did not get squandered.

Genesis 41:46–57

Working hard during the first seven years to ensure that Egypt remained nourished, as Joseph looked after the future of his countrymen, he began to think about the future of his own life—which led to the arrival of two sons.

The births of his sons, Manasseh and Ephraim, were opportunities for Joseph to showcase where his blessings came from. Humbled by the gift of children, Joseph thanked God for the way *He* had provided. It was because of God's great faithfulness that he was able to rejoice in a land that had threatened to destroy him. And Joseph was doing his part to make sure his family never forgot how gracious God was.

Under his leadership, Egypt was well prepared for the ensuing famine. Had Joseph not been present during those fourteen years, there is no telling how Egypt's history might have played out. Perhaps their seven years of bounty would have inspired short-term extravagant living and a squandering of their abundance. People would have run out to lavish themselves with bigger barns, newer cows, and more sheep. Then, when the seven years of famine struck, the nation would have be in an uproar. Their massive barns would have sat empty, their expensive cows would have no longer been affordable, and they would have realized that their sheep were actually a luxury they could have gone without. But thanks to God working through Joseph, that's not what happened. God knew the people needed accountability, and Joseph provided just that.

Then, on cue, as the calendar turned, ending the seventh and final year of prosperity, a famine began to sink its claws into the land—and Egypt felt the squeeze. As the people began to realize that the famine wasn't about to ease up and their food supply was low, they cried out to Pharaoh for provision and answers. As it turned out, one man had exactly what they were looking for. So Pharaoh sent them to Joseph.

On bended knees, people approached Joseph. In order to survive, they relied on him for the food he had stored. Before long, everyone in Egypt was coming to seek his grace. In fact, before long, the famine hit so hard that it was felt throughout the entire known world. The devastation slowly led every surrounding country in the direction of Egypt, searching for aid. Upon arrival, each weary traveller found himself at the feet of Joseph, bowing down

IN REVERENCE, RESPECT, HONOUR, AND NECESSITY.

CHAPTER 60

AS THE FAMINE SPREAD OUT LIKE A WAVE ON THE WATER, NO nation in the known world seemed to escape its threat. Moving east and affecting countries that we now know as Israel, Jordan, Lebanon, Syria, Iraq, and Saudi Arabia, it wasn't long until the famine endangered the lives of millions. At a time when the world seemed to be in need of sustenance, one man was set apart, possessing what they desired—Joseph. Rushing to Egypt like there was a Black Friday sale, sizable crowds began forming, each person hoping for an audience with Joseph, desperate to get their hands on what he had to offer. Understanding the responsibility that had been thrust upon Joseph makes it clear why it was important for his character to be tested

BEFORE HE EMBRACED
HIS POSITION OF AUTHORITY
(Psalm 105:19 NLT).

" Their journey to Egypt forced them to face
the reality of what they had done "

The world market seemed to hinge on how Joseph would respond to the cries of his neighbours. It was well within his power to dictate who lived and who died, who received grain and who didn't. He could have demanded any price he wanted for the goods Egypt had stored. Joseph had a monopoly, not just over the people of Egypt, but also over people from surrounding nations. Included in those numbers were Joseph's father and brothers.

Although he could treat people however he desired, Joseph was gracious to those who came. He was gracious because he knew what it was like to be in need, having to rely on the decency of someone else. God had always provided for him through people above him and supplied for all his needs in seasons of hardship. Now God was using Joseph to do the same for others. He was even going to call him to show grace to the ones who had offended him the greatest.

At the hands of his brothers, Joseph had been dropped to the lowest of lows in life. He had suffered as an alien slave in a foreign land and then had been launched to the highest position attainable. In time, Joseph began to realize that what had happened in life went far beyond what his brothers had done to him. Despite how easy it would have been to resent them for their actions, he had reached a place of forgiveness towards his brothers, knowing that what they meant for harm, God meant for good. The pain of his past did not haunt him.

Genesis 42 turns our attention back to Hebron, where Joseph's family still lived (south of modern-day Jerusalem). Although at the start of the famine it had been over twenty years since Joseph had been removed from his family, we discover that, unlike Joseph, the brothers still seemed haunted by the events of their past as their search for food eventually led them to Egypt.

 Genesis 42:1-26

As expected, the famine had been a time of hardship for Joseph's family, just like for everyone else. As they sat around with empty plates and few options, the famine affected more than their stomachs. With no food to eat and no crops to grow, the brothers had little to do other than watch themselves and their livestock fade away. Life seemed to come to a standstill. Moving to an area where crops were growing was out of the question. They didn't have the supplies or the energy to make the journey. Besides, none of the brothers knew of a single place on earth where food was not scarce. That was, of course, other than Egypt.

The family's decision to travel to Egypt was not made easily. Though they travelled for the purpose of retrieving food, the trek to Egypt would be costly. Tight on food and light on money, whoever travelled to Egypt would need to take a decent supply of food with them. They would likely need more food to stay adequately nourished during travel, leaving those at home even shorter on resources. Not to mention, with the world facing a food crisis, there was no guarantee that they would not encounter many dangers and threats as they crossed paths with other hungry people stuck in tough times. Joseph's brothers, and ultimately his father, Jacob, had a lot to consider before setting off.

Today, sending your kids off on a journey like this would be similar to a father from the southern states weighing the risk of his sons driving down to Mexico City in search of food. In the meantime, everyone in Mexico is starving, and no one is guaranteeing a safe return or that they'll even get food.

A lot could go wrong on the journey to Egypt, but with his family in need of sustenance and having little time to waste, Jacob made the executive decision to send his sons to Egypt—sans Benjamin.

As the brothers began their journey to Egypt filled with uncertainty, it's possible that the fear they experienced caused them to reflect on the day Joseph was taken. Though none of them uttered a word, perhaps they moved in silent contemplation, identifying with the feelings Joseph must have had when he was separated from family, scarce on food, low on money, and without much hope of a future.

Twenty years earlier, they had sold their brother and sent him down that road with strangers. *What kind of terror had he faced as he traversed the land?* With no one to talk to, no one to listen, and no one on his side, the terror of his travel would have far exceeded their current discomfort, and they knew it. The concern they carried in a group of nine was shocking enough, but they only tasted a morsel of the fear they had thrust upon Joseph. Their journey to Egypt forced them to face the reality of what they had done.

After days of travel, exhausted, dusty, hungry, and more desperate than ever, the brothers arrived in Egypt. All the anxieties they'd had previously only heightened. With people from all over flocking to the country in pursuit of an audience with the man who governed the land, the fusion of unfamiliar sights, smells, languages, and customs overwhelmed the brothers. They couldn't imagine what it would be like to navigate the chaos alone, as a slave.

Struggling to communicate and find their way around, eventually the brothers found themselves in line, awaiting their turn with the man who would decide their fate. What little conversation the brothers had shared ended completely.

Like a family in the hospital waiting to hear if surgery was a success or not, in nervous silence the brothers stood, each making prayers and hoping the outcome would be a favourable one. Glancing into one another's eyes, hearts pounding, hands shaking, and minds racing, before they knew it, their time had come. Timidly they entered into the court of their new master.

" Once a pack of ravenous wolves, they appeared before him now like sheep. "

Meanwhile, seated on a golden throne with guards and servants on every side, Joseph was going about his daily routine. With droves of people searching for food, translators helping him make sense of the different dialects he was hearing and attendants asking him questions in between, the days were hectic for Joseph. Realizing that the next band of travellers was awaiting his attention, as Joseph turned to observe what dishevelled wanderers stood before him this time, instantly his pulse quickened. Caught in an unblinking stare for a moment, unable to form a thought, Joseph sat silent before his brothers, frozen in time as his mind screamed, *This cannot be true!*

Doing his best to regain his composure as he embraced the reality that his brothers stood before him, Joseph began eyeing up each of them. Identifying their names, their ages, and how the years had changed their features, his mind flooded with memories. His thoughts took him back to the last time he'd seen their faces. They hadn't looked nearly as sombre back then. The last time he had seen them, their faces had been bent with anger, eyes filled with rage. Once a pack of ravenous wolves, they appeared before him now like sheep—lost, without a shepherd, and in need of nourishment. As all these thoughts tore through his mind, Joseph finished his inventory and noted that there were only ten brothers. He began to wonder where the other might be. *What has happened to Benjamin?*

Led by Reuben, one by one the brothers dropped to their knees in admiration—and Joseph knew they were at his mercy. Aware that they did not recognize him, Joseph composed himself, addressed them in Egyptian, and used their unsuspecting mindset to his advantage. Possessing the upper hand, he tested their resolve, badgered them with questions, and pinned them with accusations. Slowly, as they defended themselves, they offered insight into their lives, talking about their father and absent brother. Even though he obtained some answers, Joseph was not done his testing. Placing his brothers in prison and holding them for three days, he was curious to know if their hearts had changed after all these years.

After he took time to subtly reacquaint himself with his brothers, after a number of days Joseph sent them back home to their father. But not without keeping Simeon in jail, hoping that his stay in Egypt would ensure their return.

JOSEPH WAS NOT GOING TO LOSE HIS FAMILY AGAIN.

CHAPTER 61

RELEASED FROM CUSTODY AND ALLOWED TO GO HOME, NINE of the ten brothers walked away from Egypt. Leaving with more questions than when they arrived, they were almost unsure about whether or not their trip had been a success. Yes, they had grain, but it had come at the cost of leaving Simeon bound in jail. As they made their way back home and stopped at a location where they would spend their first night, the brothers continued to analyze the events that had taken place over the past week.

After they discussed the outlandish accusations of the Egyptian governor, his demands to see their younger brother, and then his choice to keep Simeon as collateral, their conversation transitioned into wondering how their father was going to react and whether or not

THEY WERE BEING PUNISHED FOR WHAT THEY HAD DONE TO THEIR LONG-LOST BROTHER, JOSEPH.

As conversation wound down and they prepared to call it a night, they found it reasonable to agree that, despite the momentary displacement of Simeon, with food for their families and nobody dead, they had found success. All they needed to do now was get back home, show Dad the goods, and convince him it was okay to take Benjamin back, and all would be well. Things didn't appear so bad after all; that was, until one brother went to feed his donkey and realized that things were far worse than they ever imagined.

 Genesis 42:27–38

Unbeknownst to his brothers, before sending them home Joseph ordered his servants to pack their sacks with provisions, as well as the pouches of money they paid for their grain with. When the brothers learned that *every* pouch of money they had given was still in their possession, they realized they had just stolen from Egypt—albeit involuntarily. Regardless, the brothers feared Egypt, and they feared the man who controlled it even more.

Distressed over their encounter and befuddled as to how the money found its way back into their belongings, upon their arrival at home the brothers did the best they could to explain to their father everything that happened. Telling him about the accusations they had faced and sheepishly informing him that they had been forced to leave Simeon behind, by the time they got around to asking their dad if they could take Benjamin back, Jacob answered with a resounding *"No!"* Counting Simeon as good as lost, Jacob refused to sacrifice another son to the fool's errand of bartering with the lord of Egypt. He would not take the risk of losing Benjamin. The death of Benjamin, the last-born child of his most cherished love, Rachel, would be the death of Jacob.

At the insistence of their father, the brothers remained in Hebron. With no immediate plan of returning for Simeon, they were forced to make do with the grain they'd been given. They settled in and did what they could to ride out the famine—a noble plan, except for the fact that the famine was far from over. The grain they had would soon be stretched thinner than any of them hoped, they would have no choice but to return to Egypt, and Jacob would be forced to risk the life of Benjamin.

The situation the family was in only made sense; Joseph would never have sent his brothers home with enough food to survive the duration of the famine. He wanted to make sure they returned to Egypt—

AND RETURN THEY WOULD.

CHAPTER 62

AS THE FAMINE MAINTAINED ITS CONTROL OF THE LAND, JOSEPH'S family found themselves without grain—again. Back to square one and desperate for nourishment, it was obvious that Egypt was their only hope for survival.

With a sour taste still lingering in their mouths from their last journey, the brothers were hesitant to return, at least not without meeting the demands of the Egyptian lord. He still had their brother Simeon in custody. If they did not bring Benjamin on their return trip, the remaining nine would simply be walking to their graves. Faced with a decision, they only had two options: stay home and starve or take Benjamin to Egypt. Everyone knew that both options carried great risk.

 **Genesis 43:1-34**

After much deliberation, Jacob finally conceded and agreed to let them return to Egypt with Benjamin. The boys prepared for their trip and loaded up their donkeys with gifts for the lord of Egypt. The family caravan—not the Dodge kind—began its journey back to Egypt, Joseph, and Simeon. Carrying the best of what they had to offer, with double the silver to compensate for the error made on their first journey, they did all they could to prepare for their meeting, hoping to appease the master of Egypt.

Arriving in Egypt, the brothers were scheduled to appear before the lord of Egypt early the following morning. Unlike on their first trip down, they no longer feared what they did not know;

RATHER, THEY FEARED WHAT THEY DID KNOW— THE MAN WHO RULED.

"He had longed for this moment. This was a desire that his heart had never thought to ask for and far beyond anything he had ever imagined."

Upon seeing his brothers, Joseph was taken with excitement. His plan of keeping their brother and shorting their supply in order to force them back had worked—and they had brought Benjamin. The sight of his younger brother was a delight he never thought he'd behold. The emotions that accompanied their second arrival were even more overwhelming than those before.

Placed in the private care of Egypt's lord, the peculiar treatment and favour they were shown unnerved the brothers. His act of kindness had them stricken with fear. Not knowing how they would be treated and if the kindness was simply a ploy, they made sure they would respond with the utmost respect and honour.

As they prepared gifts that they hoped would appease the master of Egypt, the conversation they had would have been panicked. Laying out pistachios, jars of honey, spices, and almonds in an arrangement that would appear just perfect, they were desperate for approval. When the lord entered the room, they took to the ground with bended knees, showing the greatest level of respect they could to the man who controlled their future.

Responding carefully to each question they were asked, like a terrified sixteen-year-old getting pulled over by a cop for the first time, each time they spoke they dipped low to show respect. As the brothers acted with caution, Joseph slowly approached Benjamin.

Standing before Benjamin, Joseph sensed deeply that the man in front of him was his brother—his own flesh and blood, born of the same mother and most intimately connected to him. Though he sensed it, Joseph continued his charade and asked if this truly was the younger brother they had spoken of. Hearing them consent and knowing it in his heart to be true, Joseph studied his little brother with great interest. Of all his brothers, the change in Benjamin's physical features were the most prominent. At the time Joseph had been sold, Benjamin had been tender in age when he had been told about the "death" of his big brother. Now, standing face to face, the severity of emotions was too much for Joseph to suppress. Overcome, he made an abrupt exit.

After Joseph charged from the room in an unanticipated manner, the brothers stood, alone, more confused than ever, wondering if they had done something to offend him. *Maybe he hates pistachios?* The concern they already carried grew.

As Joseph fled to a place of solitude, he let his emotions control him for a moment. Flooded with countless thoughts of thankfulness, joy, excitement, and belonging, he knew that his world was never going to be the same again. He knew he hadn't been a mindless dreamer after all.

Returning to his brothers to join them for lunch, Joseph had a tough time maintaining his composure as the food was served. As he sat eating his meal, with his brothers in his home, his father alive, and his youngest brother present, it took everything in him to keep from jumping up and revealing the truth. He had longed for this moment. This was a desire that his heart had never thought to ask for and far beyond anything he had ever imagined. As the years had ticked on and on, he had continually wondered about each of them, and now they were reunited, even if they were unaware.

Though they ate and drink freely for a short time, another test awaited the brothers. The time for all truth had not yet come. Still curious about their hearts, Joseph would not let them escape so easily. To the horror of the brothers, the worst possible scenario would soon become a reality—

BENJAMIN WOULD NOT BE MAKING THE TRIP HOME.

CHAPTER 63

THOUGH THE BROTHERS HAD RECEIVED THE ROYAL TREATMENT, they were confused over *why*. Suspicious of why they were greeted so warmly, the whole time they ate they couldn't stop thinking, *Perhaps this is our last supper?*

Despite their fear and uncertainty, after they filled themselves with food and drink, their host prepared them to be on their way. As it turned out, they were going to make it out of Egypt alive. *Maybe the lord of Egypt isn't such a bad guy after all.* What they didn't know was that

JOSEPH WASN'T GOING TO LET THEM GET AWAY THAT EASILY.

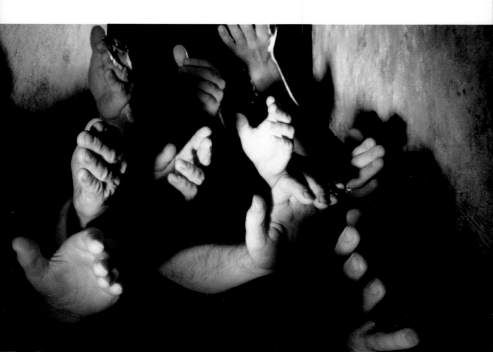

As Joseph had his servants pack his brothers' belongings for their journey home, he made sure that all the silver his brothers paid with was returned to their bags. Sending them home with all of their money and more free grain, this time Joseph added one more item to their inventory. Completely unaware, the brothers had no idea that Joseph had planted a cup in their belongings. Their journey home would soon prove to be *far* more than any of them could handle.

 Genesis 44:1–45:15

Loaded with as much food as their donkeys could carry, the brothers began their journey wondering if the animals' knees wouldn't buckle under the weight. Slowly, as they put distance between themselves and Egypt, conversations started to fill the air as the brothers discussed their amazing treatment, the lord of Egypt's interest in their family, how they had been arranged from oldest to youngest, and the peculiar conduct they had witnessed. *Did the lord of Egypt actually run from the room with tears in his eyes?* Though some of it seemed odd, nevertheless, with all eleven brothers together and no one stranded in jail, there wasn't a question in anyone's mind—this had been a successful journey.

"This was Benjamin's funeral procession."

As the conversations continued, as good brothers do, they badgered one another, primarily Simeon. When they quizzed him about his time in jail and what it was like to be in an Egyptian prison, Simeon teased that he was a changed man after doing hard time, proclaiming that they knew nothing about hard life. Laughing and carrying on, their minds stopped racing and their hearts rejoiced. For the first time in a while, the brothers shared a moment of untroubled existence, paying no attention to the figures racing towards them in the distance.

Continuing their slow saunter east, after a while they couldn't ignore the fast-moving dust cloud headed in their direction. As the celebration died down, the brothers strained to see who was in such a hurry, until they recognized the figure headed their way—it was the steward of Pharaoh's house. And he was closing in fast.

Unsure of what caused the steward to give chase, they did the best they could to carry on and act natural. As if a cop car with its lights flashing had shown up in their rear view mirrors, the brothers looked straight ahead, placed both hands on the reins, and hoped and prayed that the steward would pass by in pursuit of someone else. They wouldn't be so fortunate.

The brothers did their best to greet the steward cordially as he pulled up beside them in a cloud of dust and frustration. It didn't take them long to learn that he hadn't come for small talk. Taken back by the accusations that he set before them, some of the brothers responded in outrage, while others thought, *I knew this was too good to be true!* Regardless of how they responded, each of the brothers agreed on one thing—they were confident of their innocence.

Without hesitation, the eleven brothers put their lives on the line as a bold statement of their integrity, having no idea they had just dug a grave for their youngest brother, Benjamin.

After Joseph's cup was found in Benjamin's sack, they reloaded their camels and made the short trek back to the house of Joseph. Suddenly, the same steps they had taken moments earlier, ones that had been filled with joy and celebration, turned into a death march. This was Benjamin's funeral procession.

How could this happen? What's going on? Where did the cup come from? They were innocent of this crime. Framed and wrongly accused, now they would die. Incapable of controlling the outcome, the future looked so stark that the best-case scenario appeared to be living out their lives as slaves in Egypt. Undeserved slavery. What kind of life was that? They would spend the rest of their days separated from their families, suffering innocently for *nothing!* And they knew, no matter how much they would yell, fight, or beg for mercy, they would have no voice in the matter. With that realization, during the short trek back to Joseph's house each brother tasted *all* the pain and worry that ten of them had inflicted on their brother years earlier.

When they arrived, the brothers begged for mercy and sought an escape from their impending doom. On their knees, knowing that their words carried no weight in Egypt, some of the brothers started to surrender to the hopelessness. Realizing that this would likely be their undoing, a few of the brothers couldn't help but feel as if they were finally getting what they deserved. After all they had done to their brother so many years before, it felt painfully ironic that they would now face the same uncertain future they had sold Joseph into. Their sins had found them out.

They had spent the last twenty-plus years looking over their shoulders in constant fear, petrified of when they would have to answer for what they had done. Every cough of their children or injury to someone they loved caused them to think, *This is it. Now I will pay the price for what I did.* Kneeling in front of the master of Egypt without an explanation, it seemed as if that day had finally come. Their guilt had worked its way to the surface like a pimple, and now the lord of Egypt would put the squeeze on them. And amidst the fear and sadness, there was a small hint of relief. They wouldn't have to carry the heavy burden of their guilt and shame any longer.

> **"** They would finally face the music for what they had done. A small part of them was ready to accept their punishment and move on. **"**

Waiting for what came next, the brothers then caught a bit of a break, learning that they would not *all* face punishment for the actions of one man. Only the guilty would need to suffer for his crime. The rest of them could return home—but Benjamin, the thief, would remain.

Instantly, Judah realized that this was no break at all, especially for his father. In a fit of desperation, Judah pleaded with Joseph. Begging for understanding, offering to do whatever it would take to return Benjamin to their father, he knew any agreement that didn't result in Benjamin's freedom would only bring pain to their father.

Standing over his brothers and sensing their fear, Joseph watched the scene play out in disbelief. His brothers had come far over the years. Now united in an effort to free Benjamin, twenty years earlier they had worked with the same unity to rid themselves of a sibling. Wanting to destroy him, they once functioned as one body in hopes of appeasing their jealous rage. Now he watched as they fought for the life of his only full-blood brother, desperate to keep him in their lives.

Even though they knew Benjamin was greatly loved by their father, they did not reject him like they had Joseph. Perhaps it had been the way their father suffered for so long after the loss of Joseph. Perhaps it was the thought of what it would be like to lose the children many of them now had. Joseph was not sure. But as they begged, he saw that most of them were willing to die to save their own brother, the youngest of their clan.

Benjamin was a man cut from the same cloth as Joseph, yet they fought to save him from the life of slavery they had willingly thrust *him* into. Observing all of this, in that moment the dam that held back Joseph's feelings burst. A mighty surge of emotions crashed over his body, sweeping him away in its power. Tears sprang from his eyes with such force that he could not fight them. He began to sob with such intensity that his rib cage heaved, his body shook, and he joined his brothers on his knees. The charade was finally over. Through the sobs Joseph revealed that he was their brother.

The moment he disclosed his identity, Joseph saw the whole story from beginning to end. He hadn't always understood why God allowed so many confusing things to happen, but now he couldn't deny His presence in the good and the bad. Through everything, God had positioned Joseph in a place where he would be able to preserve his family. In His sovereign and perfect will, God had orchestrated each moment of Joseph's days with precision. He led them all back together in His mercy and grace.

All the pain Joseph had endured—the rejection, the confusion, the hurt, and frustration—disappeared in an instant. With a richer understanding of what he had endured, each moment of his life, including the pain, shone with brilliance and carried a new sense of purpose. *Everything,* from the tears he had cried when he was incarcerated unjustly by Potiphar and onward, made sense. God had been at work the entire time. Joseph's life had been a picture—a collage of God's amazing work. He understood that even though, at times, some of the pictures were dark and terrifying, in the end, God had arranged each one in its proper place. The finished product of pain and triumph was now the most beautiful collage imaginable.

> **"** God's work in Joseph's life, arranged as He had desired from beginning to end, was an absolute masterpiece. **"**

Joseph also understood that God's work in his life had implications *far* beyond what had taken place for him. The purpose of his story wasn't just that he would prosper and overcome. His story was about God. His story was about what God was doing with his family and the plans that God had for the nation of Israel. Joseph was being used in a major way so God could continue to carry out His plan of restoration for the entire world through the people He had chosen. The revelation of it all was too much to contain. All along, Joseph had trusted that God was doing something amidst the pain, and now he saw. It was beautiful! He knew no other way to respond than with powerful tears of joy, thankfulness, and praise. *God is good, all the time,* Joseph thought.

ALL THE TIME, GOD IS GOOD.

CHAPTER 64

WHEN JOSEPH FINALLY IDENTIFIED HIMSELF, THE CELEBRATION that followed lasted deep into the night. Sitting and discussing the days gone by, everyone was hungry to hear the news regarding each other's lives. Joseph wanted to know about everyone.

HE BURNED WITH THE DESIRE TO LEARN MORE ABOUT HIS FAMILY.

Sitting in shock over the unexpected disclosure, Joseph's brothers conversed in disbelief. They answered each of Joseph's pressing questions mechanically, with an air of reverence and respect that flowed naturally after their previous encounters with their brother. As they tried to uncover what had brought Joseph from where they had left him to where he was now, their minds spun out of control. None of them, in their wildest imaginations, was able to come up with an explanation that progressed from *sold into slavery* to *lord of Egypt*. When Joseph finally told them his life's journey, it was even more heartbreaking and fantastic than they could have dreamt.

Despite their inability to fully comprehend what Joseph had been through and all God had done, the brothers knew one thing for sure: they were in the company of one of the most powerful men on earth. Joseph's dreams *had* come true, and each of them recalled the taunting words of their once-little brother. Many years ago, the suggestion that they would bow down to him had driven them to hate, but they'd never been so wrong. Their greatest nightmare had become their salvation. God was good.

 **Genesis 45:16–28**

As reports about the reunion between Joseph and his family spread, the news eventually reached Pharaoh. A Joseph enthusiast, Pharaoh was moved by the latest developments in Joseph's life and didn't hesitate to offer Joseph's family the best of the land. Adamant that they come to Egypt at once and join their brother, Pharaoh instructed the family not to waste time with packing their belongings, as they would have all they needed and more awaiting them in Egypt. Supplying them with carts so their children and wives wouldn't have to walk, Pharaoh looked to speed the arrival of this immigrating family any way he could.

Their donkeys loaded to their breaking point with goods, Joseph's brothers aimed their caravan (not the Dodge) east, and for the third time in a short time, they began the trek back to their father.

Blessed beyond their wildest dreams and caught up in a sovereign act of God, as they left Egypt it was heartily agreed upon that they had found favour. Their father's prayer had most definitely been heard (**Genesis 43:14**). Having come to Egypt in terror and remained in the city in fear, they left with an indescribable peace and the blessing of the two most powerful men in the known world.

Travelling as quickly as they could and taking no unnecessary stops, the brothers could not get home fast enough, anxious to explain to their father the dramatic events that had taken place. Bursting at the seams, they couldn't wait to share the greatest news of all—Joseph was alive.

As his sons arrived home, Jacob couldn't help but notice that they somehow seemed to be louder than normal—if it were possible. Boisterous and joyful, his sons erupted into his presence with a volume more suited for times of celebration and prosperity, not a famine. The delight they wore on their faces was a comforting yet unnerving sight, considering the times. Quickly making note that Benjamin was with them, Jacob then counted the trip a success. Content with this discovery, the words he heard next paralyzed him like a scream in the darkness. *My sons must be mistaken. Their claim cannot be true!*

Overwhelmed by the fact that everything they told him hinged on the survival of his dead son, Joseph, in disbelief Jacob listened to his sons' report of lavish living, elegant lifestyles, and the riches of Egypt. But he rejected their claims. Especially the statement that Joseph was alive. Never in his life had Jacob expected to hear such words, and now that he had, he didn't believe them. Though his heart longed for it to be true—and had longed for it since the day of Joseph's reported demise—Jacob was no fool. His dream would never be a reality; he had seen Joseph's bloodied coat. *That* was his reality.

His sons continued their profession that Joseph was alive and prosperous, and their insistence almost seemed torturous. Jacob wanted to believe them and ignore what he knew to be true—ignore that Joseph was dead and had been gone for the last twenty years. A part of Jacob ached to believe them with all his heart, but he couldn't allow himself. He had barely survived the news of Joseph's death the first time and had spent years wrestling with the fact that his son was gone. His absence still hurt. To actually believe the outlandish claims his sons were making would mean letting down walls he had built up. If he believed them and the claims turned out to be false, the reminder of his son's absence would cut too deeply.

Sensing their father's struggle to embrace their enthusiasm, the brothers urged him to follow them outside to the donkeys. Leading him by the hand and listing off the inventory they had been sent home with, they drew their father's attention to the newly acquired clothes, carts for their families, and food for a journey *back* to Egypt. Slowly, at the sight of all the goods, Jacob's denial was swayed by what his eyes saw. Then noting the extra gifts bestowed upon Benjamin, he thought, *Perhaps it is true. Joseph has even given extra blessings to his only full-blood brother!*

Slowly Jacob's countenance changed as he allowed himself, for the first time in many years, to dream that Joseph was alive. He thought about his son, his survival, how he might look, and how it would feel to wrap his arms around him again. Surrendering to his excitement, Jacob knew he could not waste another day without his son. Declaring his acceptance of all he had been told, he ordered his family to pack. They were moving to Egypt.

THE CELEBRATION WOULD BEGIN.

CHAPTER 65

MOVING WITH AN EDGE OF YOUTHFUL DELIGHT THAT HIS FAMILY had not seen in years, Jacob, with his sons, their wives, and their children, loaded up the donkeys, piled into the carts, and headed off for Egypt. As eager as they all were, no one could match Jacob's excitement.

Like his sons before him, Jacob tried to picture all the scenarios that could have led his son from the grave to his seat of power in a foreign country. Incapable of making sense of it, he agreed that no matter *how* it had happened, God had woven the story together like a magnificent tapestry that

WOULD SOON INCLUDE THEIR REUNION.

The thought of seeing Joseph triggered a warmth in Jacob's heart. It spread through his chest and sent a shiver up his spine. Like fireworks, the sensation peaked at the nape of his neck, where it seemed to hang for a split second before bursting into a brilliant smile he dared not fight. Tears of joy formed in his eyes, and Jacob quickened his pace. The God of Abraham and Isaac had done it again.

 Genesis 46:1-27

Departing from his last noted location, Hebron (**Genesis 35:27**), Jacob stopped at Beersheba to offer sacrifices to God, praising Him for all He had done. As Beersheba was a location that had been used by his grandfather, it's possible that Jacob stopped at the same tamarisk tree Abraham planted and called to God from (**Genesis 21:33**).

Although he was anxious to get down to Egypt, Jacob made time to focus on the One who orchestrated the reunion. And as he did, he may have also sought God's direction regarding whether or not he should stay in Egypt.

Earlier, God had warned Jacob's father, Isaac, that he wasn't supposed to go down to Egypt (**Genesis 26:2–3**). Perhaps, recalling this encounter, Jacob had misgivings. But during Jacob's time of worship, God removed any hesitations he had. Quieting Jacob's heart, He assured him that He would be with him and his family the entire way.

God's words were a comforting reminder of what Jacob had been told earlier in life (**Genesis 28:13–15**). God's plan to expand his family and bless them with their own land was being carried out. He would bring them back from Egypt, and at that time, the sixty-plus descendants he had at the moment would seem like a paltry number.

Comforted about going to Egypt and the future of his family, Jacob knew that everything that had transpired was in accordance with the promises that he trusted God with. Even though it did not always make sense, it was precisely how God had planned. At the instruction of the Lord, Jacob and his family moved on as an amazing transition took place. Years after being robbed of his own son and enduring the pain of losing a child, Jacob found comfort in knowing that now

THIS SON WOULD BURY HIM.

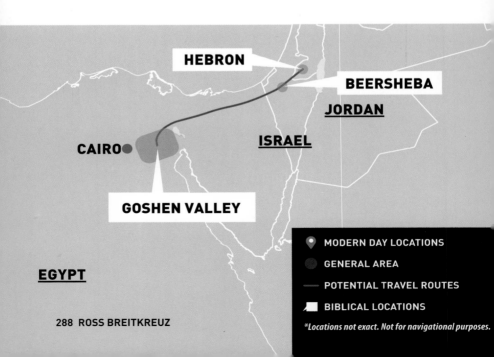

HEBRON

BEERSHEBA

JORDAN

ISRAEL

CAIRO

GOSHEN VALLEY

MODERN DAY LOCATIONS

GENERAL AREA

POTENTIAL TRAVEL ROUTES

BIBLICAL LOCATIONS

Locations not exact. Not for navigational purposes.

EGYPT

CHAPTER 66

THE JOURNEY FROM BEERSHEBA DOWN TO EGYPT WOULD HAVE required travelling over 300 kilometres (around 190 miles). Making their way across the desert terrain, Jacob's family would take no less than a week before finally arriving at the borders of Egypt.

As the days passed, excited conversations floated through the air as everyone discussed their new home and how it might look. Children ran around the knees of their parents and in between rolling carts, giggling playfully and taking turns pretending to be Uncle Joseph, *the mightiest ruler in the land*. Smiling over the carefree joy of the children, and hardly better at containing their excitement, the adults walked in boisterous contemplation, elaborating and occasionally embellishing reports they had heard from the eleven brothers. The dreams and visions of luxury grew with each step as they discussed the potential lifestyle shift, the culture, the people,

AND THEIR LONG-LOST RELATIVE.

" Before long, Jacob and his family would have a new home. "

At the centre of the cluster of travellers walked Jacob. Observing the excitement of his family, he couldn't help but reflect on what a quick transition it had been from their famine-inflicted, downtrodden state to the joy they now shared. Engulfed by the beauty of it, for Jacob, the best was yet to come.

As they finally neared their destination, Jacob sent his oldest son, Judah, ahead of the family to inform Joseph of their arrival and to receive instructions on where to settle. Before long, Jacob and his family would have a new home.

 Genesis 46:28–47:12

Arriving in the Goshen region of Egypt, Jacob was met with the embrace of his son. Before even hugging Joseph, his eyes were filled with tears. The two men held one another and wept for joy. They had twenty lost years to make up for.

Caught in a moment where no one else seemed to exist, their embrace was an opportunity to familiarize themselves with one another's touch and long-forgotten scent. Jacob knew he could die in peace. Joseph felt like he belonged. *This* was home.

Along with the peace that he had in the presence of Joseph, Jacob also found himself under the blessing of Pharaoh. Settling in Goshen, their plot of land was located in some of the most beautiful and fertile territory Egypt had to offer. The security they found in Egypt could not have come at a better time. We discover through his conversation with Pharaoh that Jacob was now 130 years old, and it's apparent that his time on earth was winding down. In his old age, he would die prosperous, with a large family and unity among his sons. Jacob's age also reveals promise He made back in **Genesis 3:15**. Provided with more detail and direction with each generation, the three men chosen to pursue God's riches had seen many joys. But now, nearing his final days, Jacob had more kids than his forefathers, greater prosperity, an affiliation with the most powerful man on earth, and a son who was a great governing authority. For Jacob, the promises that had been passed down for 215 years seemed more tangible than ever.

Though we are never told Joseph's age at the time of all this, considering Jacob's age and the location of our story, we can establish a concrete number. The reunion that was taking place with the family was said to have begun in the second year of the seven-year famine (**Genesis 45:6**). Seven years of prosperity had taken place *before* the famine, and Joseph was hired by Pharaoh at the age of thirty (**Genesis 41:46**). This means Joseph was *around* age thirty-nine when his father moved to Egypt, which means Joseph had spent nearly twenty-two years separated from his family after being sold around the age of seventeen (**Genesis 37:2**). Though the years were long, they saw no shortage of adventure, as Joseph had ventured from home, to slavery, to master of Potiphar's house, to jail, and then to provider for the known world.

Much like his son Joseph's, Jacob's years had been busy as well. Born the younger twin of his brother, Esau, after tricking his father into blessing him he had run from his brother to save his own life. In the company of relatives, he, like Joseph, had spent over twenty years separated from his family, all because of an angry sibling. Working for his shrewd Uncle Laban over those years, he was mistreated and tricked into working fourteen years to marry the woman he loved, as well as having his wages changed numerous times. When Jacob finally left Laban to return to his family, he did so with great apprehension. Terrified over his brother's reception, Jacob's anxiety led to sleepless nights and a plea for forgiveness. Though Esau met him with a gracious embrace, their reunion was quickly followed by the death of his love, Rachel, his father, Isaac, and his son Joseph. Joseph had always carried the memory of Rachel, and with his "death," Jacob felt like he lost Rachel all over again. For the rest of the family, losing Joseph had led to the loss of Jacob.

Though he remained with his family physically, Jacob had lived in pain and misfortune during those twenty-two years. But now, the years of brokenness ended. His final days would be filled with the peace that comes from being in the safety and security of the ones you love. It was a blessing given to Jacob

BECAUSE OF GOD'S GRACE AND PROVISION.

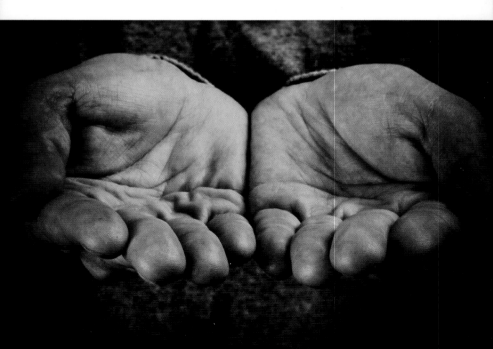

CHAPTER 67

SETTLED IN GOSHEN UNDER JOSEPH'S CARE, JACOB AND HIS growing family found stability amidst the famine.

As for Joseph, he truly felt at home in Egypt with his family close by. Their presence was an ongoing reminder of God's goodness, and he spent as much time as he could afford with them, even though the famine maintained a horrifying grip on the land for the next four to five years,

ENDANGERING NATIONS AND THREATENING LIFE IN EGYPT AND CANAAN (the area Joseph's family moved from).

Joseph faced a continual onslaught of starving residents who begged him for nourishment and relief. Despite the fact that he had known these days were coming and had worked hard to prepare for them, the famine's merciless impact still gave him chills. It was devastating. Had the country not prepared for its arrival, there's no telling how many people would have faced tragic deaths during the seven years. Even with food in storage, the people suffered.

The ongoing famine and pursuit of sustenance left everyone in Egypt dependent on Joseph's food reserves. As the people emptied their pockets and used anything they could as leverage for buying food, the unrelenting famine left almost everyone poor and hungry. Doing what he could to sustain them, Joseph struck up a deal with the people of Egypt that saw them trading in their money, livestock, land, and future income. Before the famine ended, Pharaoh owned Egypt and its people.

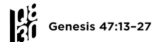 **Genesis 47:13–27**

The famine hit the people in Egypt hard, forcing everyone to dish out every penny they could find. The people emptied their couches and the ashtrays on their camels in an effort to scrounge up what they had left. Desperate for food, they emptied their pockets in front of Joseph, sheepishly offering everything they had. They stood before Joseph like a six-year-old boy at the candy shop, placing a few pennies, some lint, and a runaway Tic Tac onto the counter, then asking, "Sir, what can I get with this much?"

After draining their piggy banks and realizing they had nothing left to offer in exchange for grain, the people's desperation led them to trading in cattle and land. Liquidizing all their assets, they were forced into bankruptcy. Selling off their toys, their homes, and their land, they did whatever it took to survive.

By the time the seven years of famine ended, Pharaoh owned every inch of land throughout Egypt (with the exception of the land that the priests owned). Pharaoh became landlord and boss. The people were his tenants and employees.

The insight and wisdom God had given Joseph for navigating the drought set Pharaoh and his nation on a pedestal. The contracts Joseph established remained in place for hundreds of years. Despite the citizens having to trade in what they owned, compared to how things *could* have gone Egypt flourished in the famine, and in due time, just as God had said, the famine eventually relented.

The survival of the Egyptian people, compared to the nations around them, firmly established them as a powerful nation. Pharaoh's insurmountable riches and even loftier stature gave him and the leaders that followed great power.

Meanwhile in Goshen, where Joseph's family lived, Jacob and his family benefited greatly from the food that was provided. Flourishing like the other residents in Egypt, they continued to grow in numbers. Before they realized, seventeen years had passed by in Egypt, and they had experienced security and wealth unlike any other time in their lives. With the passing of an additional seventeen years, Jacob reached the age of 147,

A WELL-TRAVELLED OLD MAN WHOSE PILGRIMAGE WOULD COME TO A CLOSE.

CHAPTER 68

IT SEEMS AS IF JACOB'S TIME IN EGYPT HAD BEEN PLEASANT, A tranquil season in life. Though he had enjoyed the refuge he'd found in the Goshen Valley, his heart had remained in Canaan, back in the Promised Land.

Hesitant to go to Egypt in the first place, at least not without God's full consent (**Genesis 46:3-4**), Jacob had never stopped thinking about returning to the land where he grew up. He was well aware that his family's current address was not inside the borders of the land God had promised. Despite the prosperity and lavish lifestyle, Jacob had not been distracted from God's plan for His people. In fact, the thought of how great life was in Egypt made him that much more desperate for the Promised Land, as he thought to himself, *If life in Egypt is this good and God has an even better land for our descendants, I can't imagine how amazing it will be!*

Though Jacob knew in his heart he wouldn't live to see the fulfillment of all he'd been promised, he still longed for Canaan to be his final resting place. His faith in God's unwavering commitment to do exactly what He said left Jacob with a deep desire to be laid to rest in Canaan, in the Promised Land his family would inherit, next to his wife. Even though at the time of his death he would still be an alien in Canaan,

HIS FAITH IN GOD TOLD HIM THAT ONE DAY IT WOULD BE HOME.

 **Genesis 47:28–48:22**

"Jacob's failing eyes beheld a sight he had never dreamt of seeing: Joseph's children."

Swelling inside over the blessings in his life (or from the water retention that can accompany old age), Jacob's failing eyes beheld a sight he had never dreamt of seeing: Joseph's children.

At the sight of his grandsons, he embraced the two boys as if they were his own, making it clear that they would share in the rich inheritance God had for the family. Ephraim and Manasseh were now part of the mighty nation God was raising.

As Jacob proceeded to pour out the blessing onto his grandkids, there appeared to be a miscommunication between him and Joseph. Thinking his father must have been confused when Jacob chose Ephraim over Manasseh, Joseph tried to correct him. Perhaps choosing to bless the younger over the older because it was the blessing he had received, Jacob insisted that what he was doing was right, placing Ephraim ahead of his brother, Manasseh. Both brothers received a new and rich promise—

A PROMISE GIVEN TO THEM NOT ONLY FROM GRANDPA BUT FROM GOD.

CHAPTER 69

As his words washed over his grandsons and Joseph, Jacob must have seemed like he was on a bit of a blessing-offering roll. When he invited the rest of the family to join them and receive the forecast for their lives, the words Jacob uttered to his sons were *not* spoken on a whim. His words were not rooted in gut feelings and inklings; they were a display of wisdom and God-given insight as

JACOB ADDRESSED HIS TWELVE SONS WITH WORDS OF CORRECTION AND GRACE.

By the time their dad finished talking, each brother had been addressed. Some of them walked away encouraged, while others remained slightly mystified. For others, their meeting with Dad turned into an uncomfortable occasion as their dirty laundry got laid out and family secrets surfaced.

> **"** One by one Jacob catalogued some of the grievances his sons had put him through... **"**

 Genesis 49:1–50:3

Not knowing what to expect at their family gathering, as word had spread among the brothers that Dad's health was waning and he was handing out blessings, perhaps some of the brothers assumed their father had forgotten some of their blunders from the past. Men like Reuben certainly would have hoped for this. However, the brothers discovered that even in his old age, their father hadn't forgotten the things they had done. Recalling some of their events with an uncomfortable level of detail, one by one Jacob catalogued some of the grievances his sons had put him through, and he offered insight into how the family would function in years to come.

As Jacob began his address with his oldest, Reuben's eyes popped from his head as his father called him out for sleeping with his concubine (**Genesis 35:22**). Leaving his eldest son stammering in disbelief, Jacob then rebuked Simeon and Levi, again, for the vengeance they had sought against the Shechemites (**Genesis 34**). Reprimanding his three oldest sons for their conduct, Jacob revealed that none of them were fit for leadership, which explains why, in the future, Judah (the fourth son born of Jacob) would take such a prominent position of leadership among his brothers (**Genesis 43:3-10; 44:16; 44:18-34; 46:28**). Ultimately, Judah received the richest inheritance of all his brothers, as Jacob informed Judah that he would be a leader among his brothers. Judah's descendants would always hold a position of authority. It would be through his family that the promised seed of God (**Genesis 3:15**) would come (**Genesis 49:10**). From his family line, the greatest leader of all would be born. God was choosing Judah's family to deliver the one who would crush Satan, sin, and death. Judah would take part in the restoration of mankind's relationship to his Creator. The whole point behind all of God's promises rested in the family of Judah—this was a family that would be watched with great anticipation.

Considering all that was pronounced over Judah, it could feel like the rest of the family blessings were inconsequential. Though Judah was given the promise of the One to come, each brother, and their growing families, would still have a *great* impact inside the Promised Land.

Jacob's words to the rest of his sons painted a dynamic picture of the diversity that would be found in his family. He provided insight into how broad the giftings would be, spanning various trades and roles. In summary, their family's future could be broken down as follows:

Zebulun would become a people of the water. Establishing ports along the ocean, this family would give birth to beautiful oceanside communities, with harbours that everyone would love to visit. They just might grow up to be a nation of sailors.

Issachar was going to be the kind of family that was known for its ability to work hard. These guys would work their donkeys off. Unfortunately, their hard work was perhaps going to come through slavery.

Dan would be a man of great discernment and judgment. He would sit as an arbitrator for his family—a family of lawyers and judges.

Gad wouldn't go down without a fight. He might not be the biggest kid on the block, but that wouldn't stop him. Gad and his descendants would have the heart and valour of a superhero. Unfortunately, they would be stuck with the physique of someone built for desk work.

Asher would be a master in the kitchen. His people were going to hammer out delicate carb-loaded pastries that everyone would want.

Naphtali was going to be a pretty boy. It's not entirely clear what line of work their delicate features would score them. The "fawns" he would give birth to were likely going to have an Orlando Bloom-esque look about them.

From what we read, the breakdown of the family's blessings were fairly straightforward—that is, until Jacob reached Joseph.

Joseph received a blessing so gargantuan that Jacob had trouble putting it into words. Like trying to stuff a barrel of jelly filling into a single donut, there was so much goodness in one place that it was hard to contain.

Eventually, as Jacob wound down, leaving some brothers sitting quietly in anger while others were content and joyous, he ended with his youngest son, Benjamin. With words that were once again straightforward, Jacob explained to Benjamin that he and his family would be like ravenous wolves, hunters, who killed in the morning and feasted at night.

With each of his twelve sons receiving a word, when all was said and done, we look back at an absolute menagerie of personalities. A dynamic and colourful future awaited Jacob's twelve sons or, as they'd soon be known, the twelve tribes of Israel.

Having spoken with Yoda-like wisdom, in epic fashion, with perfect timing, Jacob then curled up into his bed and took his last breath. In the end, whether they had received a blessing or a reprimand, with the passing of their father each brother was left with a contrite heart.

Grieved by his passing, the boys mourned Jacob's death and prepared to fulfill his final request—to be buried with his wife in the land God had promised. However, as the brothers got ready for the journey, they soon discovered that transporting their father's body back to Canaan

WASN'T GOING TO BE THEIR ONLY CONCERN.

CHAPTER 70

AFTER JACOB'S PASSING, OUT OF RESPECT FOR JOSEPH AND HIS family the entire nation of Egypt entered a time of mourning. Though Egypt had never been fully introduced to Jacob, they were undoubtedly thankful for his son who had guided them through such difficult times.

During the time of mourning, which lasted over one month, Egyptian morticians attended to Jacob's vacated body. The process of mummification and embalming was no easy task, and they didn't take grieving lightly either. By the time the season of lamenting and celebrating Jacob's life ended,

**NEARLY TWO-AND-A-HALF MONTHS
HAD GONE BY.**

As the time of mourning eventually wound down, Joseph and his brothers realized it was time to make preparations for their journey back to the land of Canaan. They had to fulfill their father's wish of burying him in their homeland. It was going to be an act of service to their father as well as a symbol of their own faith in God.

 **Genesis 50:4–14**

> **"**When was God going to give them the inheritance He had long ago called them to?**"**

In a large procession, Joseph, his brothers, and numerous Egyptian dignitaries made the journey to Canaan.

As they traversed the land between Egypt and Canaan, eventually they reached the Jordan River. There, on the borders of Canaan, they stopped to say goodbye to their father one last time. Then, after seven days, they carried his body into Canaan and placed him where he'd requested. Three generations that had carried God's promise now lay in the cave. Abraham and Sarah; Isaac and Rebekah; and now Jacob and Leah. Their final resting place was a declaration of their confidence in God's promise. This was their home.

As they turned around and made their way back to Egypt, the return trip was undoubtedly a sombre one. Moving across land that was once their home, the brothers reflected on the fact that it had been almost twenty years since they had relocated to Egypt. Joseph had been gone from that area for over forty years.

Being back in their ol' stomping grounds caused the brothers to wonder when they were going to return to Canaan permanently. When was God going to give them the inheritance He had long ago called them to? It had been over 225 years since their Grandpa Abraham had been promised this land (**Genesis 12**), and the brothers' return to Egypt after burying their father only heightened their curiosity about *how* God would make this land their home.

Not only were they wondering about the future, their travels caused many memories from their past to resurface. As they thought about what it was like growing up in Canaan, soon a new question grew in their minds—one that sparked an anxiety they thought they had escaped. As they journeyed back to Egypt, the brothers found themselves reflecting on their betrayal of Joseph, and eventually they wondered, had their father's death opened up a door for Joseph's revenge?

With their father dead and Joseph embraced as Egyptian royalty, there was no telling what the future held. Who was to say that Joseph had not placed a mark on their heads? Without Dad around to mediate and keep everyone in check, would Joseph act out vengefully? As the brothers considered this, the long-forgotten fear of retribution for their actions crept back into their lives. Haunted all over again by the choice they had made, they tried to assure themselves that Joseph would never treat them poorly. *Surely he has forgiven us and means us no harm?* But the mere fact that they had to ask themselves that question left them unsettled and concerned. The brothers had to do something—anything—to avoid a grievous outcome. There had to be a way to ensure that Joseph would not

COME LOOKING TO SETTLE THE SCORE.

CHAPTER 71

IT'S CLEAR THAT JACOB'S PRESENCE WITH HIS DRAMATIC FAMILY of twelve had been an adhesive between his sons, binding them together. His life had brought security to each of their minds, knowing that no matter what, Dad would always defend them—

BUT NOW, HE WAS GONE.

In Jacob's absence, the closet that housed many of the brothers' skeletons seemed to burst open. The choice they had spent their entire lives running from was once again back on display. As they journeyed back from the gravesite in Canaan, they grew terrified over the thought that maybe, just maybe, Joseph had been anticipating this shift in family leadership for a long time.

Concerned that Joseph had been spending his time awaiting the perfect opportunity to remind them of their mistakes, they started to view his kindness over the years as preparation—as if he had been fattening them up like a calf for a feast. The brothers grew nervous, terrified that behind Joseph's words of forgiveness was a heart filled with vengeful excitement, longing to make them relive his pain. With Dad gone, it appeared as if Joseph was free to repay them all, with little recourse. He controlled an entire nation and could essentially do whatever he desired.

Realizing that Egypt might not be the place of rest they thought it was, in an effort to save themselves Joseph's brothers frantically devised a plan. As they travelled together like a herd of frightened deer, they cooked up a plan to ensure their own comfort. Working in unison in a manner eerily similar to their earlier team effort (the one that got them in trouble in the first place),

> **"** ...once again they discussed how to remove the threat of Joseph from their lives. **"**

 Genesis 50:15-26

When his brothers said that their father had *strongly* encouraged him *not* to seek retribution on them, Joseph's heart broke. Although it's unclear whether he knew his brothers had fabricated the story or sincerely believed that the message had come from his father, it seared Joseph's heart.

Had he truly been that misunderstood? Were they all so blind that they did not understand that he had forgiven them? Did they view his character as fickle and wavering? He had loved his family and ached for them during their time apart. He had no intention of harming them. Clearly, his brothers had failed to see the greater picture in what had taken place. They had missed out on God's grand design amidst everything that had happened. Now the "words of warning" were nothing short of a sword to his spirit—an attack on his character.

Through this encounter, it was once again made very clear that Joseph didn't see things the way his brothers did. He had embraced each scenario in life as a blessing, even the rough ones. As he looked back at God's mighty work in his life, he saw how everything that transpired had led him to where he was. Joseph knew that anger and resentment towards his brothers' decisions wouldn't reveal a frustration with them; it would show resentment towards the work God had been doing. Of course, God never wanted bad things to happen to Joseph. He never wanted the brothers to beat Joseph and sell him. But He had taken each error and done something marvellous with it. Joseph was thankful for the manner in which his story had unfolded. He held no grudge against his brothers, and he was forever grateful to God for the way He had worked out His will against all odds and despite the blunders of others.

As Joseph reaffirmed his brothers and insisted that the message was unnecessary, the story of Genesis comes to an end, with no further disclosure on Joseph's life and the years spent in Egypt with this family. At the age of 110 Joseph died, and the Genesis portion of the story closes, roughly 2,370 years after it began with Adam.

Surveying all that had transpired in and through this family as they pursued the promises God had for them, it's hard to ignore how beautifully dynamic the story is. The families of Abraham, Isaac, and Jacob lived out stories filled with triumph, suffering, trials, and pain. But most importantly, they lived lives of grace, mercy, love, faith, and promise.

AND THEIR STORY WAS *FAR* FROM OVER.

EPILOGUE

THE BOOK OF GENESIS CLOSES 2,370 YEARS AFTER THE BIRTH OF mankind. During those years, it seemed as if mankind had come up with every way imaginable to ignore God and reject His instruction. Mankind lost sight of their history and purpose. They forgot their original design, the relationship they were created for, and the perfect garden they were meant to experience. Humanity spread across the earth unaware and unconcerned with God's desire for them. Though most people would remain oblivious, God never gave up on the ones He created. He was using each moment of joy and heartache

TO FULFILL HIS PLAN OF REDEMPTION.

The words God spoke in **Genesis 3:15** had powerfully stunned creation. His plan to fix everything that *had* gone wrong and *would* go wrong in the world was the first mighty display of His grace. Redeeming His fallen creation was the heartbeat behind the promises He carried with Abraham, Isaac, Jacob—and now Jacob's twelve sons, the nation of Israel. God was pursuing His plans through this family.

As Genesis ends with the family settled in Egypt, with a level of prosperity no one in the family had experienced before, the family tree expanded just as God had promised (**Genesis 13:16**). A mighty nation grew inside the borders of Egypt, seeming to pop up out of nowhere. With each new addition to the family, the story moved one step closer to the promised seed that would bring peace on earth. One step closer to God's ultimate promise. One day, their King would come, but before He did, the nation of Israel would discover that the prosperity of their family wasn't always going to be celebrated.

In the chapters to come, this great nation was going to need God's deliverance more than ever before. Not far on the horizon, a day was coming when a new pharaoh would come to power—one who did not know about Joseph and what he had done for Egypt. For this pharaoh, the large family growing in his kingdom would be nothing more than a threat that needed to be handled. With no one from their family seated in a position of power, the entire family would eventually be forced into slavery, trapped as aliens in a strange land.

Entire generations of God's chosen people would live and die as slaves. Many of the Israelites would never know or witness a *glimpse* of God's promise for their people. God's presence in their lives would, at times, seem like a figment of their imaginations. His great promises would sound more like childish naive optimism from the past—a belief they knew better than to trust. For many, the expectations of a vibrant future would feel dead, unrealistic, and not worth hoping for. Their large numbers would bring them no more confidence in a bright future than Sarah's barren belly had. Life would seem dark. Their faith would grow cold.

But God will *never* ignore His people—especially in a time of suffering. As the pain of slavery mounted, so would their desperation for God to intervene—and He would. Crying out in surrender, desperate for release, Israel would beg for an escape from their suffering, clinging to the promise that started it all: "You are My creation, and I will never abandon you. I created you for Myself, and I will fix what you have done. In My time, I will provide One who will make right all that has gone wrong. I will never leave you nor forsake you. I love you, My child" (**Genesis 3:15**).

Though Genesis ends with Israel living in comfortable prosperity, the next part of the story, Exodus, will begin with the nation backed into an inescapable corner, where God reveals that He remains faithful even when we are faithless (**2 Timothy 2:13**). He will remember His love for Israel (**Psalm 98:3**). He will remember His promise to the earth. Though their burdens would seem too heavy to carry, God had a plan to free them from their yoke of slavery. A time was coming when Israel would leave Egypt. A time was coming when they would journey home. A time was coming when the world would move one step closer to receiving the child who would change their hearts, remove their pain, soothe their sorrows, and love them to death.

TO BE CONTINUED...

Lovingly dedicated to my amazing momma. I don't know where I'd be if not for your prayers and constant encouragement. Together we discussed ideas, read rough drafts, made edits, and prayed. You longed to see this book completed and told everyone you knew about it. Q830 was just as much your passion as it is mine. The writing process will never be the same without you. You're a good oma, and I'll always miss you.

Darcy Elaine Breitkreuz
1953-2014